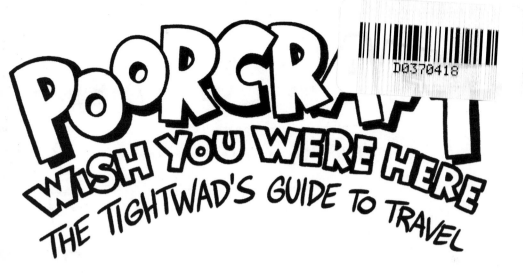

POORCRAFT
WISH YOU WERE HERE
THE TIGHTWAD'S GUIDE TO TRAVEL

Writer	Ryan Estrada
Artist	Diana Nock
Editor	C. Spike Trotman
Cover Colors	Amanda Lafrenais
Book Design	Matt Sheridan
Proofreader	J.K. Hilbert

Published by Iron Circus Comics
ironcircus@gmail.com
www.ironcircus.com

First Edition: February 2015
ISBN 978-0-9794080-5-2
Printed in Canada

TABLE OF CONTENTS

Prologue

Vacation Time!

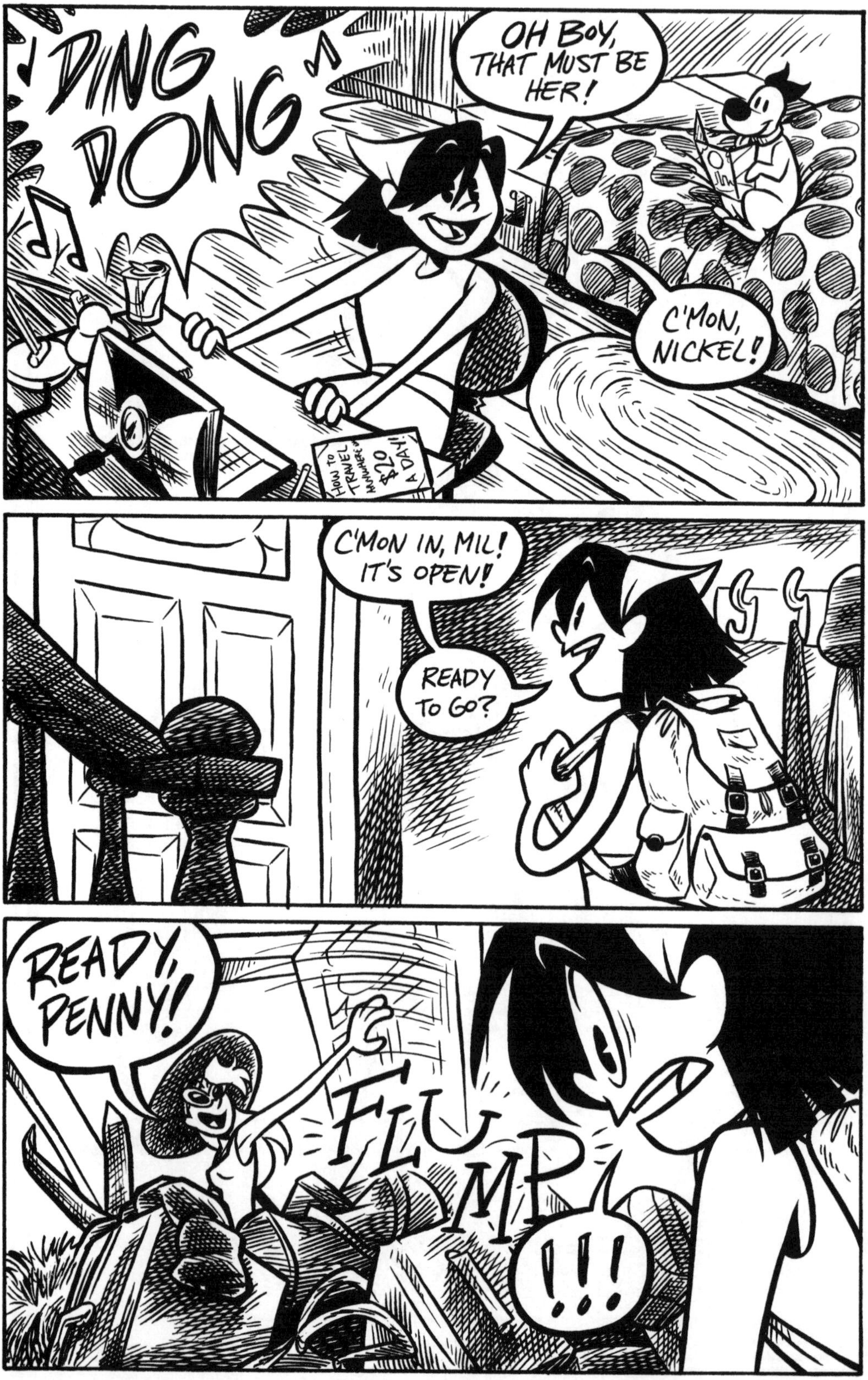
DING DONG
OH BOY, THAT MUST BE HER!
HOW TO TRAVEL ANYWHERE ON $20 A DAY!
C'MON, NICKEL!
C'MON IN, MIL! IT'S OPEN!
READY TO GO?
READY, PENNY!
FLUMP
!!!

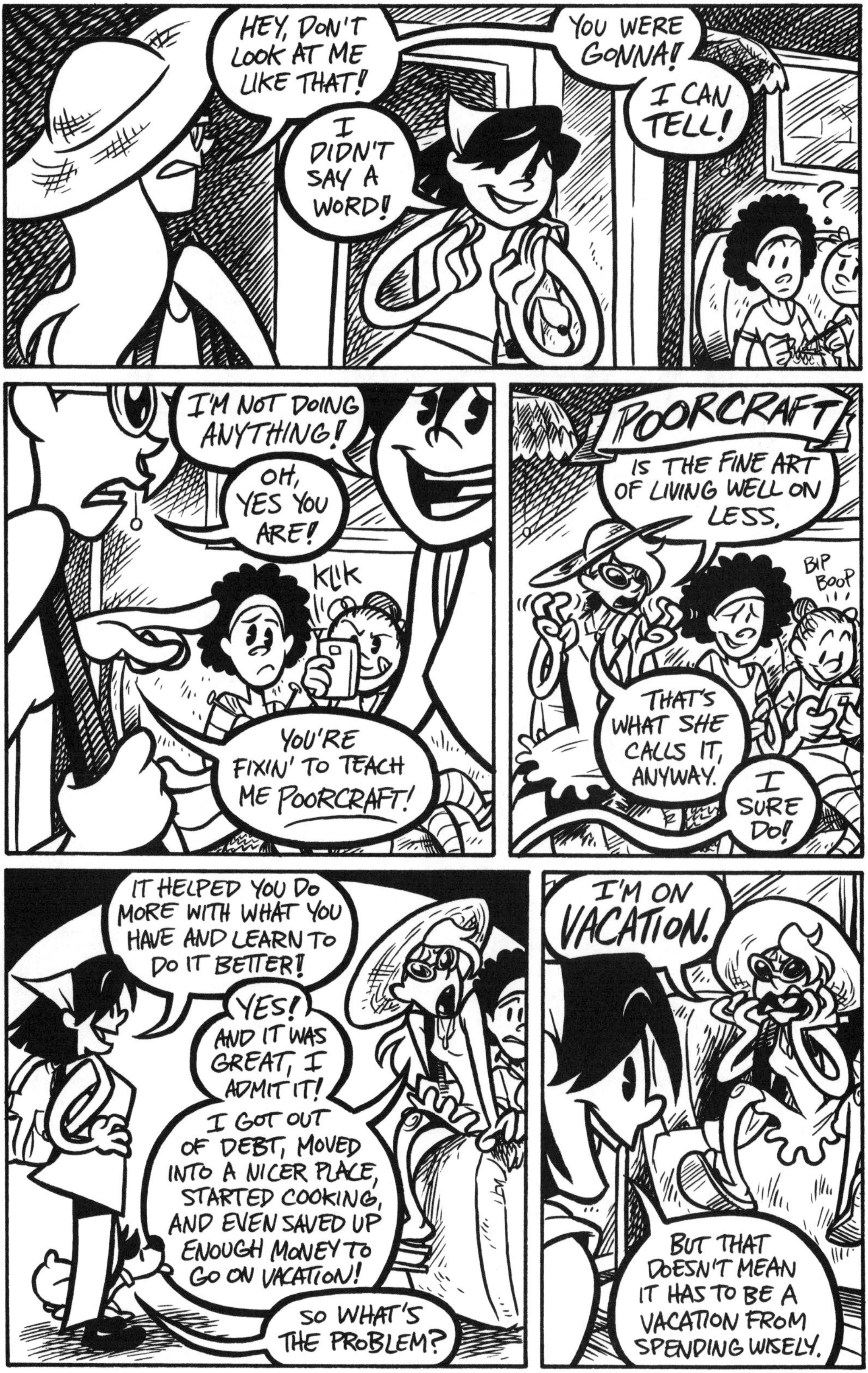
HEY, DON'T LOOK AT ME LIKE THAT!
I DIDN'T SAY A WORD!
YOU WERE GONNA!
I CAN TELL!
?
I'M NOT DOING ANYTHING!
OH, YES YOU ARE!
KLIK
YOU'RE FIXIN' TO TEACH ME POORCRAFT!
POORCRAFT
IS THE FINE ART OF LIVING WELL ON LESS.
BIP BOOP
THAT'S WHAT SHE CALLS IT, ANYWAY.
I SURE DO!
IT HELPED YOU DO MORE WITH WHAT YOU HAVE AND LEARN TO DO IT BETTER!
YES! AND IT WAS GREAT, I ADMIT IT!
I GOT OUT OF DEBT, MOVED INTO A NICER PLACE, STARTED COOKING, AND EVEN SAVED UP ENOUGH MONEY TO GO ON VACATION!
SO WHAT'S THE PROBLEM?
I'M ON VACATION.
BUT THAT DOESN'T MEAN IT HAS TO BE A VACATION FROM SPENDING WISELY.

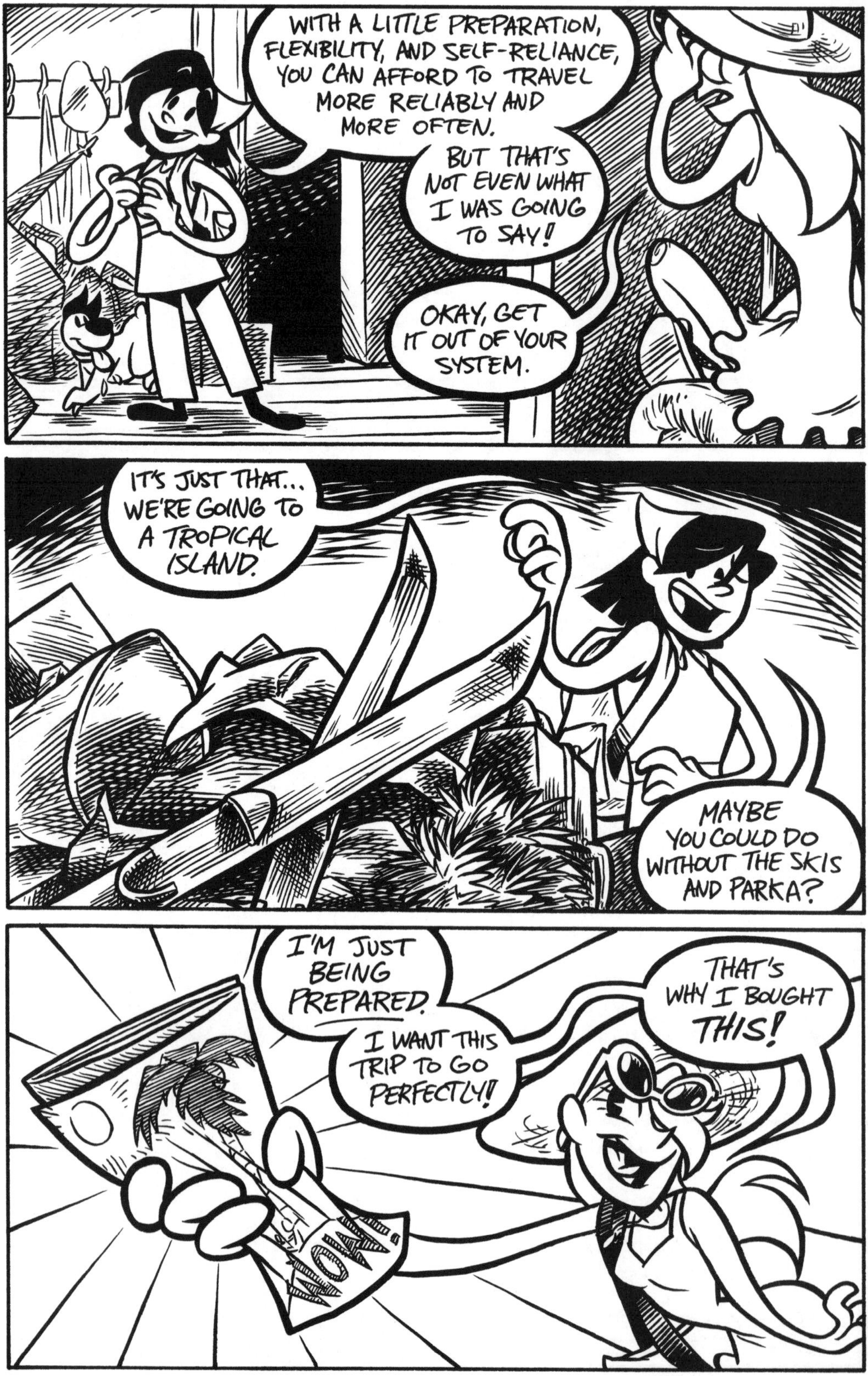
WITH A LITTLE PREPARATION, FLEXIBILITY, AND SELF-RELIANCE, YOU CAN AFFORD TO TRAVEL MORE RELIABLY AND MORE OFTEN.
BUT THAT'S NOT EVEN WHAT I WAS GOING TO SAY!
OKAY, GET IT OUT OF YOUR SYSTEM.
IT'S JUST THAT... WE'RE GOING TO A TROPICAL ISLAND.
MAYBE YOU COULD DO WITHOUT THE SKIS AND PARKA?
I'M JUST BEING PREPARED.
I WANT THIS TRIP TO GO PERFECTLY!
THAT'S WHY I BOUGHT THIS!
WOW!

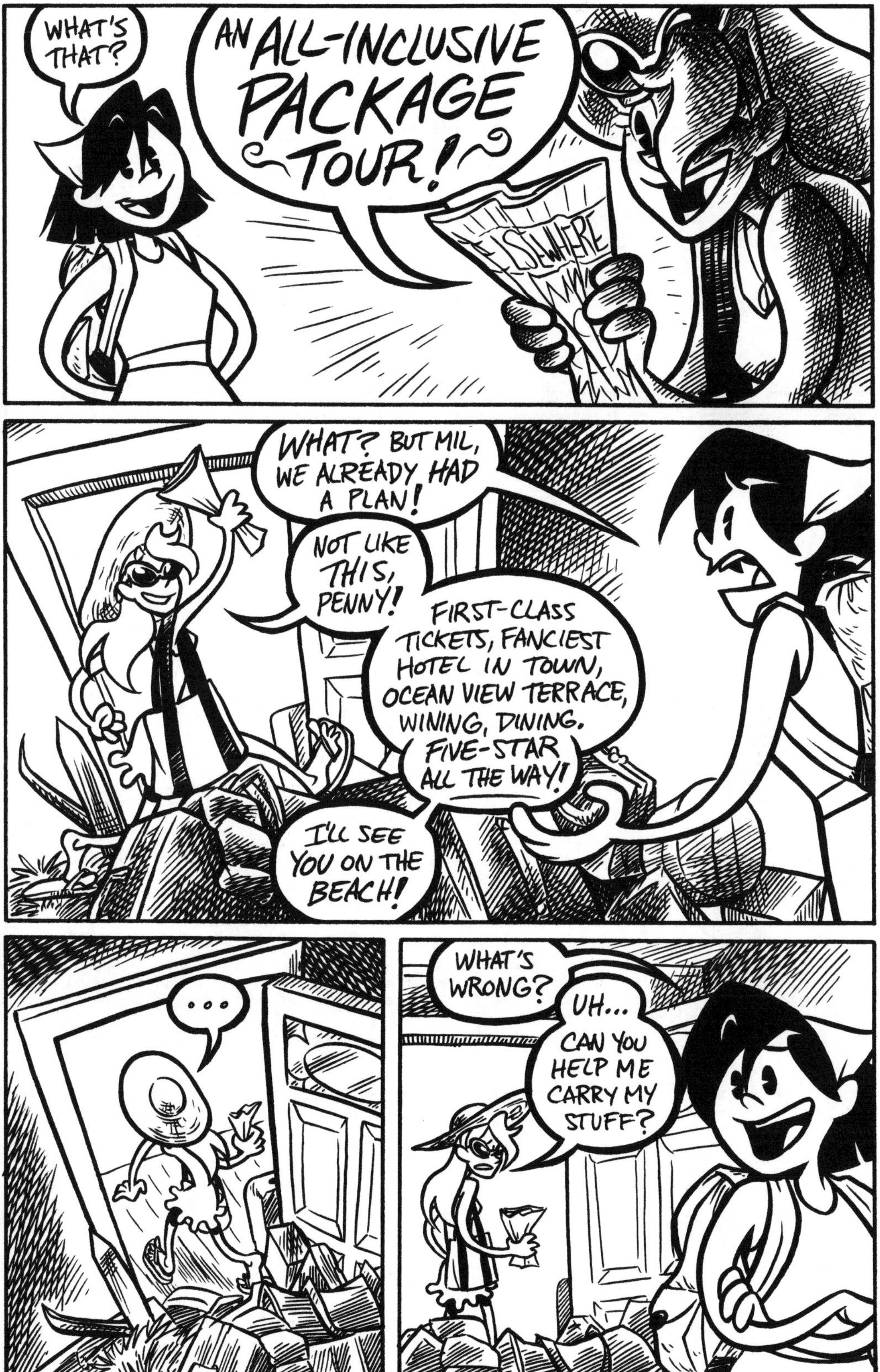
WHAT'S THAT?
AN ALL-INCLUSIVE PACKAGE TOUR!
ELSEWHERE
WHAT? BUT MIL, WE ALREADY HAD A PLAN!
NOT LIKE THIS, PENNY!
FIRST-CLASS TICKETS, FANCIEST HOTEL IN TOWN, OCEAN VIEW TERRACE, WINING, DINING. FIVE-STAR ALL THE WAY!
I'LL SEE YOU ON THE BEACH!
...
WHAT'S WRONG?
UH... CAN YOU HELP ME CARRY MY STUFF?

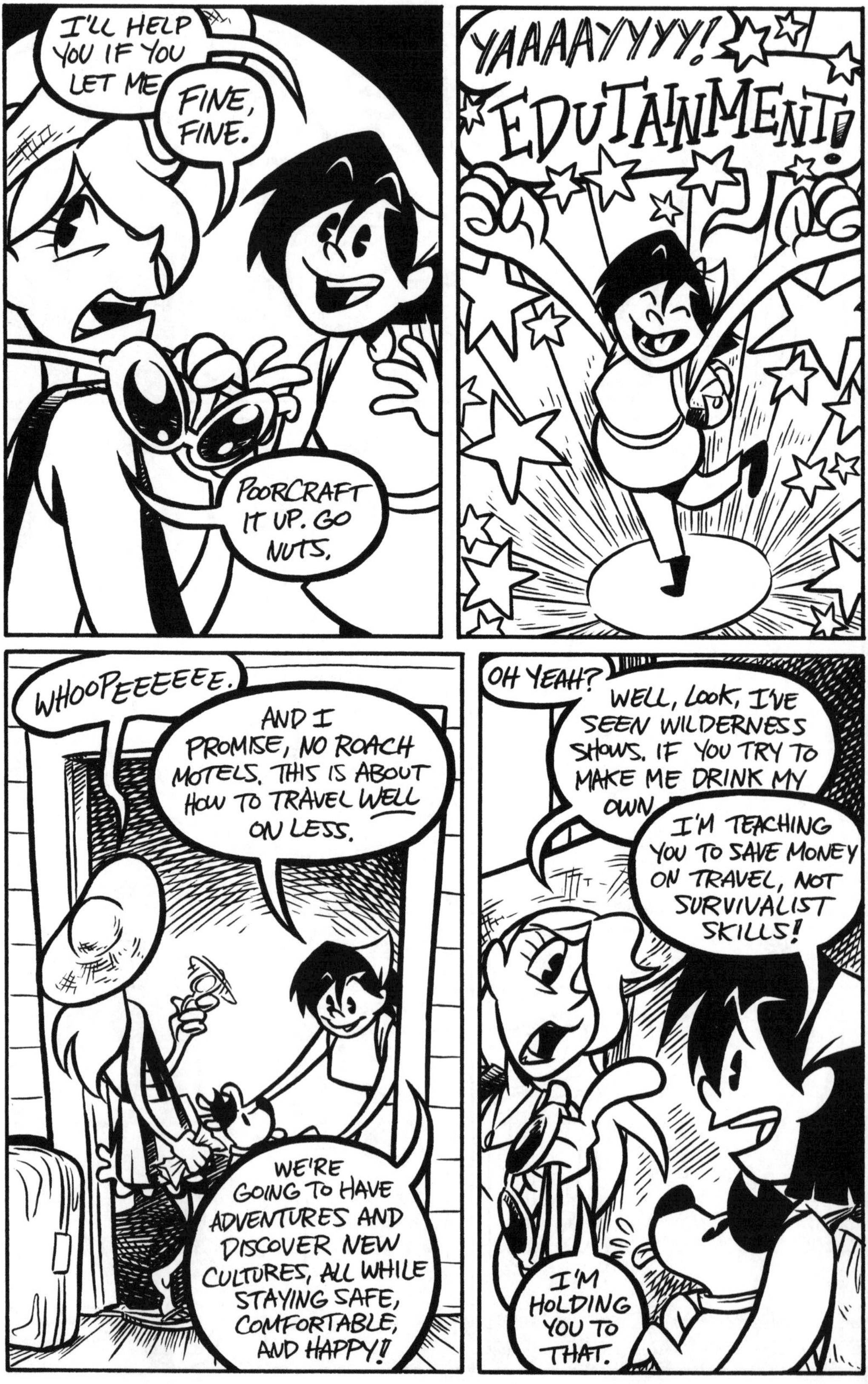
I'LL HELP YOU IF YOU LET ME.
FINE, FINE.
POORCRAFT IT UP. GO NUTS.
YAAAAYYYY!
EDUTAINMENT!
WHOOPEEEEEE.
AND I PROMISE, NO ROACH MOTELS. THIS IS ABOUT HOW TO TRAVEL WELL ON LESS.
WE'RE GOING TO HAVE ADVENTURES AND DISCOVER NEW CULTURES, ALL WHILE STAYING SAFE, COMFORTABLE, AND HAPPY!
OH YEAH?
WELL, LOOK, I'VE SEEN WILDERNESS SHOWS. IF YOU TRY TO MAKE ME DRINK MY OWN
I'M TEACHING YOU TO SAVE MONEY ON TRAVEL, NOT SURVIVALIST SKILLS!
I'M HOLDING YOU TO THAT.

Chapter One
Packing

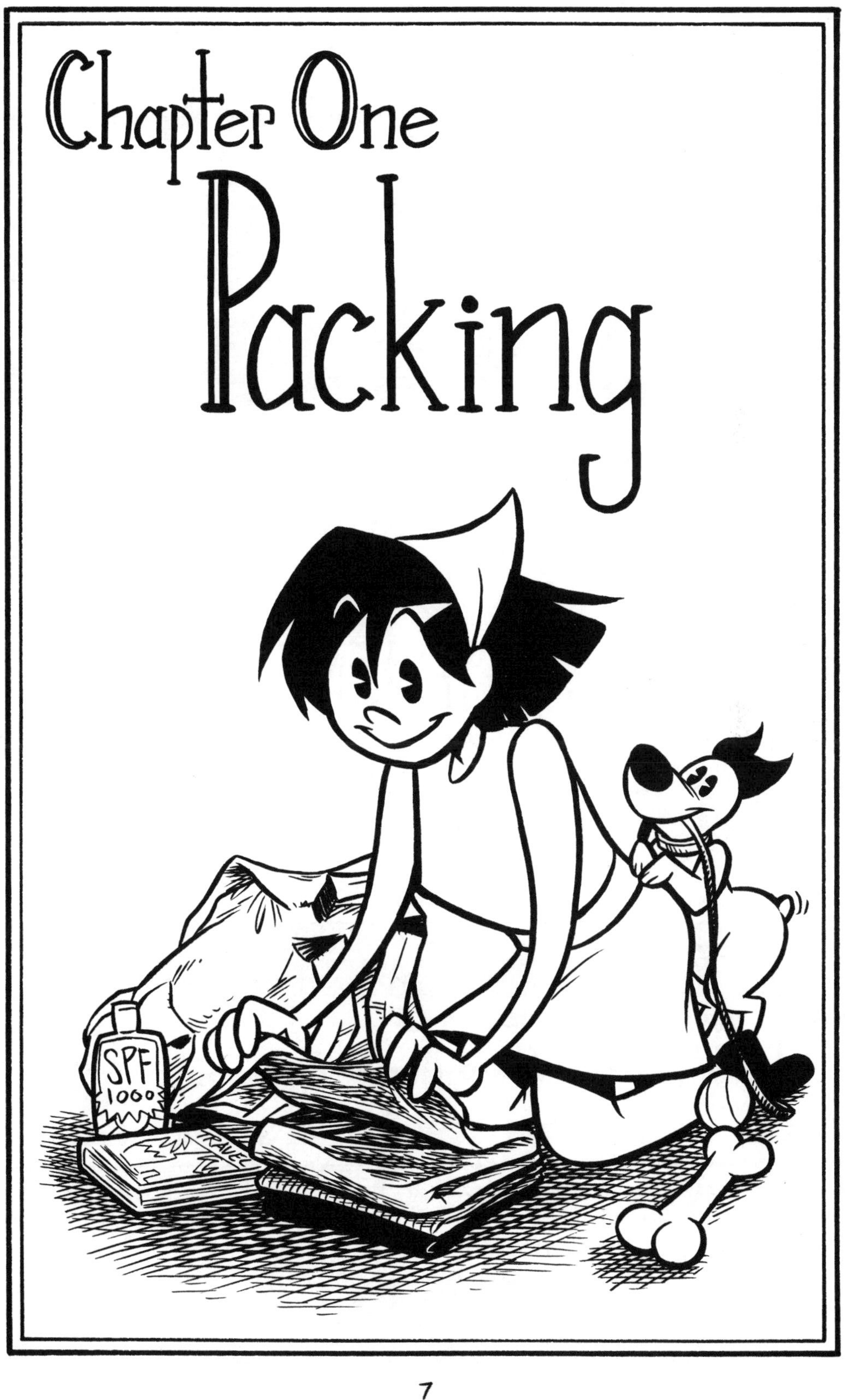
SPF
1000
TRAVEL

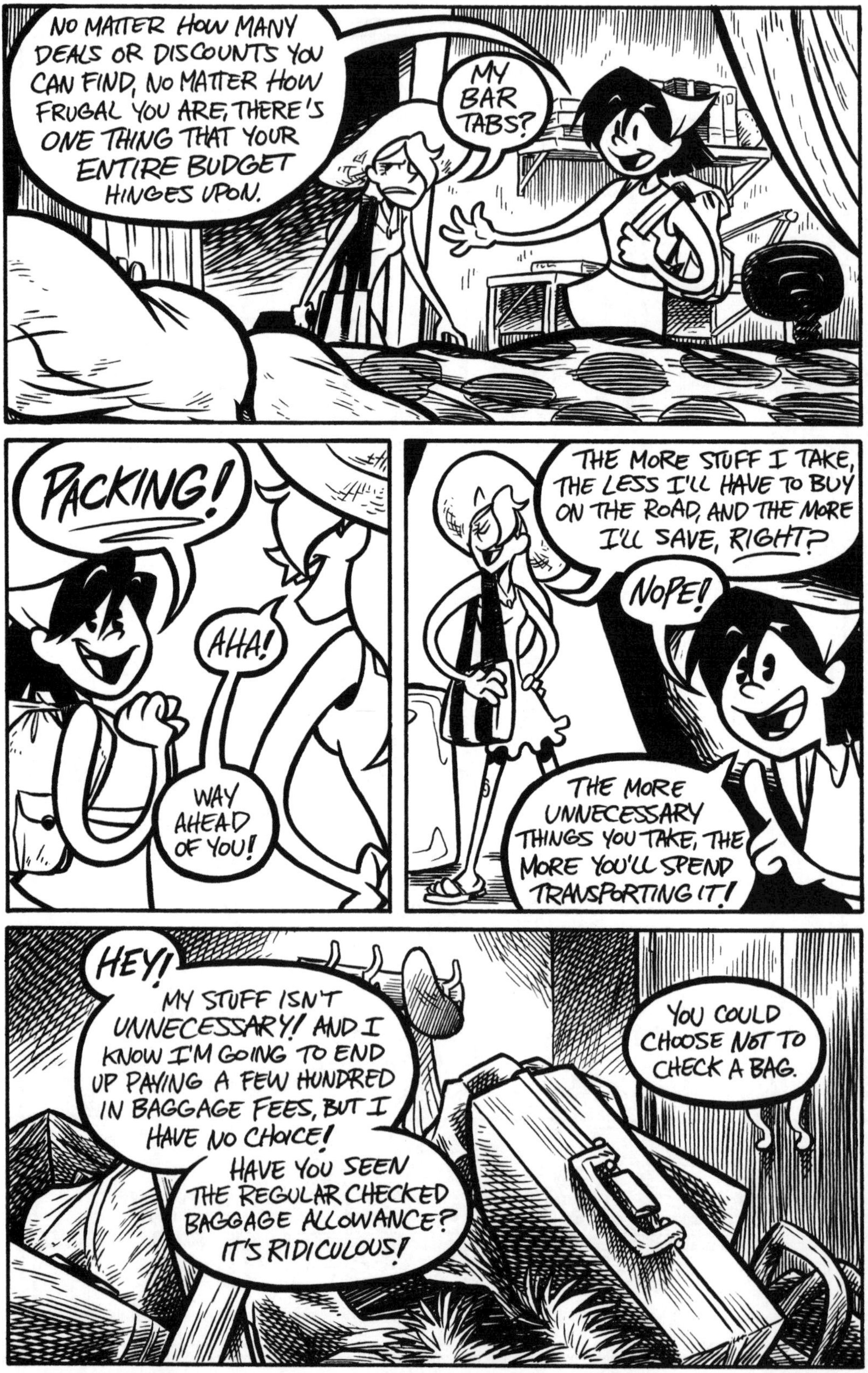
NO MATTER HOW MANY DEALS OR DISCOUNTS YOU CAN FIND, NO MATTER HOW FRUGAL YOU ARE, THERE'S ONE THING THAT YOUR ENTIRE BUDGET HINGES UPON.
MY BAR TABS?
PACKING!
AHA!
WAY AHEAD OF YOU!
THE MORE STUFF I TAKE, THE LESS I'LL HAVE TO BUY ON THE ROAD, AND THE MORE I'LL SAVE, RIGHT?
NOPE!
THE MORE UNNECESSARY THINGS YOU TAKE, THE MORE YOU'LL SPEND TRANSPORTING IT!
HEY!
MY STUFF ISN'T UNNECESSARY! AND I KNOW I'M GOING TO END UP PAYING A FEW HUNDRED IN BAGGAGE FEES, BUT I HAVE NO CHOICE!
HAVE YOU SEEN THE REGULAR CHECKED BAGGAGE ALLOWANCE? IT'S RIDICULOUS!
YOU COULD CHOOSE NOT TO CHECK A BAG.

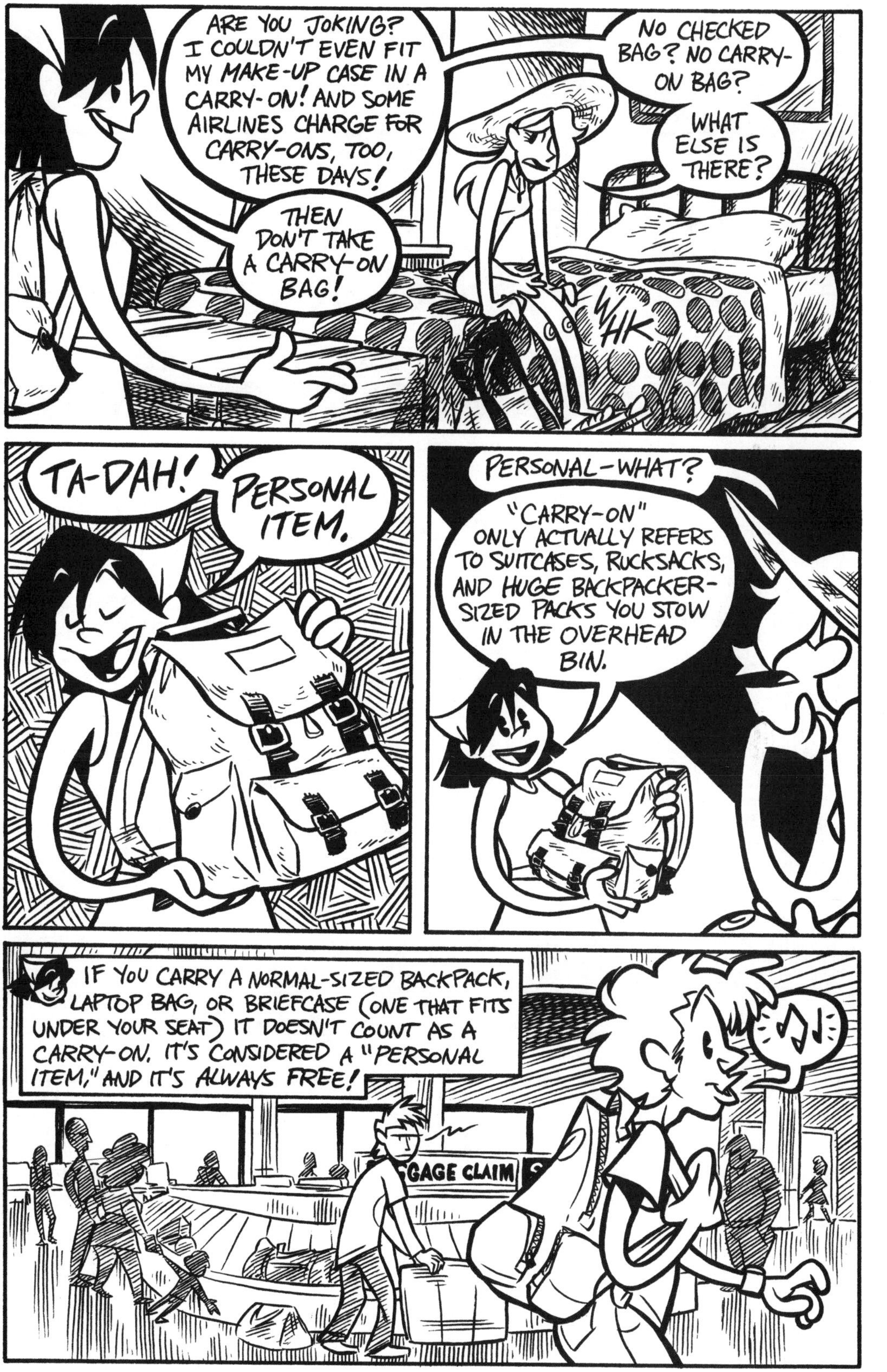
ARE YOU JOKING? I COULDN'T EVEN FIT MY MAKE-UP CASE IN A CARRY-ON! AND SOME AIRLINES CHARGE FOR CARRY-ONS, TOO, THESE DAYS!
THEN DON'T TAKE A CARRY-ON BAG!
NO CHECKED BAG? NO CARRY-ON BAG?
WHAT ELSE IS THERE?
WHK
TA-DAH!
PERSONAL ITEM.
PERSONAL-WHAT?
"CARRY-ON" ONLY ACTUALLY REFERS TO SUITCASES, RUCKSACKS, AND HUGE BACKPACKER-SIZED PACKS YOU STOW IN THE OVERHEAD BIN.
IF YOU CARRY A NORMAL-SIZED BACKPACK, LAPTOP BAG, OR BRIEFCASE (ONE THAT FITS UNDER YOUR SEAT) IT DOESN'T COUNT AS A CARRY-ON. IT'S CONSIDERED A "PERSONAL ITEM," AND IT'S ALWAYS FREE!
GAGE CLAIM

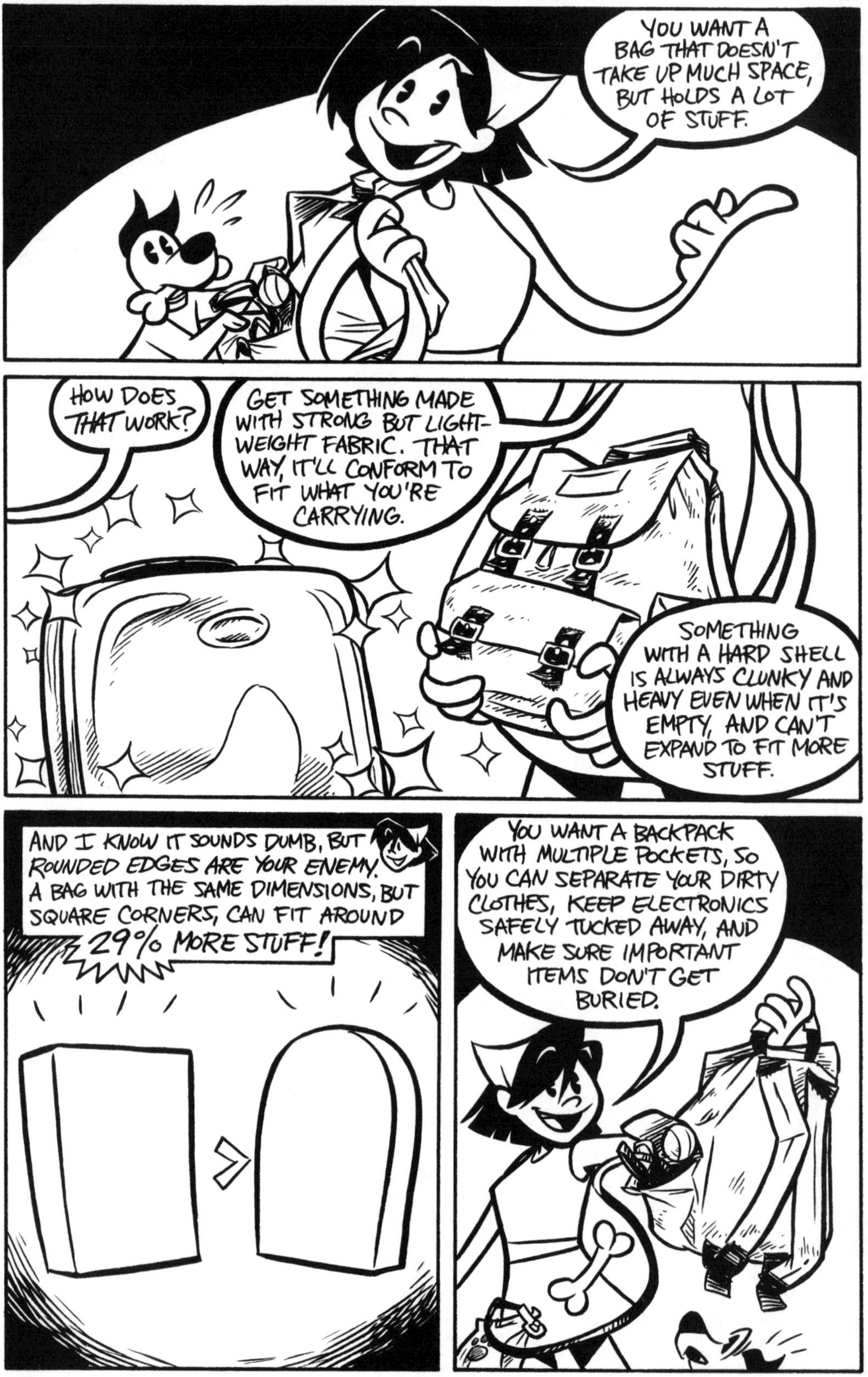
YOU WANT A BAG THAT DOESN'T TAKE UP MUCH SPACE, BUT HOLDS A LOT OF STUFF.
HOW DOES THAT WORK?
GET SOMETHING MADE WITH STRONG BUT LIGHT-WEIGHT FABRIC. THAT WAY, IT'LL CONFORM TO FIT WHAT YOU'RE CARRYING.
SOMETHING WITH A HARD SHELL IS ALWAYS CLUNKY AND HEAVY EVEN WHEN IT'S EMPTY, AND CAN'T EXPAND TO FIT MORE STUFF.
AND I KNOW IT SOUNDS DUMB, BUT ROUNDED EDGES ARE YOUR ENEMY. A BAG WITH THE SAME DIMENSIONS, BUT SQUARE CORNERS, CAN FIT AROUND
29% MORE STUFF!
YOU WANT A BACKPACK WITH MULTIPLE POCKETS, SO YOU CAN SEPARATE YOUR DIRTY CLOTHES, KEEP ELECTRONICS SAFELY TUCKED AWAY, AND MAKE SURE IMPORTANT ITEMS DON'T GET BURIED.

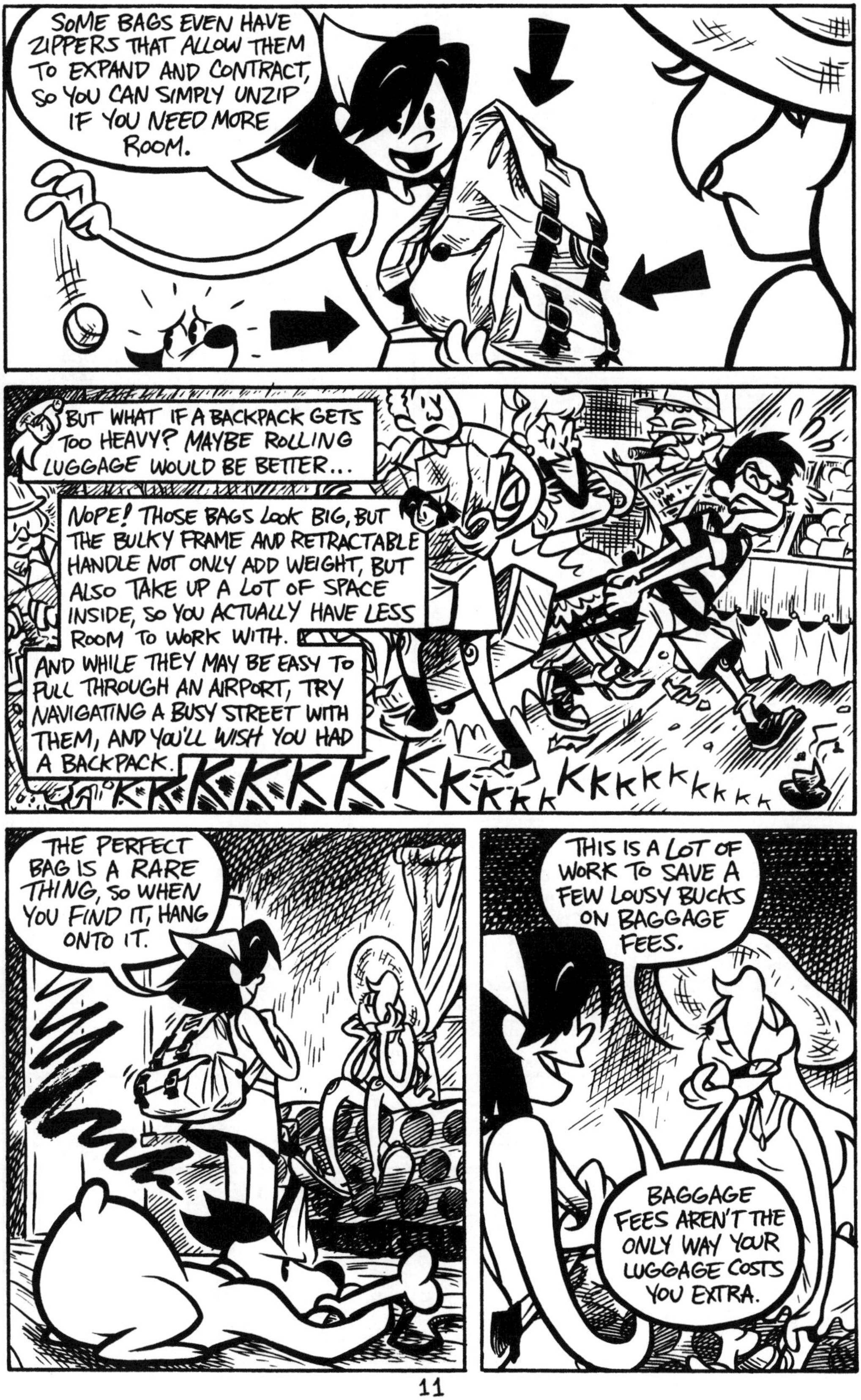
SOME BAGS EVEN HAVE ZIPPERS THAT ALLOW THEM TO EXPAND AND CONTRACT, SO YOU CAN SIMPLY UNZIP IF YOU NEED MORE ROOM.
BUT WHAT IF A BACKPACK GETS TOO HEAVY? MAYBE ROLLING LUGGAGE WOULD BE BETTER...
NOPE! THOSE BAGS LOOK BIG, BUT THE BULKY FRAME AND RETRACTABLE HANDLE NOT ONLY ADD WEIGHT, BUT ALSO TAKE UP A LOT OF SPACE INSIDE, SO YOU ACTUALLY HAVE LESS ROOM TO WORK WITH.
AND WHILE THEY MAY BE EASY TO PULL THROUGH AN AIRPORT, TRY NAVIGATING A BUSY STREET WITH THEM, AND YOU'LL WISH YOU HAD A BACKPACK.
KRKKKKKKKKKKKKKKKKKK
THE PERFECT BAG IS A RARE THING, SO WHEN YOU FIND IT, HANG ONTO IT.
THIS IS A LOT OF WORK TO SAVE A FEW LOUSY BUCKS ON BAGGAGE FEES.
BAGGAGE FEES AREN'T THE ONLY WAY YOUR LUGGAGE COSTS YOU EXTRA.

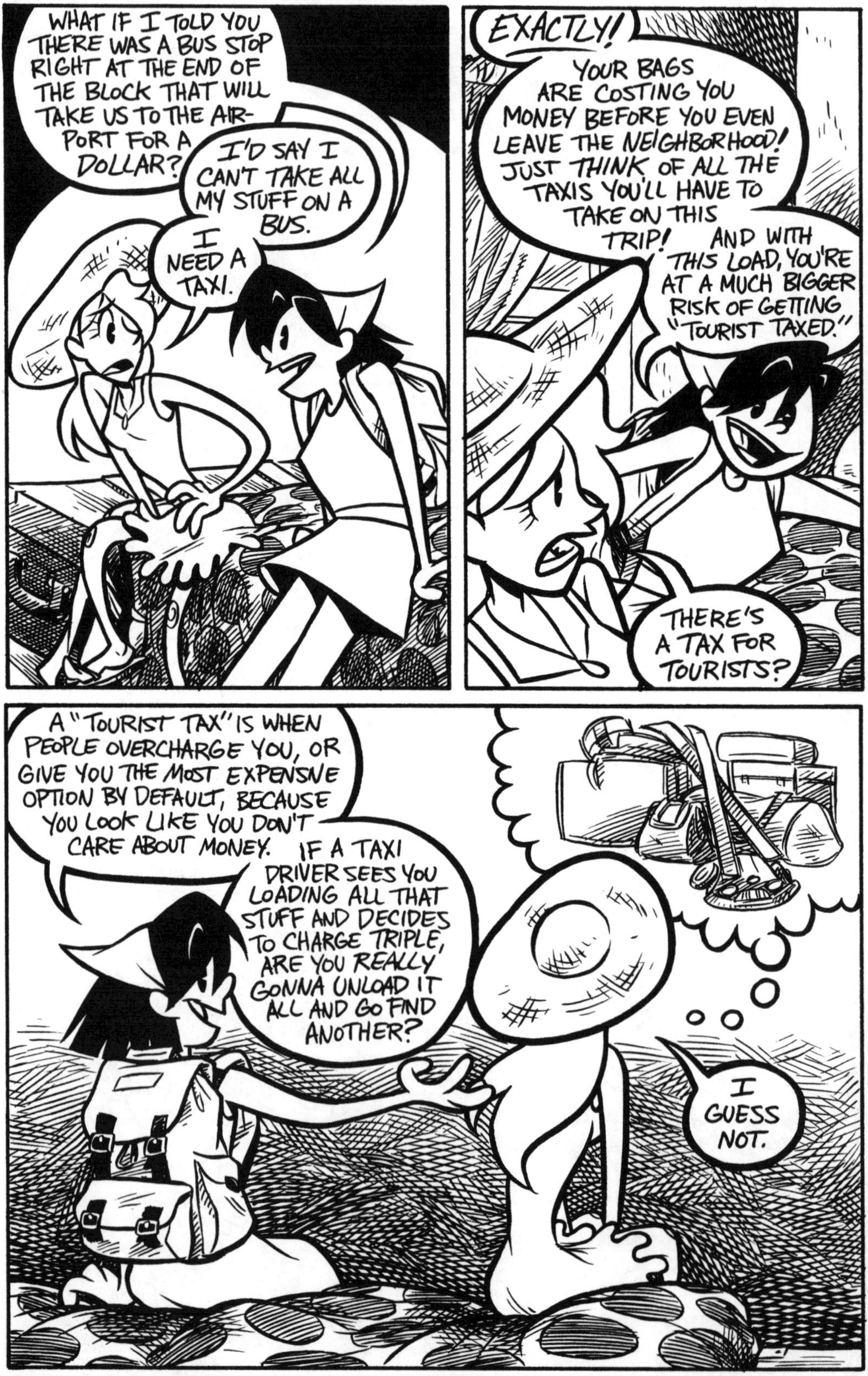
WHAT IF I TOLD YOU THERE WAS A BUS STOP RIGHT AT THE END OF THE BLOCK THAT WILL TAKE US TO THE AIRPORT FOR A DOLLAR?
I'D SAY I CAN'T TAKE ALL MY STUFF ON A BUS.
I NEED A TAXI.
EXACTLY!
YOUR BAGS ARE COSTING YOU MONEY BEFORE YOU EVEN LEAVE THE NEIGHBORHOOD! JUST THINK OF ALL THE TAXIS YOU'LL HAVE TO TAKE ON THIS TRIP!
AND WITH THIS LOAD, YOU'RE AT A MUCH BIGGER RISK OF GETTING "TOURIST TAXED."
THERE'S A TAX FOR TOURISTS?
A "TOURIST TAX" IS WHEN PEOPLE OVERCHARGE YOU, OR GIVE YOU THE MOST EXPENSIVE OPTION BY DEFAULT, BECAUSE YOU LOOK LIKE YOU DON'T CARE ABOUT MONEY.
IF A TAXI DRIVER SEES YOU LOADING ALL THAT STUFF AND DECIDES TO CHARGE TRIPLE, ARE YOU REALLY GONNA UNLOAD IT ALL AND GO FIND ANOTHER?
I GUESS NOT.

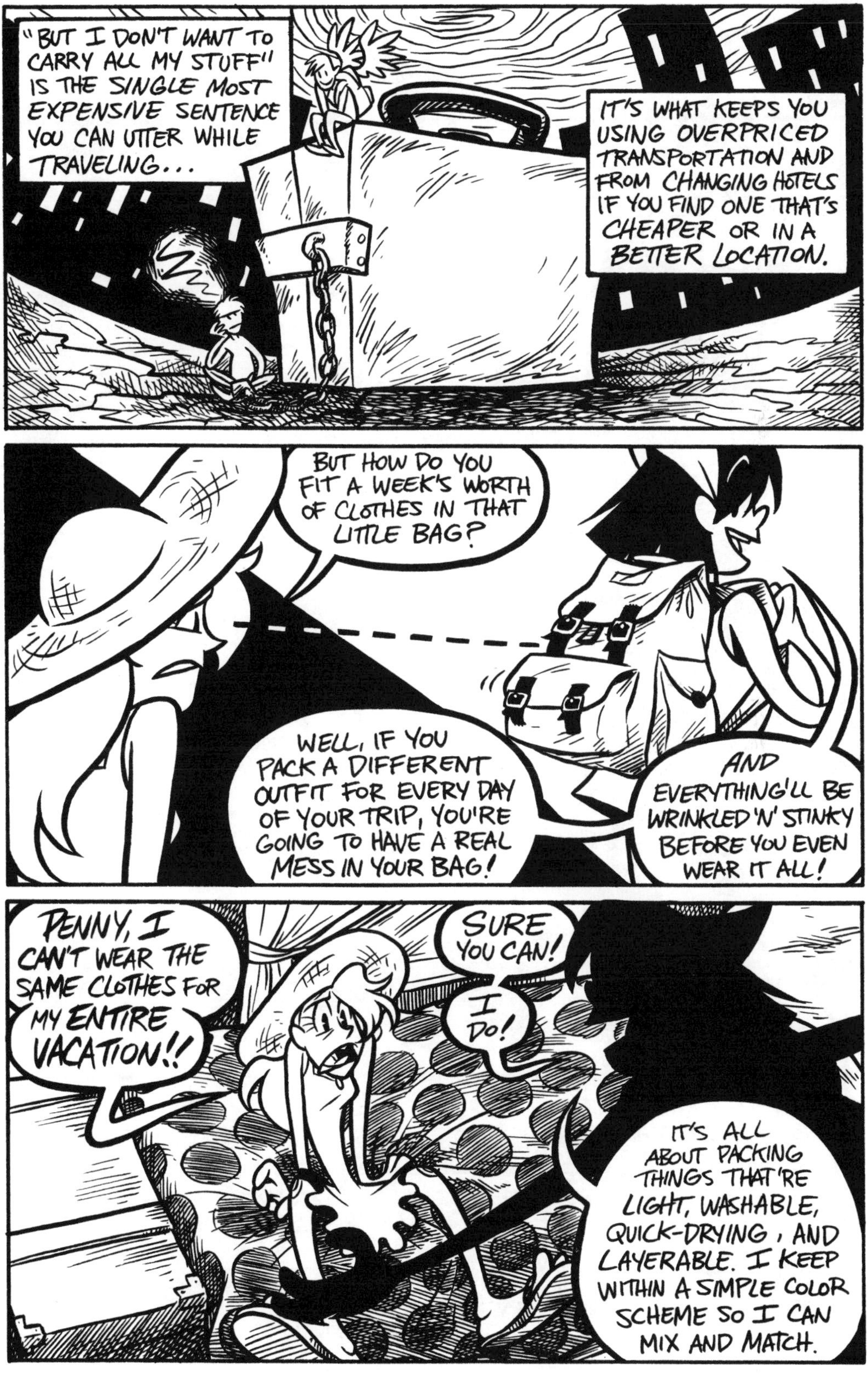
"BUT I DON'T WANT TO CARRY ALL MY STUFF" IS THE SINGLE MOST EXPENSIVE SENTENCE YOU CAN UTTER WHILE TRAVELING...
IT'S WHAT KEEPS YOU USING OVERPRICED TRANSPORTATION AND FROM CHANGING HOTELS IF YOU FIND ONE THAT'S CHEAPER OR IN A BETTER LOCATION.
BUT HOW DO YOU FIT A WEEK'S WORTH OF CLOTHES IN THAT LITTLE BAG?
WELL, IF YOU PACK A DIFFERENT OUTFIT FOR EVERY DAY OF YOUR TRIP, YOU'RE GOING TO HAVE A REAL MESS IN YOUR BAG!
AND EVERYTHING'LL BE WRINKLED 'N' STINKY BEFORE YOU EVEN WEAR IT ALL!
PENNY, I CAN'T WEAR THE SAME CLOTHES FOR MY ENTIRE VACATION!!
SURE YOU CAN!
I DO!
IT'S ALL ABOUT PACKING THINGS THAT'RE LIGHT, WASHABLE, QUICK-DRYING, AND LAYERABLE. I KEEP WITHIN A SIMPLE COLOR SCHEME SO I CAN MIX AND MATCH.

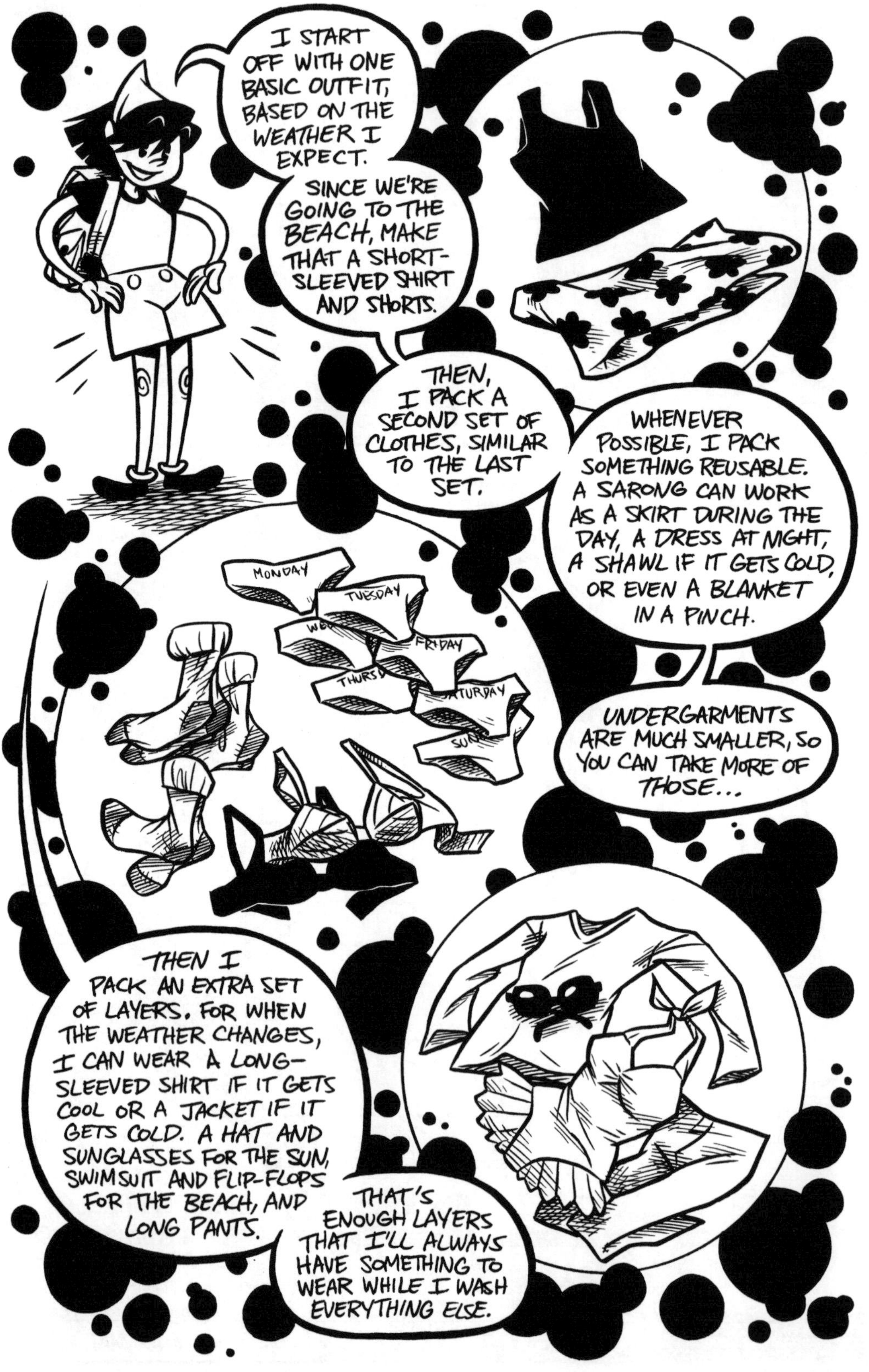
I START OFF WITH ONE BASIC OUTFIT, BASED ON THE WEATHER I EXPECT.
SINCE WE'RE GOING TO THE BEACH, MAKE THAT A SHORT-SLEEVED SHIRT AND SHORTS.
THEN, I PACK A SECOND SET OF CLOTHES, SIMILAR TO THE LAST SET.
WHENEVER POSSIBLE, I PACK SOMETHING REUSABLE. A SARONG CAN WORK AS A SKIRT DURING THE DAY, A DRESS AT NIGHT, A SHAWL IF IT GETS COLD, OR EVEN A BLANKET IN A PINCH.
MONDAY
TUESDAY
FRIDAY
UNDERGARMENTS ARE MUCH SMALLER, SO YOU CAN TAKE MORE OF THOSE...
THEN I PACK AN EXTRA SET OF LAYERS. FOR WHEN THE WEATHER CHANGES, I CAN WEAR A LONG-SLEEVED SHIRT IF IT GETS COOL OR A JACKET IF IT GETS COLD. A HAT AND SUNGLASSES FOR THE SUN, SWIMSUIT AND FLIP-FLOPS FOR THE BEACH, AND LONG PANTS.
THAT'S ENOUGH LAYERS THAT I'LL ALWAYS HAVE SOMETHING TO WEAR WHILE I WASH EVERYTHING ELSE.

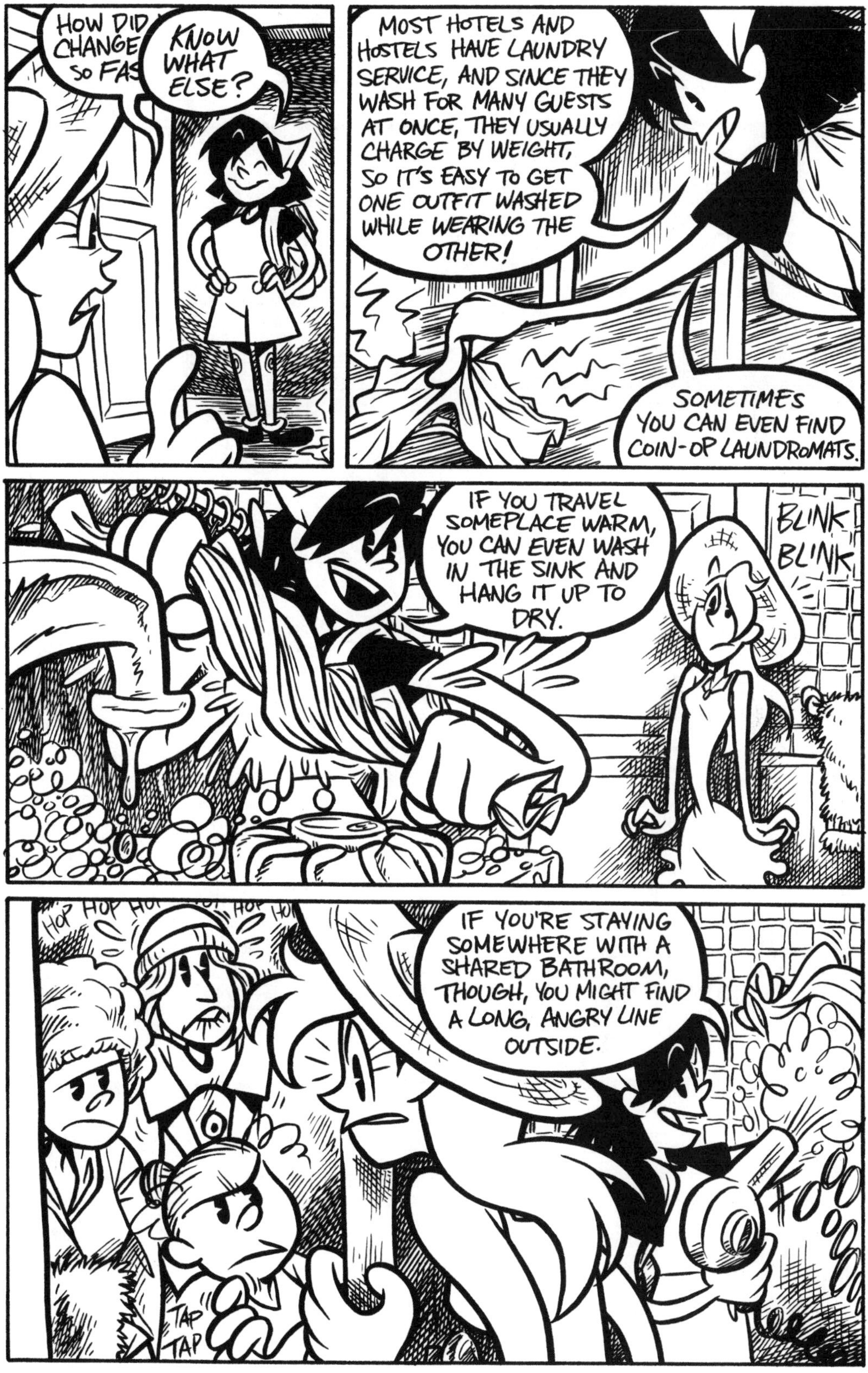
HOW DID
CHANGE
SO FAS
KNOW WHAT ELSE?
MOST HOTELS AND HOSTELS HAVE LAUNDRY SERVICE, AND SINCE THEY WASH FOR MANY GUESTS AT ONCE, THEY USUALLY CHARGE BY WEIGHT, SO IT'S EASY TO GET ONE OUTFIT WASHED WHILE WEARING THE OTHER!
SOMETIMES YOU CAN EVEN FIND COIN-OP LAUNDROMATS.
IF YOU TRAVEL SOMEPLACE WARM, YOU CAN EVEN WASH IN THE SINK AND HANG IT UP TO DRY.
BLINK BLINK
HOP HOP
IF YOU'RE STAYING SOMEWHERE WITH A SHARED BATHROOM, THOUGH, YOU MIGHT FIND A LONG, ANGRY LINE OUTSIDE.
TAP TAP

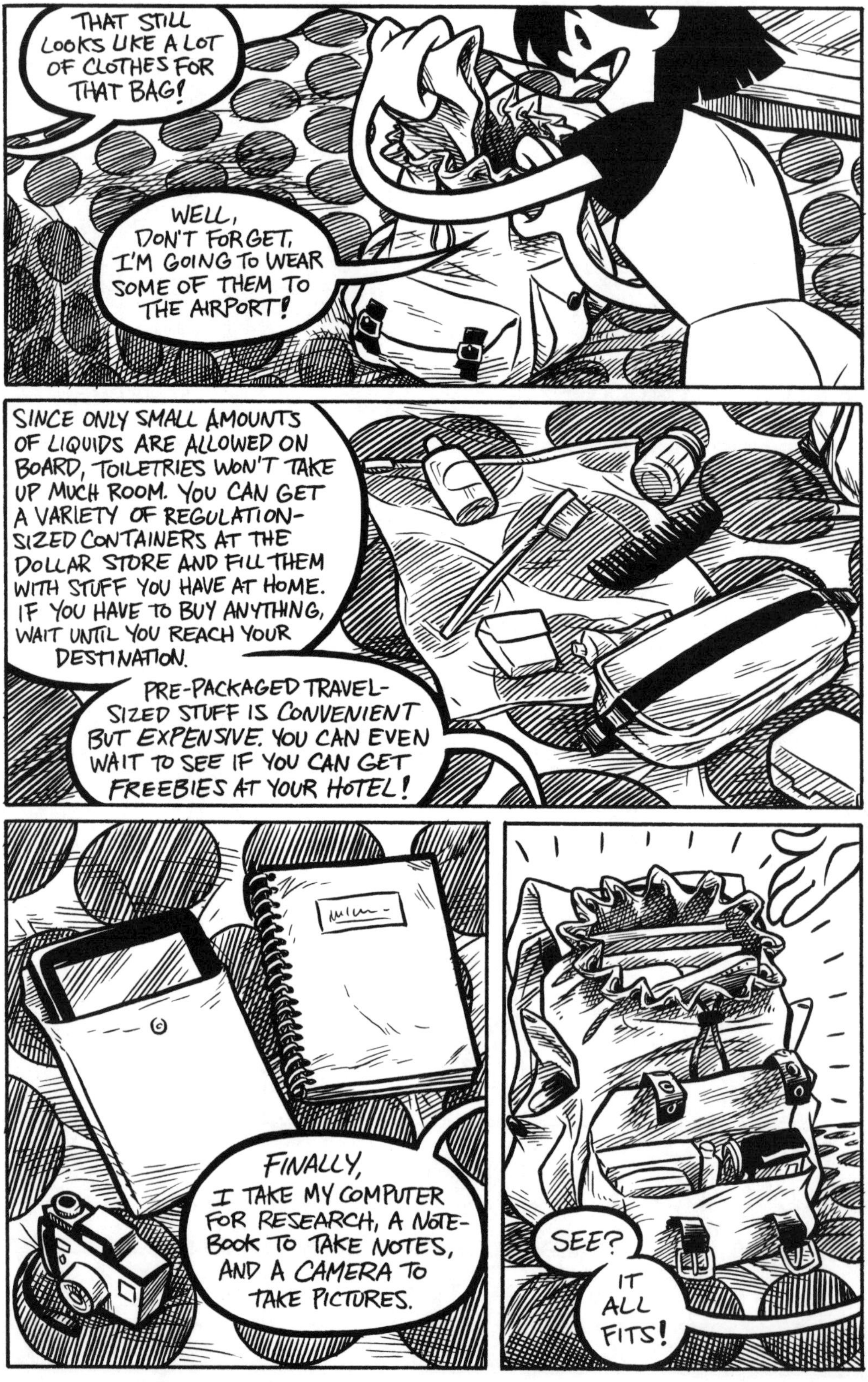
THAT STILL LOOKS LIKE A LOT OF CLOTHES FOR THAT BAG!
WELL, DON'T FORGET, I'M GOING TO WEAR SOME OF THEM TO THE AIRPORT!
SINCE ONLY SMALL AMOUNTS OF LIQUIDS ARE ALLOWED ON BOARD, TOILETRIES WON'T TAKE UP MUCH ROOM. YOU CAN GET A VARIETY OF REGULATION-SIZED CONTAINERS AT THE DOLLAR STORE AND FILL THEM WITH STUFF YOU HAVE AT HOME. IF YOU HAVE TO BUY ANYTHING, WAIT UNTIL YOU REACH YOUR DESTINATION.
PRE-PACKAGED TRAVEL-SIZED STUFF IS CONVENIENT BUT *EXPENSIVE*. YOU CAN EVEN WAIT TO SEE IF YOU CAN GET FREEBIES AT YOUR HOTEL!
FINALLY, I TAKE MY COMPUTER FOR RESEARCH, A NOTEBOOK TO TAKE NOTES, AND A *CAMERA* TO TAKE PICTURES.
SEE?
IT ALL FITS!

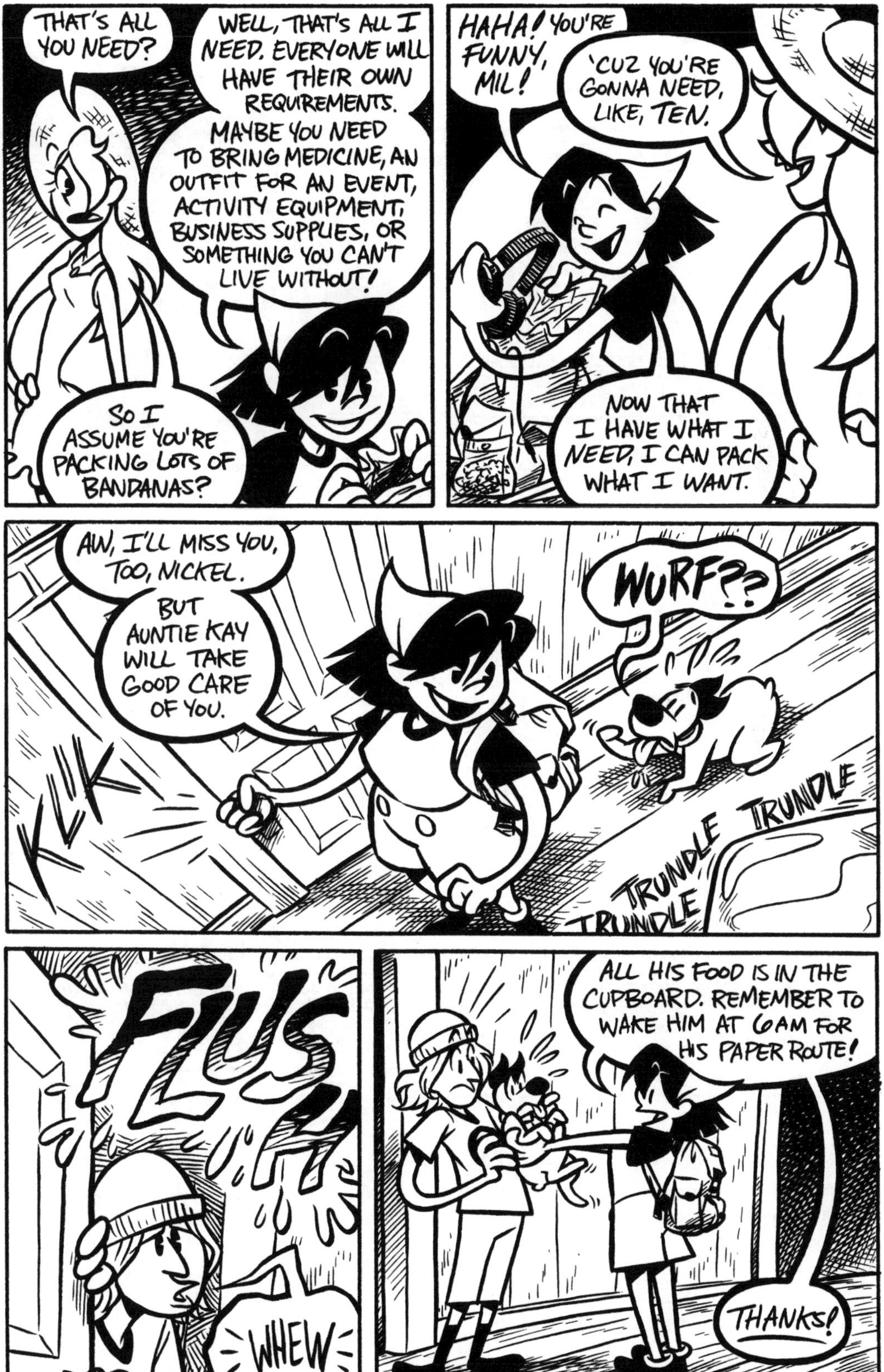
THAT'S ALL YOU NEED?
WELL, THAT'S ALL I NEED. EVERYONE WILL HAVE THEIR OWN REQUIREMENTS.
MAYBE YOU NEED TO BRING MEDICINE, AN OUTFIT FOR AN EVENT, ACTIVITY EQUIPMENT, BUSINESS SUPPLIES, OR SOMETHING YOU CAN'T LIVE WITHOUT!
SO I ASSUME YOU'RE PACKING LOTS OF BANDANAS?
HAHA! YOU'RE FUNNY, MIL!
'CUZ YOU'RE GONNA NEED, LIKE, TEN.
NOW THAT I HAVE WHAT I NEED, I CAN PACK WHAT I WANT.
AW, I'LL MISS YOU, TOO, NICKEL.
BUT AUNTIE KAY WILL TAKE GOOD CARE OF YOU.
WURF??
KLIK
TRUNDLE TRUNDLE
TRUNDLE TRUNDLE
FLUSH
WHEW
ALL HIS FOOD IS IN THE CUPBOARD. REMEMBER TO WAKE HIM AT 6AM FOR HIS PAPER ROUTE!
THANKS!

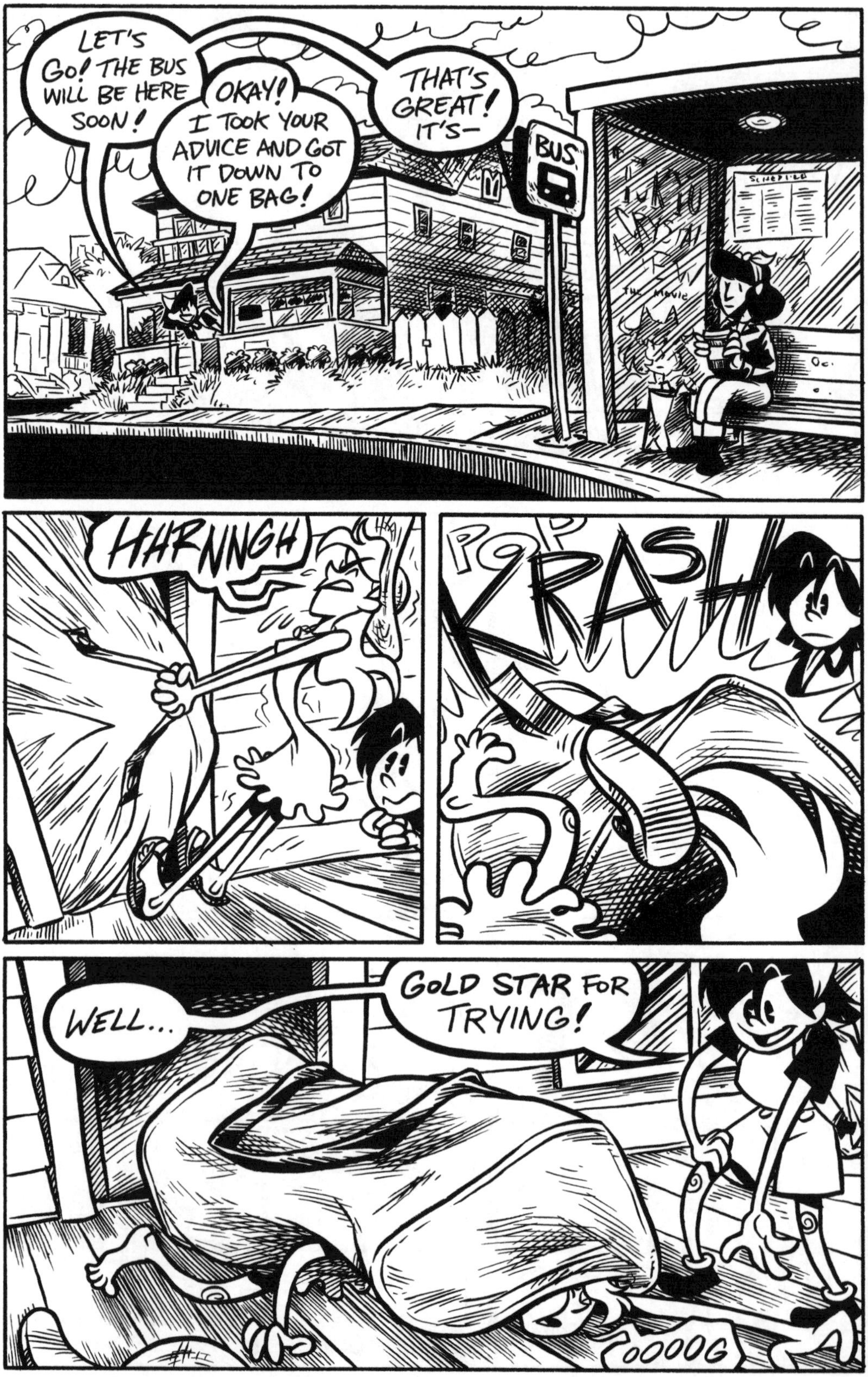
LET'S GO! THE BUS WILL BE HERE SOON!
OKAY! I TOOK YOUR ADVICE AND GOT IT DOWN TO ONE BAG!
THAT'S GREAT! IT'S—
BUS
HHRNNGH
POP
KRASH
WELL...
GOLD STAR FOR TRYING!
OOOOG

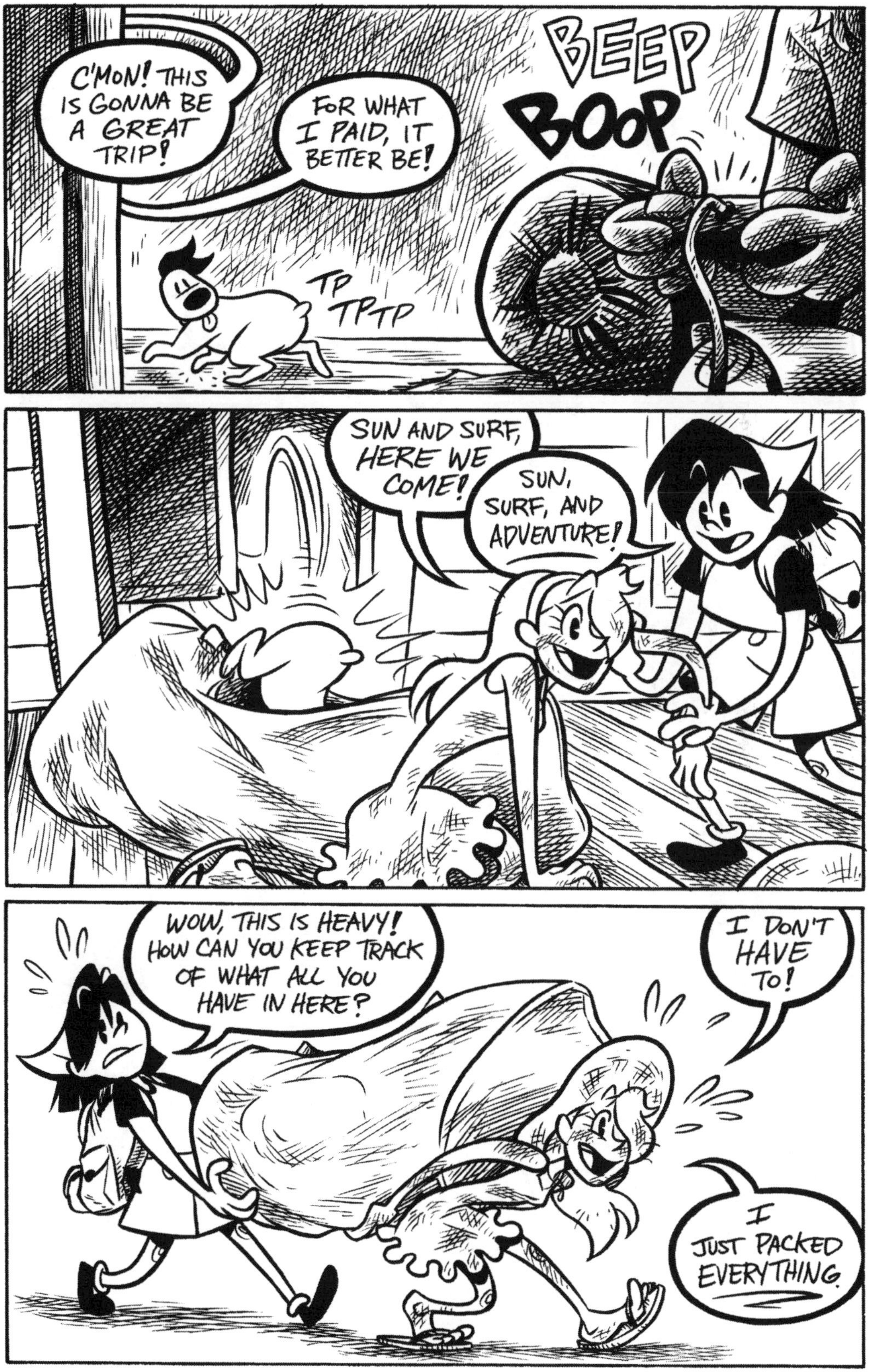
C'MON! THIS IS GONNA BE A GREAT TRIP!
FOR WHAT I PAID, IT BETTER BE!
BEEP
BOOP
TP TP TP
SUN AND SURF, HERE WE COME!
SUN, SURF, AND ADVENTURE!
WOW, THIS IS HEAVY! HOW CAN YOU KEEP TRACK OF WHAT ALL YOU HAVE IN HERE?
I DON'T HAVE TO!
I JUST PACKED EVERYTHING.

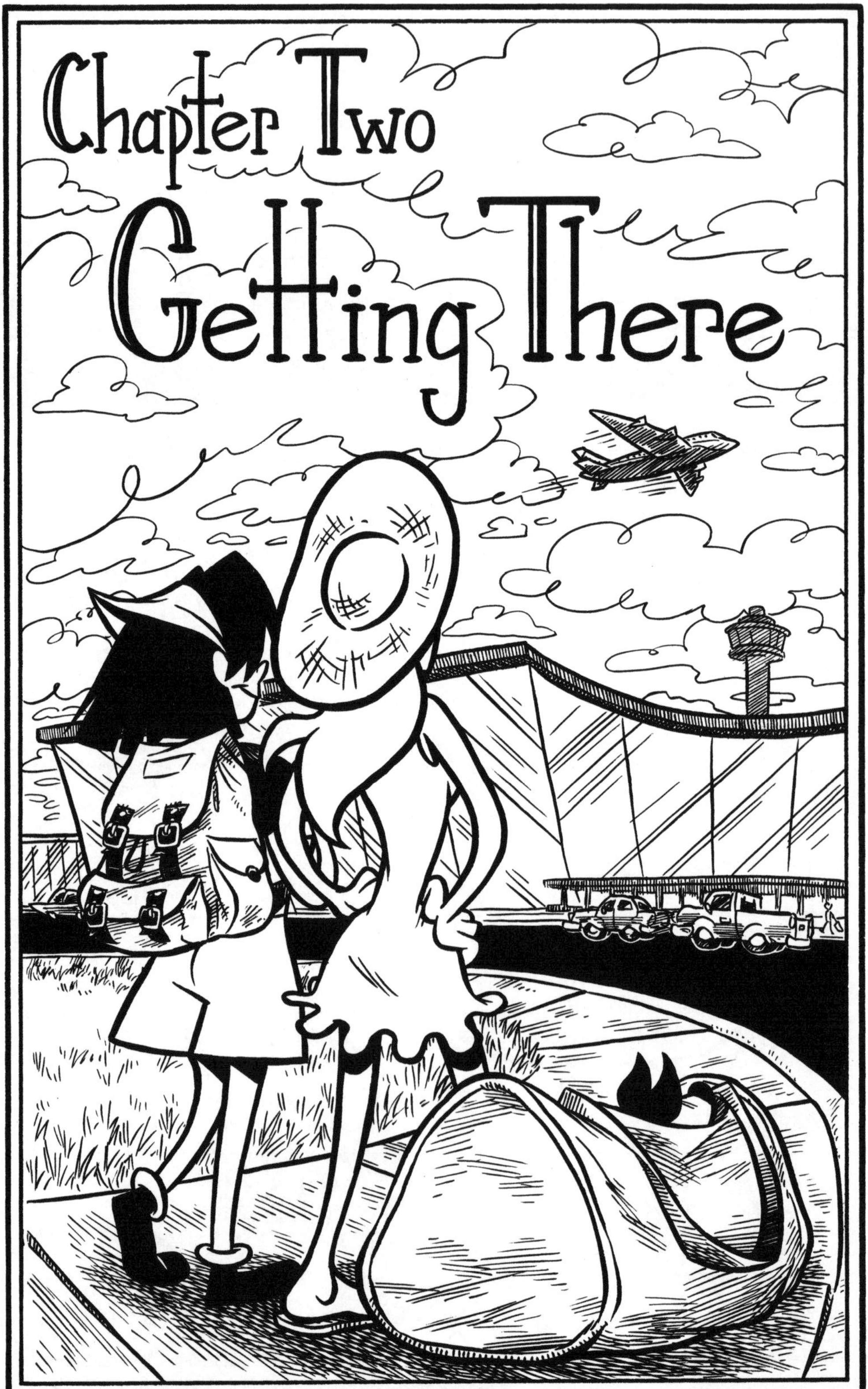

Chapter Two
Getting There

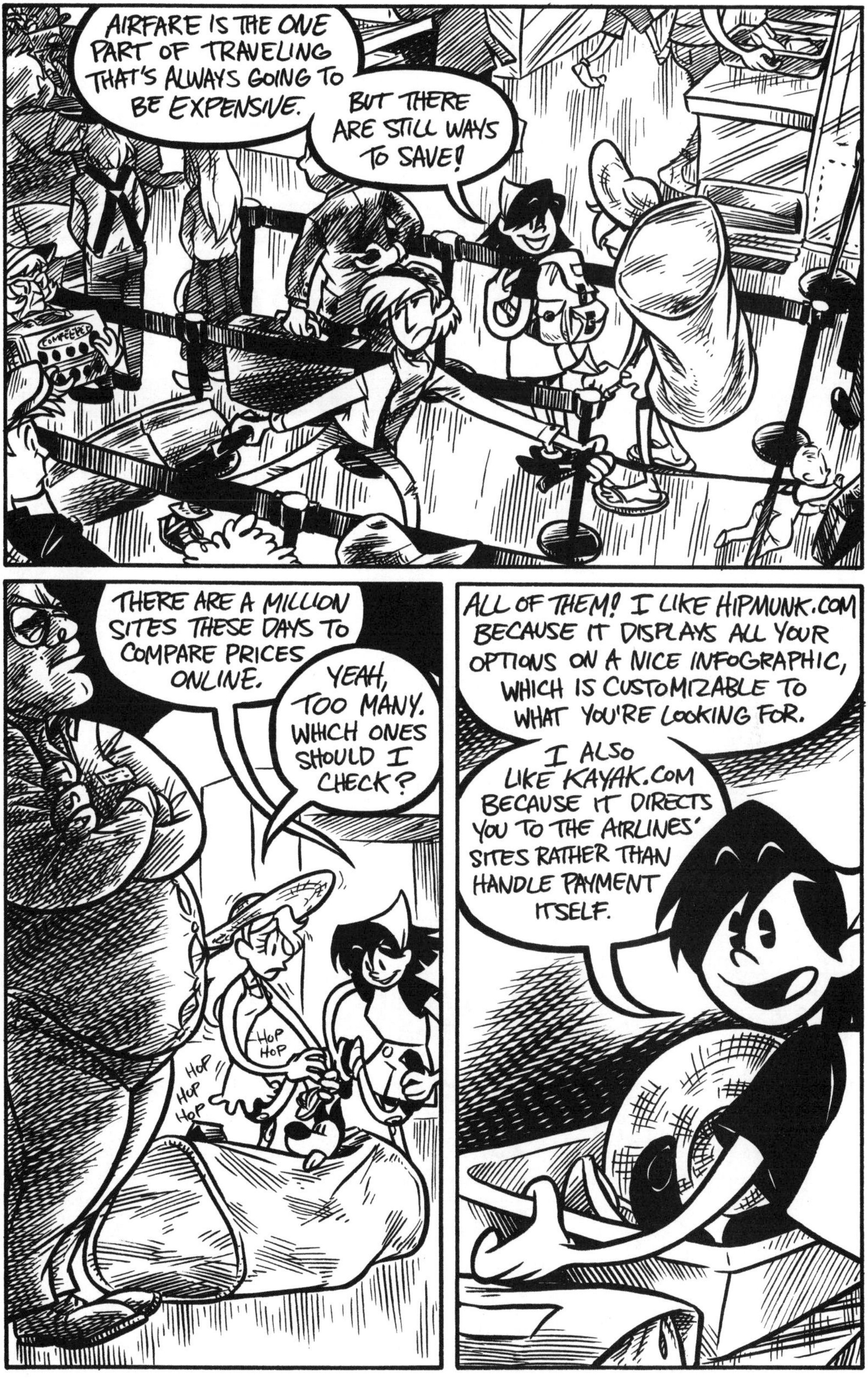
AIRFARE IS THE ONE PART OF TRAVELING THAT'S ALWAYS GOING TO BE EXPENSIVE.
BUT THERE ARE STILL WAYS TO SAVE!
THERE ARE A MILLION SITES THESE DAYS TO COMPARE PRICES ONLINE.
YEAH, TOO MANY. WHICH ONES SHOULD I CHECK?
HOP HOP
HOP HOP HOP
ALL OF THEM! I LIKE HIPMUNK.COM BECAUSE IT DISPLAYS ALL YOUR OPTIONS ON A NICE INFOGRAPHIC, WHICH IS CUSTOMIZABLE TO WHAT YOU'RE LOOKING FOR.
I ALSO LIKE KAYAK.COM BECAUSE IT DIRECTS YOU TO THE AIRLINES' SITES RATHER THAN HANDLE PAYMENT ITSELF.

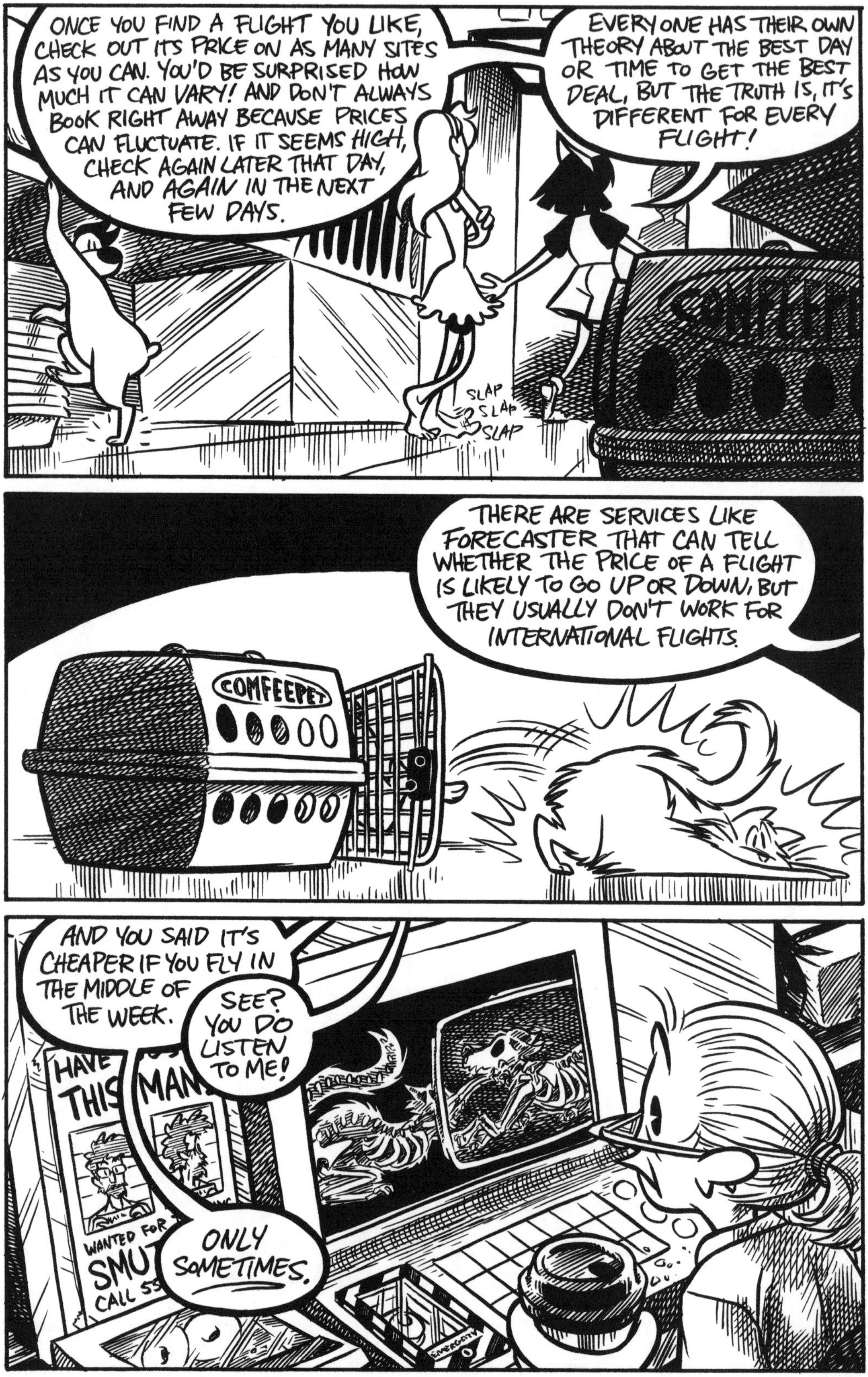
ONCE YOU FIND A FLIGHT YOU LIKE, CHECK OUT ITS PRICE ON AS MANY SITES AS YOU CAN. YOU'D BE SURPRISED HOW MUCH IT CAN VARY! AND DON'T ALWAYS BOOK RIGHT AWAY BECAUSE PRICES CAN FLUCTUATE. IF IT SEEMS HIGH, CHECK AGAIN LATER THAT DAY, AND AGAIN IN THE NEXT FEW DAYS.
EVERYONE HAS THEIR OWN THEORY ABOUT THE BEST DAY OR TIME TO GET THE BEST DEAL, BUT THE TRUTH IS, IT'S DIFFERENT FOR EVERY FLIGHT!
SLAP SLAP SLAP
THERE ARE SERVICES LIKE FORECASTER THAT CAN TELL WHETHER THE PRICE OF A FLIGHT IS LIKELY TO GO UP OR DOWN, BUT THEY USUALLY DON'T WORK FOR INTERNATIONAL FLIGHTS.
COMFEEPET
AND YOU SAID IT'S CHEAPER IF YOU FLY IN THE MIDDLE OF THE WEEK.
SEE? YOU DO LISTEN TO ME!
ONLY SOMETIMES.
WANTED FOR
SMU
CALL 55

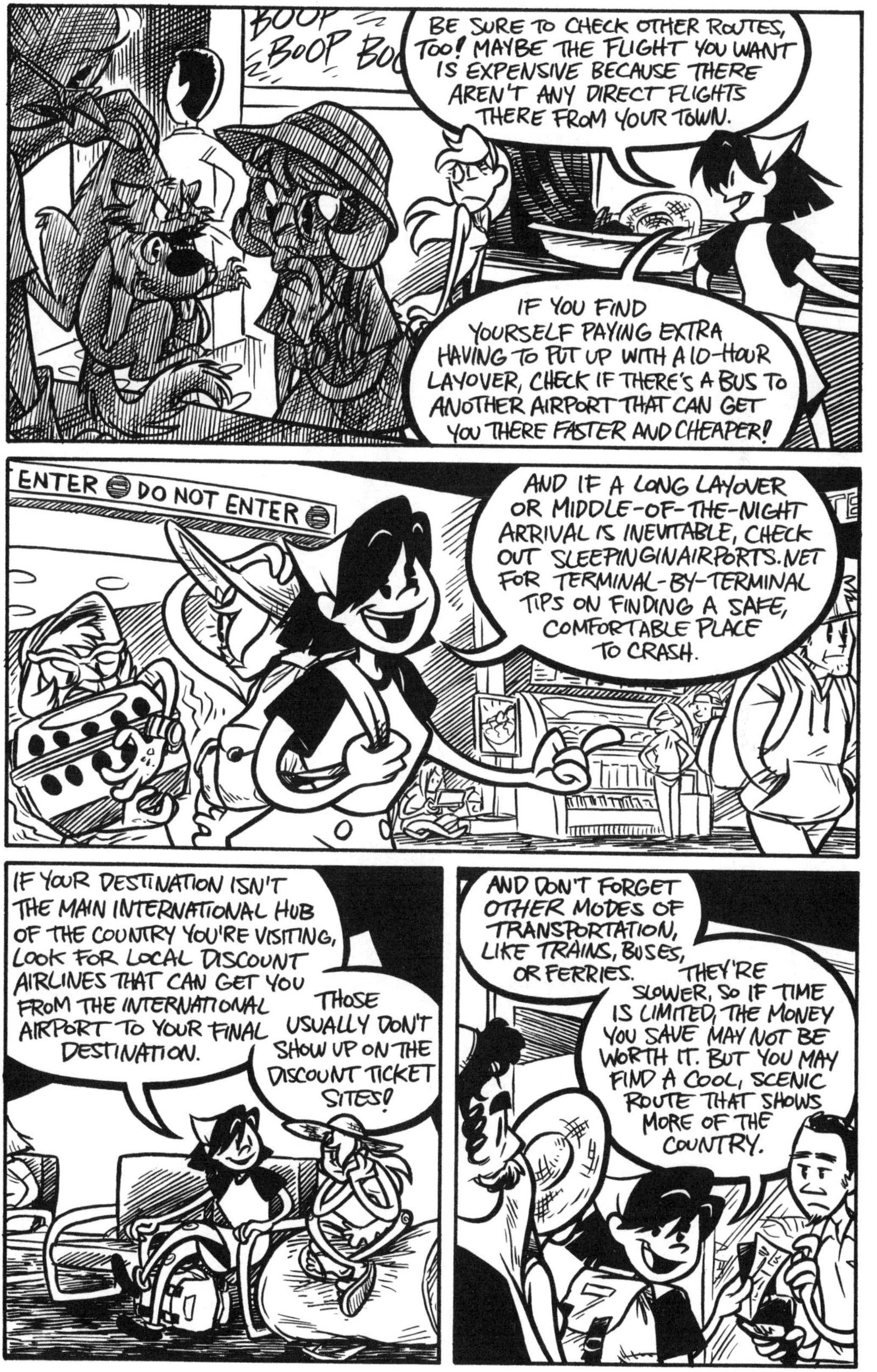
BOOP BOOP BOO
BE SURE TO CHECK OTHER ROUTES, TOO! MAYBE THE FLIGHT YOU WANT IS EXPENSIVE BECAUSE THERE AREN'T ANY DIRECT FLIGHTS THERE FROM YOUR TOWN.
IF YOU FIND YOURSELF PAYING EXTRA HAVING TO PUT UP WITH A 10-HOUR LAYOVER, CHECK IF THERE'S A BUS TO ANOTHER AIRPORT THAT CAN GET YOU THERE FASTER AND CHEAPER!
ENTER DO NOT ENTER
AND IF A LONG LAYOVER OR MIDDLE-OF-THE-NIGHT ARRIVAL IS INEVITABLE, CHECK OUT SLEEPINGINAIRPORTS.NET FOR TERMINAL-BY-TERMINAL TIPS ON FINDING A SAFE, COMFORTABLE PLACE TO CRASH.
IF YOUR DESTINATION ISN'T THE MAIN INTERNATIONAL HUB OF THE COUNTRY YOU'RE VISITING, LOOK FOR LOCAL DISCOUNT AIRLINES THAT CAN GET YOU FROM THE INTERNATIONAL AIRPORT TO YOUR FINAL DESTINATION.
THOSE USUALLY DON'T SHOW UP ON THE DISCOUNT TICKET SITES!
AND DON'T FORGET OTHER MODES OF TRANSPORTATION, LIKE TRAINS, BUSES, OR FERRIES.
THEY'RE SLOWER, SO IF TIME IS LIMITED, THE MONEY YOU SAVE MAY NOT BE WORTH IT. BUT YOU MAY FIND A COOL, SCENIC ROUTE THAT SHOWS MORE OF THE COUNTRY.

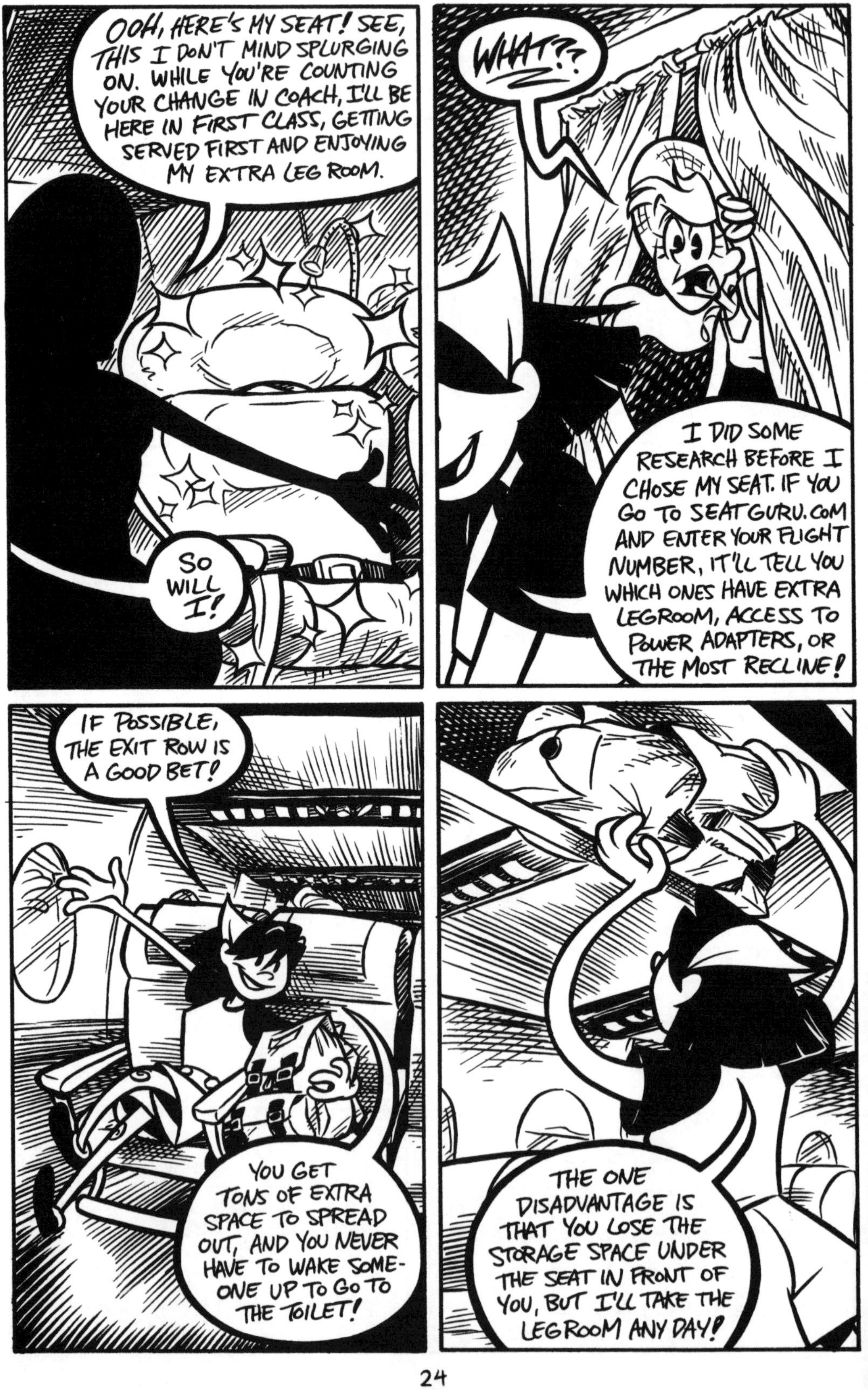
OOH, HERE'S MY SEAT! SEE, THIS I DON'T MIND SPLURGING ON. WHILE YOU'RE COUNTING YOUR CHANGE IN COACH, I'LL BE HERE IN FIRST CLASS, GETTING SERVED FIRST AND ENJOYING MY EXTRA LEG ROOM.
SO WILL I!
WHAT??
I DID SOME RESEARCH BEFORE I CHOSE MY SEAT. IF YOU GO TO SEATGURU.COM AND ENTER YOUR FLIGHT NUMBER, IT'LL TELL YOU WHICH ONES HAVE EXTRA LEGROOM, ACCESS TO POWER ADAPTERS, OR THE MOST RECLINE!
IF POSSIBLE, THE EXIT ROW IS A GOOD BET!
YOU GET TONS OF EXTRA SPACE TO SPREAD OUT, AND YOU NEVER HAVE TO WAKE SOME-ONE UP TO GO TO THE TOILET!
THE ONE DISADVANTAGE IS THAT YOU LOSE THE STORAGE SPACE UNDER THE SEAT IN FRONT OF YOU, BUT I'LL TAKE THE LEGROOM ANY DAY!

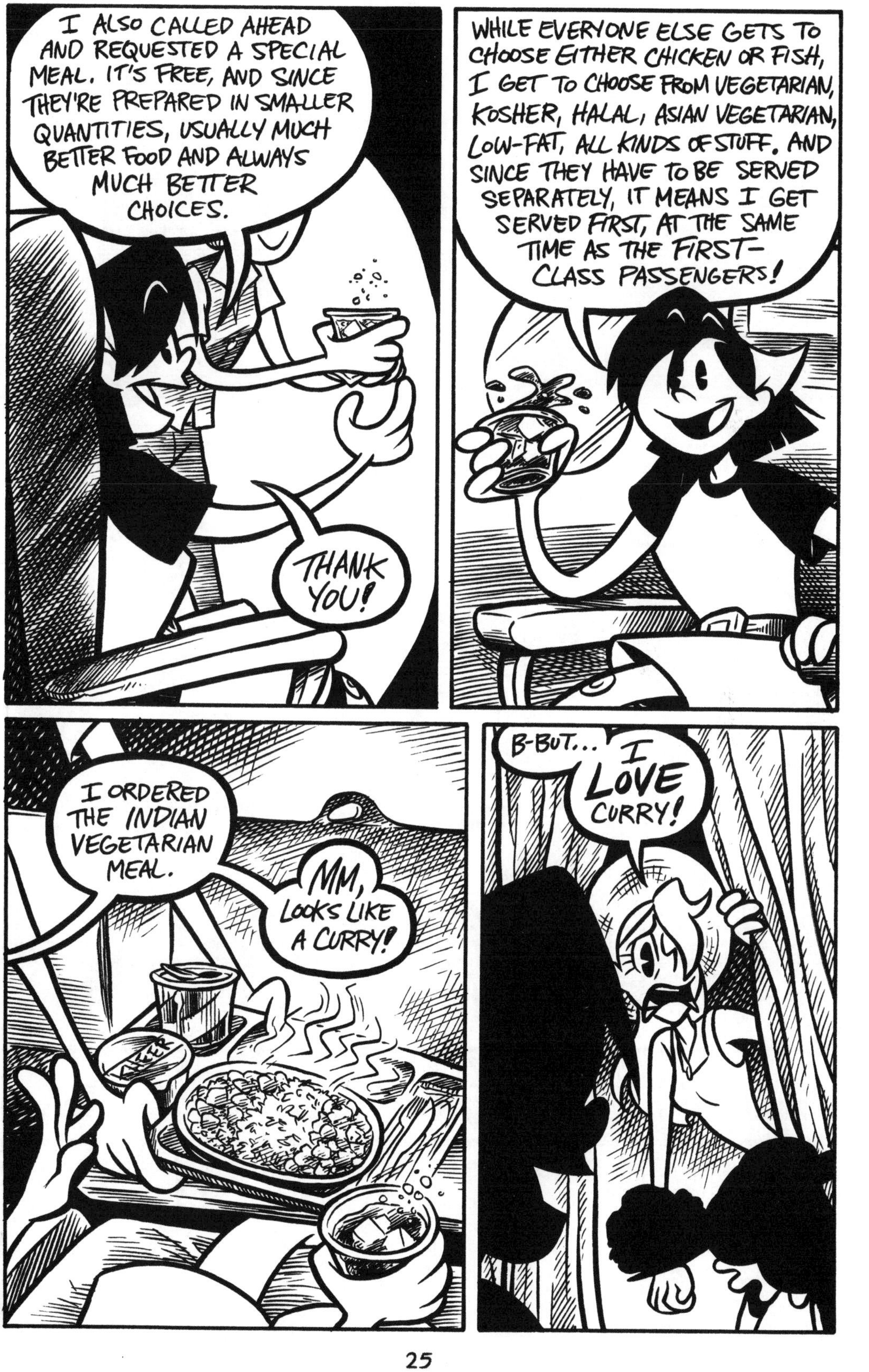
I ALSO CALLED AHEAD AND REQUESTED A SPECIAL MEAL. IT'S FREE, AND SINCE THEY'RE PREPARED IN SMALLER QUANTITIES, USUALLY MUCH BETTER FOOD AND ALWAYS MUCH BETTER CHOICES.
THANK YOU!
WHILE EVERYONE ELSE GETS TO CHOOSE EITHER CHICKEN OR FISH, I GET TO CHOOSE FROM VEGETARIAN, KOSHER, HALAL, ASIAN VEGETARIAN, LOW-FAT, ALL KINDS OF STUFF. AND SINCE THEY HAVE TO BE SERVED SEPARATELY, IT MEANS I GET SERVED FIRST, AT THE SAME TIME AS THE FIRST-CLASS PASSENGERS!
I ORDERED THE INDIAN VEGETARIAN MEAL.
MM, LOOKS LIKE A CURRY!
B-BUT...
I LOVE CURRY!

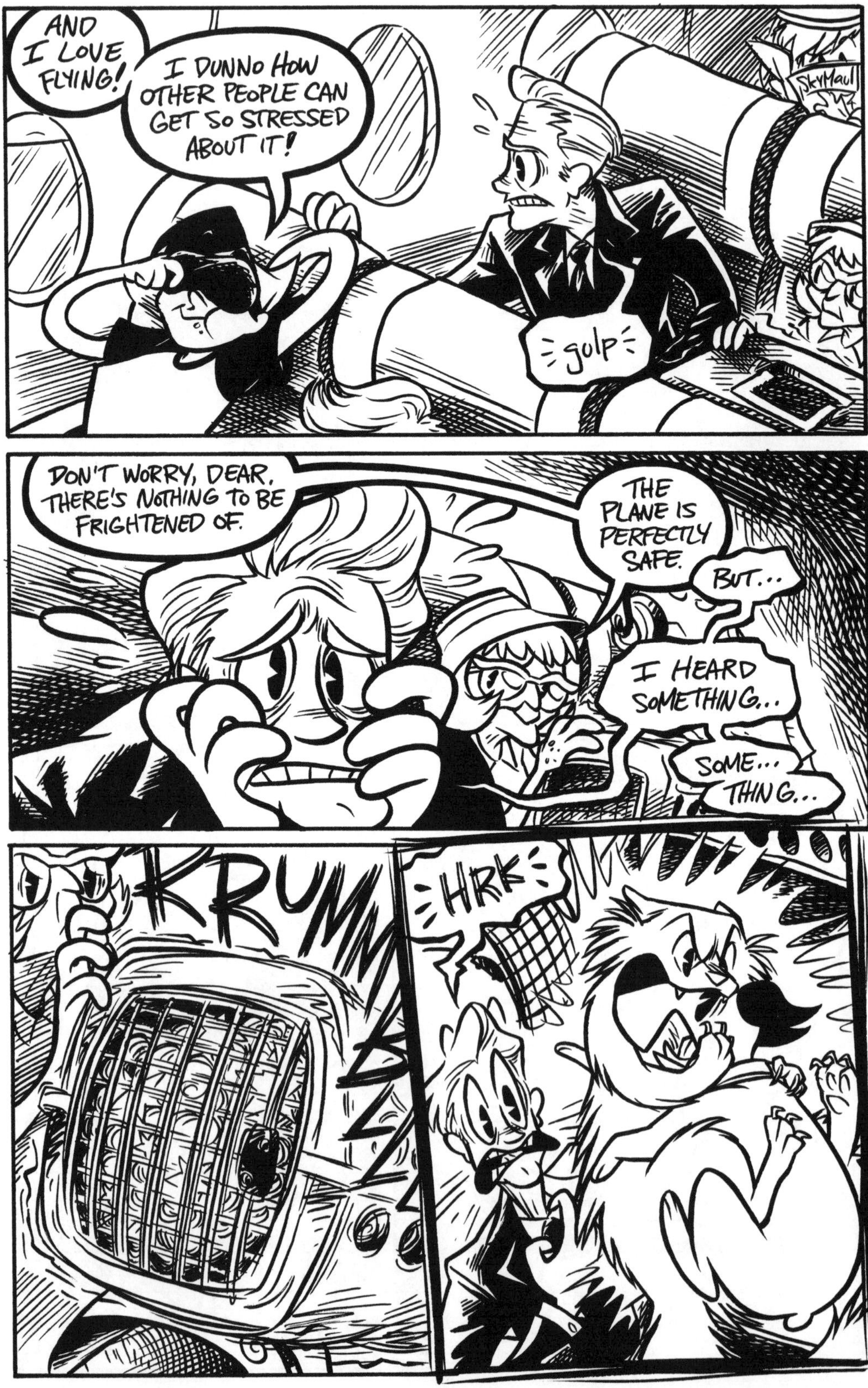
AND I LOVE FLYING!
I DUNNO HOW OTHER PEOPLE CAN GET SO STRESSED ABOUT IT!
SkyMaul
gulp
DON'T WORRY, DEAR. THERE'S NOTHING TO BE FRIGHTENED OF.
THE PLANE IS PERFECTLY SAFE.
BUT...
I HEARD SOMETHING...
SOME... THING...
KRUMM
HRK

Chapter Three

Arrival

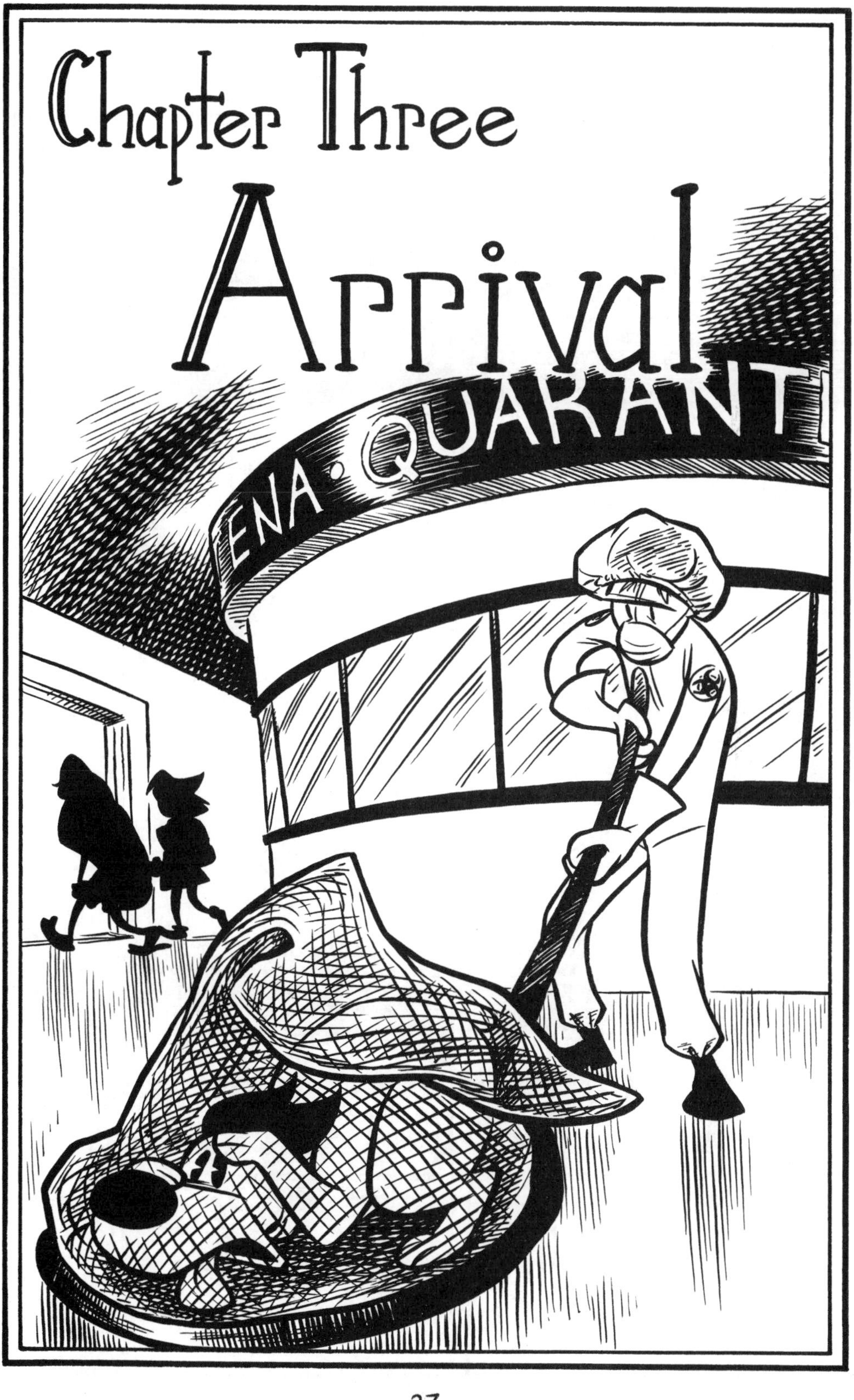
ENA · QUARANTI

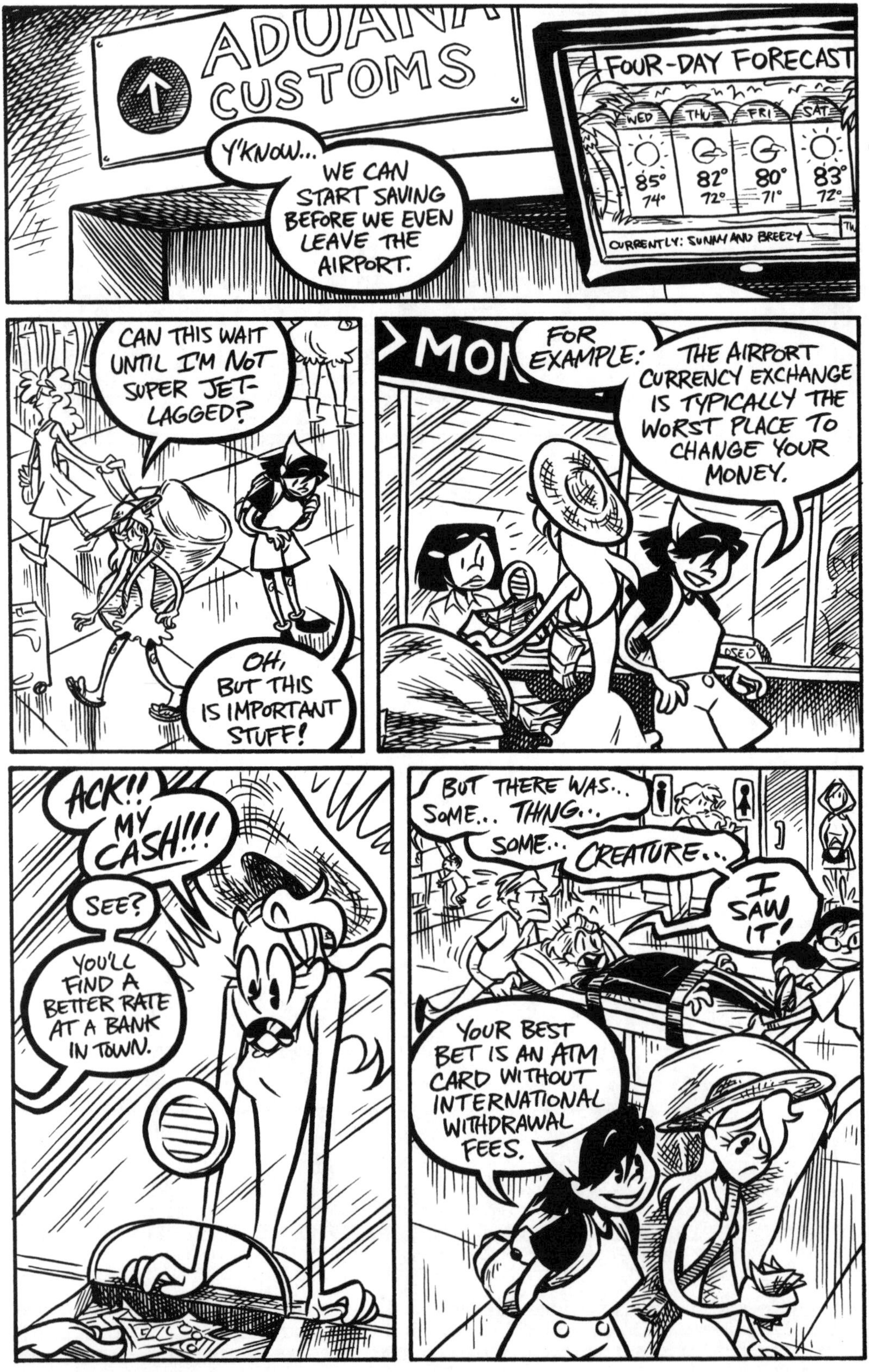
ADUANA
CUSTOMS
FOUR-DAY FORECAST
WED THU FRI SAT
85° 74° 82° 72° 80° 71° 83° 72°
CURRENTLY: SUNNY AND BREEZY
Y'KNOW...
WE CAN START SAVING BEFORE WE EVEN LEAVE THE AIRPORT.
CAN THIS WAIT UNTIL I'M NOT SUPER JET-LAGGED?
OH, BUT THIS IS IMPORTANT STUFF!
FOR EXAMPLE:
THE AIRPORT CURRENCY EXCHANGE IS TYPICALLY THE WORST PLACE TO CHANGE YOUR MONEY.
ACK!! MY CASH!!!
SEE?
YOU'LL FIND A BETTER RATE AT A BANK IN TOWN.
BUT THERE WAS... SOME... THING...
SOME... CREATURE...
I SAW IT!
YOUR BEST BET IS AN ATM CARD WITHOUT INTERNATIONAL WITHDRAWAL FEES.

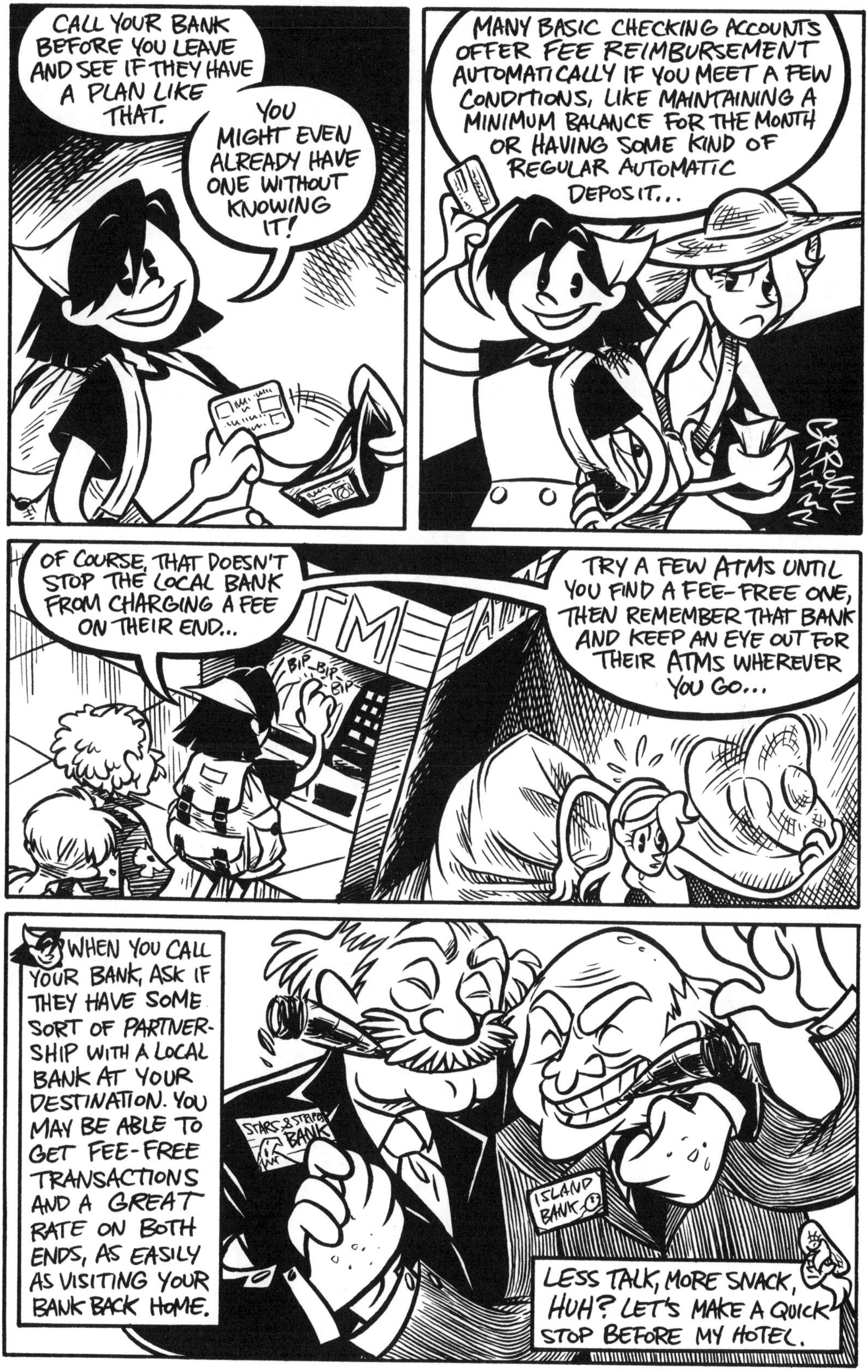
CALL YOUR BANK BEFORE YOU LEAVE AND SEE IF THEY HAVE A PLAN LIKE THAT.
YOU MIGHT EVEN ALREADY HAVE ONE WITHOUT KNOWING IT!
MANY BASIC CHECKING ACCOUNTS OFFER FEE REIMBURSEMENT AUTOMATICALLY IF YOU MEET A FEW CONDITIONS, LIKE MAINTAINING A MINIMUM BALANCE FOR THE MONTH OR HAVING SOME KIND OF REGULAR AUTOMATIC DEPOSIT...
GRROWL
OF COURSE, THAT DOESN'T STOP THE LOCAL BANK FROM CHARGING A FEE ON THEIR END...
BIP BIP BIP
TRY A FEW ATMS UNTIL YOU FIND A FEE-FREE ONE, THEN REMEMBER THAT BANK AND KEEP AN EYE OUT FOR THEIR ATMS WHEREVER YOU GO...
WHEN YOU CALL YOUR BANK, ASK IF THEY HAVE SOME SORT OF PARTNERSHIP WITH A LOCAL BANK AT YOUR DESTINATION. YOU MAY BE ABLE TO GET FEE-FREE TRANSACTIONS AND A GREAT RATE ON BOTH ENDS, AS EASILY AS VISITING YOUR BANK BACK HOME.
STARS & STRIPES BANK
ISLAND BANK
LESS TALK, MORE SNACK, HUH? LET'S MAKE A QUICK STOP BEFORE MY HOTEL.

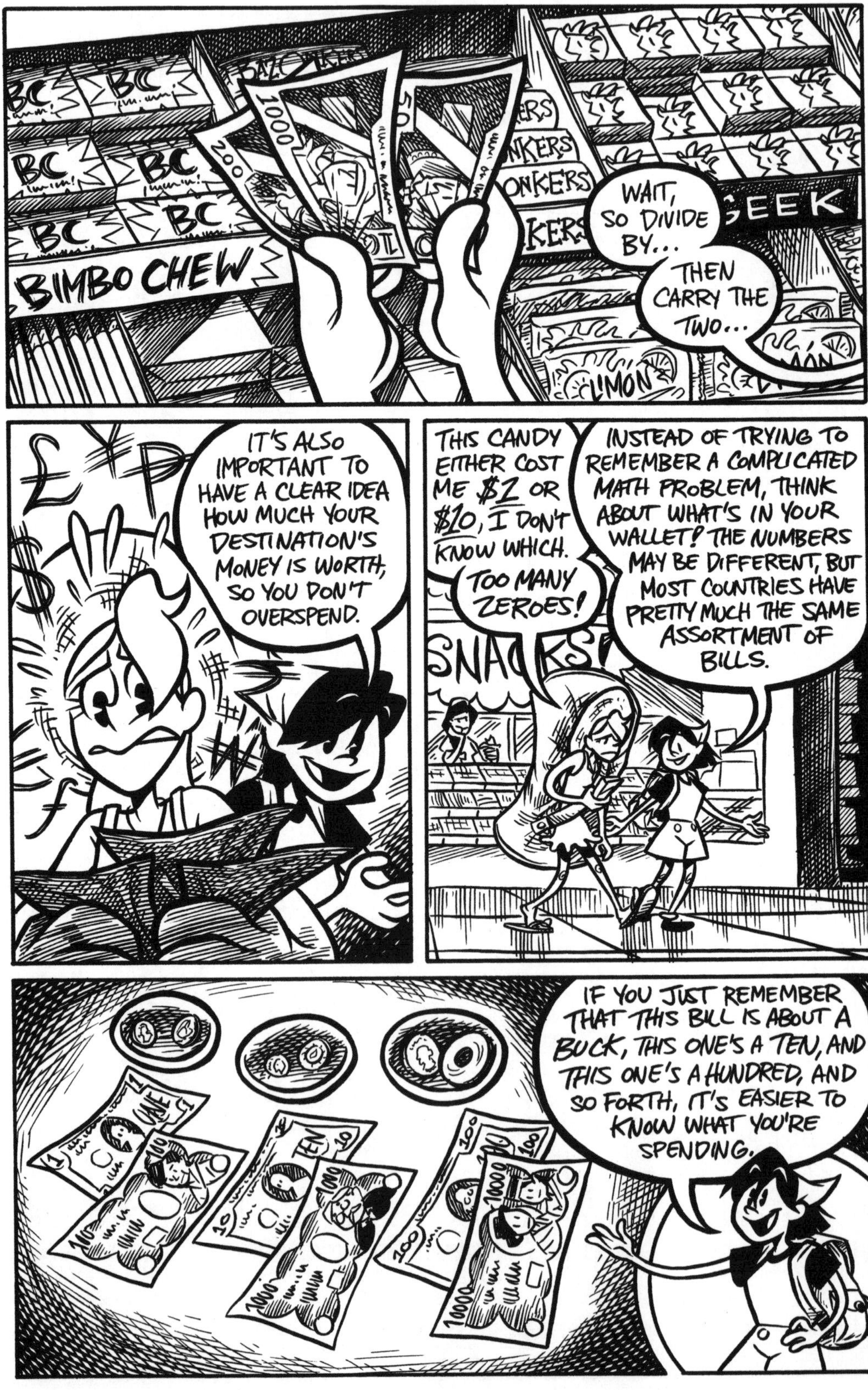
BC
BIMBO CHEW
BAZONKERS
GEEK
LIMON
WAIT, SO DIVIDE BY...
THEN CARRY THE TWO...
IT'S ALSO IMPORTANT TO HAVE A CLEAR IDEA HOW MUCH YOUR DESTINATION'S MONEY IS WORTH, SO YOU DON'T OVERSPEND.
THIS CANDY EITHER COST ME $2 OR $10, I DON'T KNOW WHICH.
TOO MANY ZEROES!
INSTEAD OF TRYING TO REMEMBER A COMPLICATED MATH PROBLEM, THINK ABOUT WHAT'S IN YOUR WALLET! THE NUMBERS MAY BE DIFFERENT, BUT MOST COUNTRIES HAVE PRETTY MUCH THE SAME ASSORTMENT OF BILLS.
SNACKS
ONE
TEN
IF YOU JUST REMEMBER THAT THIS BILL IS ABOUT A BUCK, THIS ONE'S A TEN, AND THIS ONE'S A HUNDRED, AND SO FORTH, IT'S EASIER TO KNOW WHAT YOU'RE SPENDING.

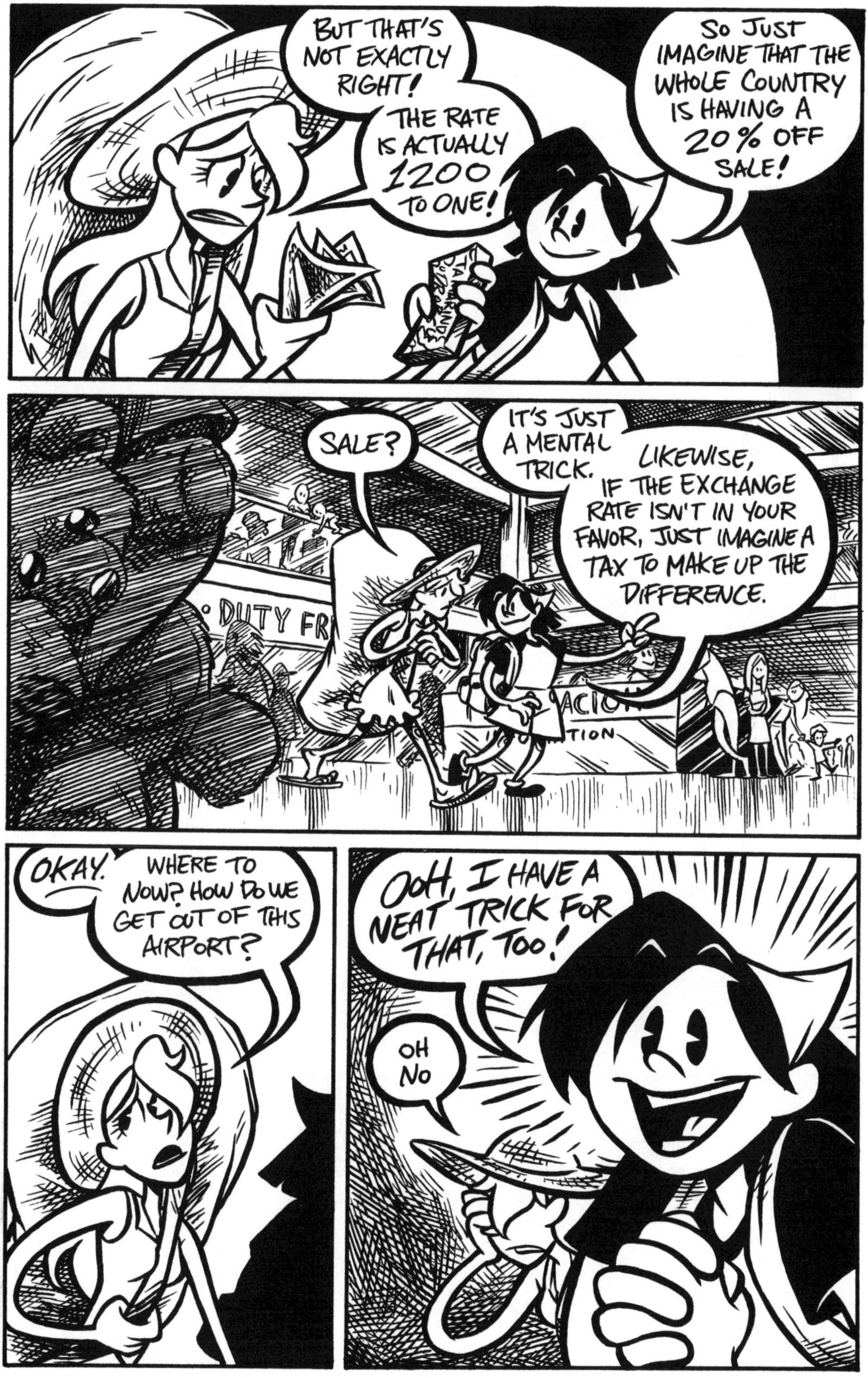
BUT THAT'S NOT EXACTLY RIGHT!
THE RATE IS ACTUALLY 1200 TO ONE!
SO JUST IMAGINE THAT THE WHOLE COUNTRY IS HAVING A 20% OFF SALE!
SALE?
IT'S JUST A MENTAL TRICK.
LIKEWISE, IF THE EXCHANGE RATE ISN'T IN YOUR FAVOR, JUST IMAGINE A TAX TO MAKE UP THE DIFFERENCE.
DUTY FR
ACION
TION
OKAY.
WHERE TO NOW? HOW DO WE GET OUT OF THIS AIRPORT?
OOH, I HAVE A NEAT TRICK FOR THAT, TOO!
OH NO

Chapter Four
Getting Around

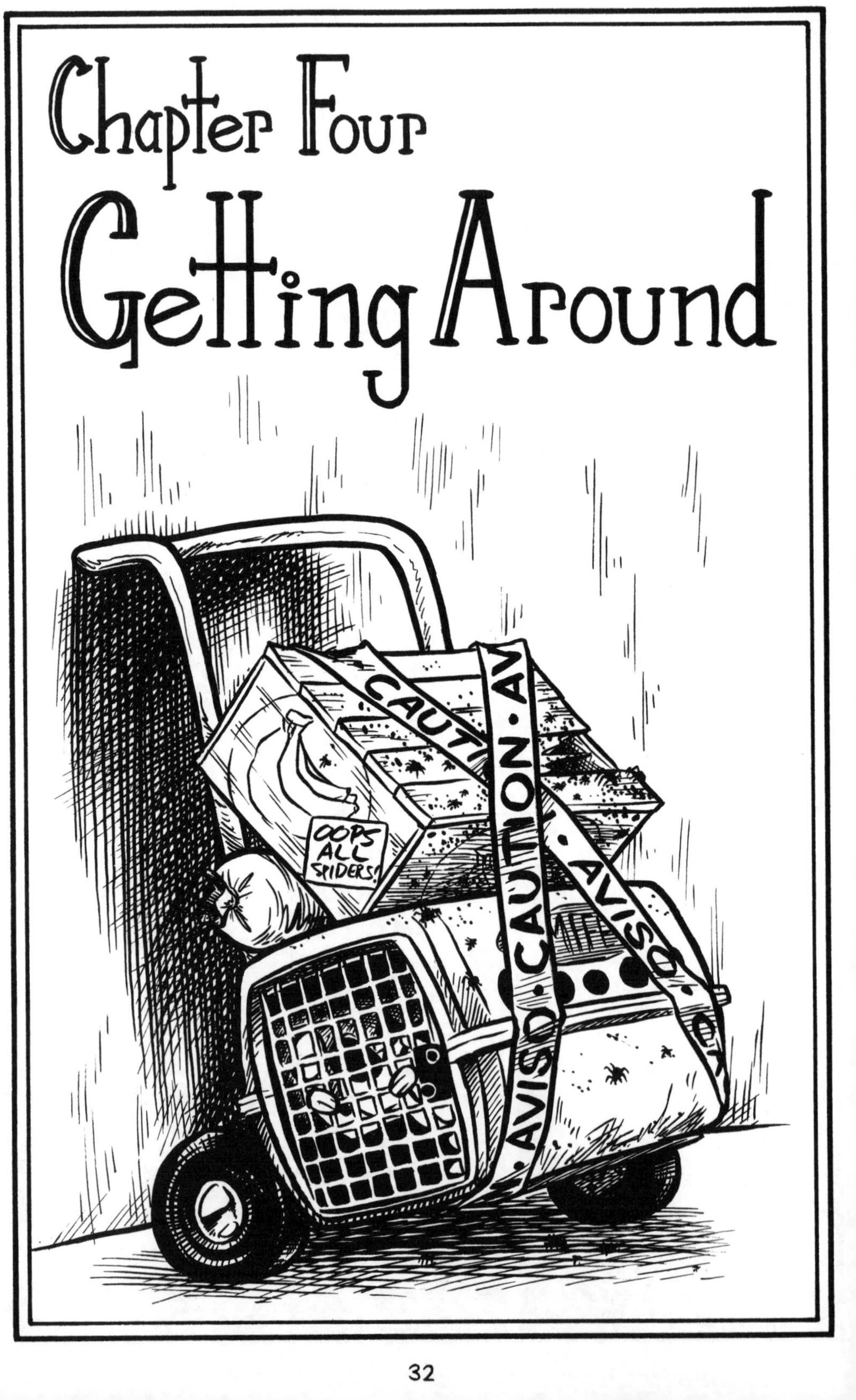

CAUTI
CAUTION · AV
AVISO · CAUTION
AVISO
OOPS ALL SPIDERS!

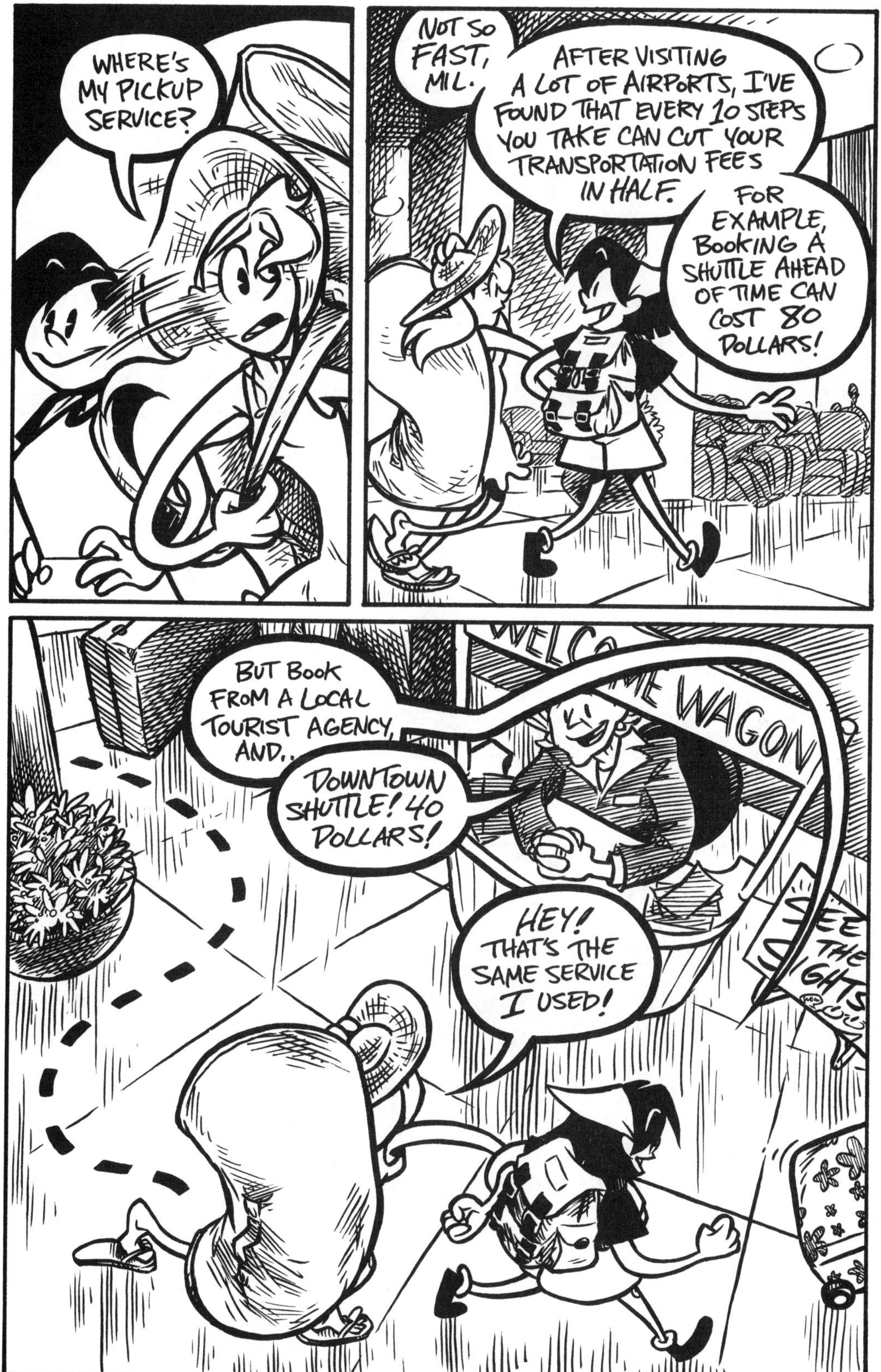
WHERE'S MY PICKUP SERVICE?
NOT SO FAST, MIL.
AFTER VISITING A LOT OF AIRPORTS, I'VE FOUND THAT EVERY 10 STEPS YOU TAKE CAN CUT YOUR TRANSPORTATION FEES IN HALF.
FOR EXAMPLE, BOOKING A SHUTTLE AHEAD OF TIME CAN COST 80 DOLLARS!
WAGON
BUT BOOK FROM A LOCAL TOURIST AGENCY, AND..
DOWNTOWN SHUTTLE! 40 DOLLARS!
HEY! THAT'S THE SAME SERVICE I USED!
SEE THE SIGHTS

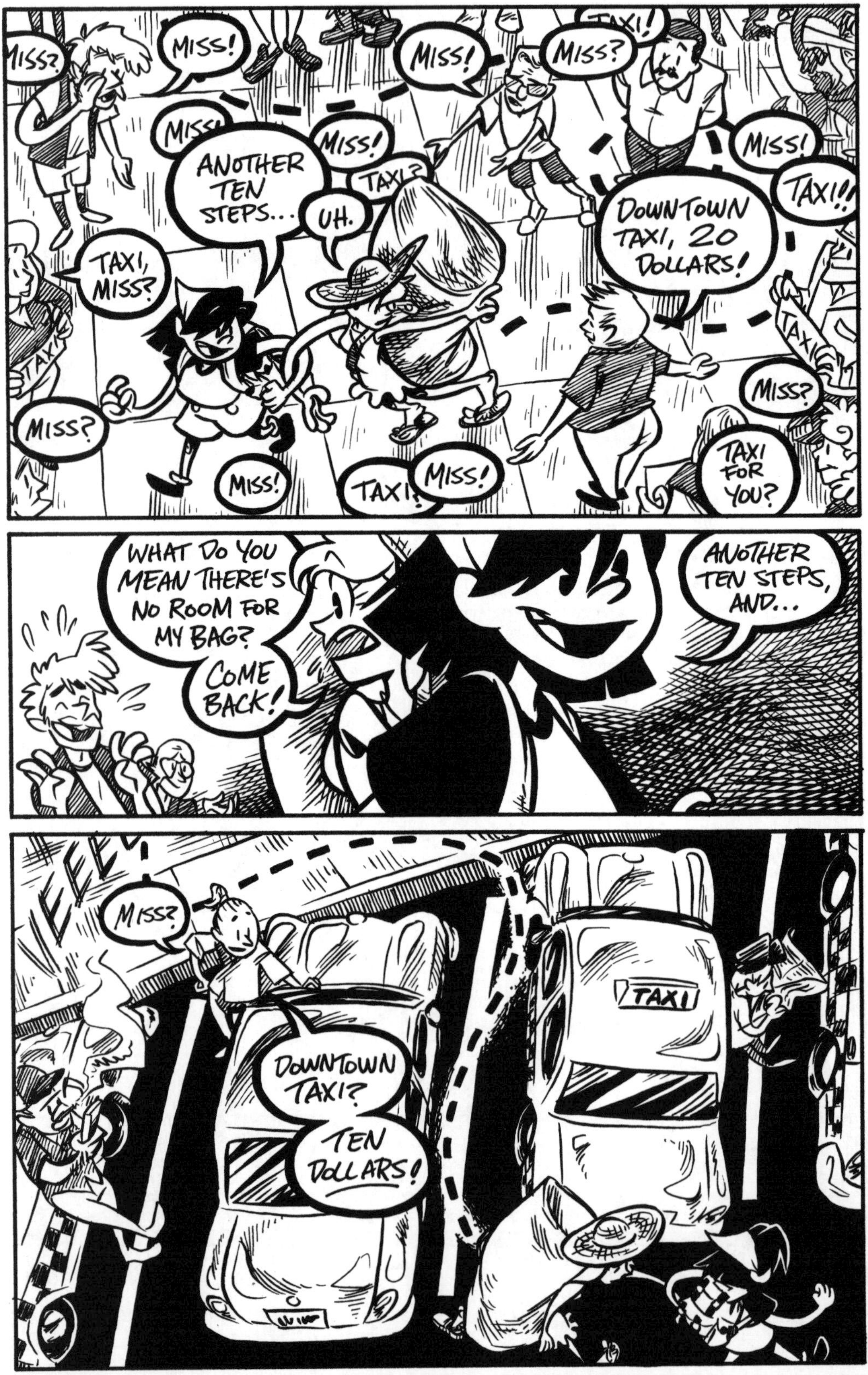
MISS?
MISS!
MISS!
MISS?
TAXI!
MISS!
MISS!
ANOTHER TEN STEPS...
TAXI?
UH.
MISS!
TAXI!!
DOWNTOWN TAXI, 20 DOLLARS!
TAXI, MISS?
TAXI
MISS?
MISS?
MISS!
TAXI!
MISS!
TAXI FOR YOU?
WHAT DO YOU MEAN THERE'S NO ROOM FOR MY BAG?
COME BACK!
ANOTHER TEN STEPS, AND...
MISS?
TAXI
DOWNTOWN TAXI?
TEN DOLLARS!

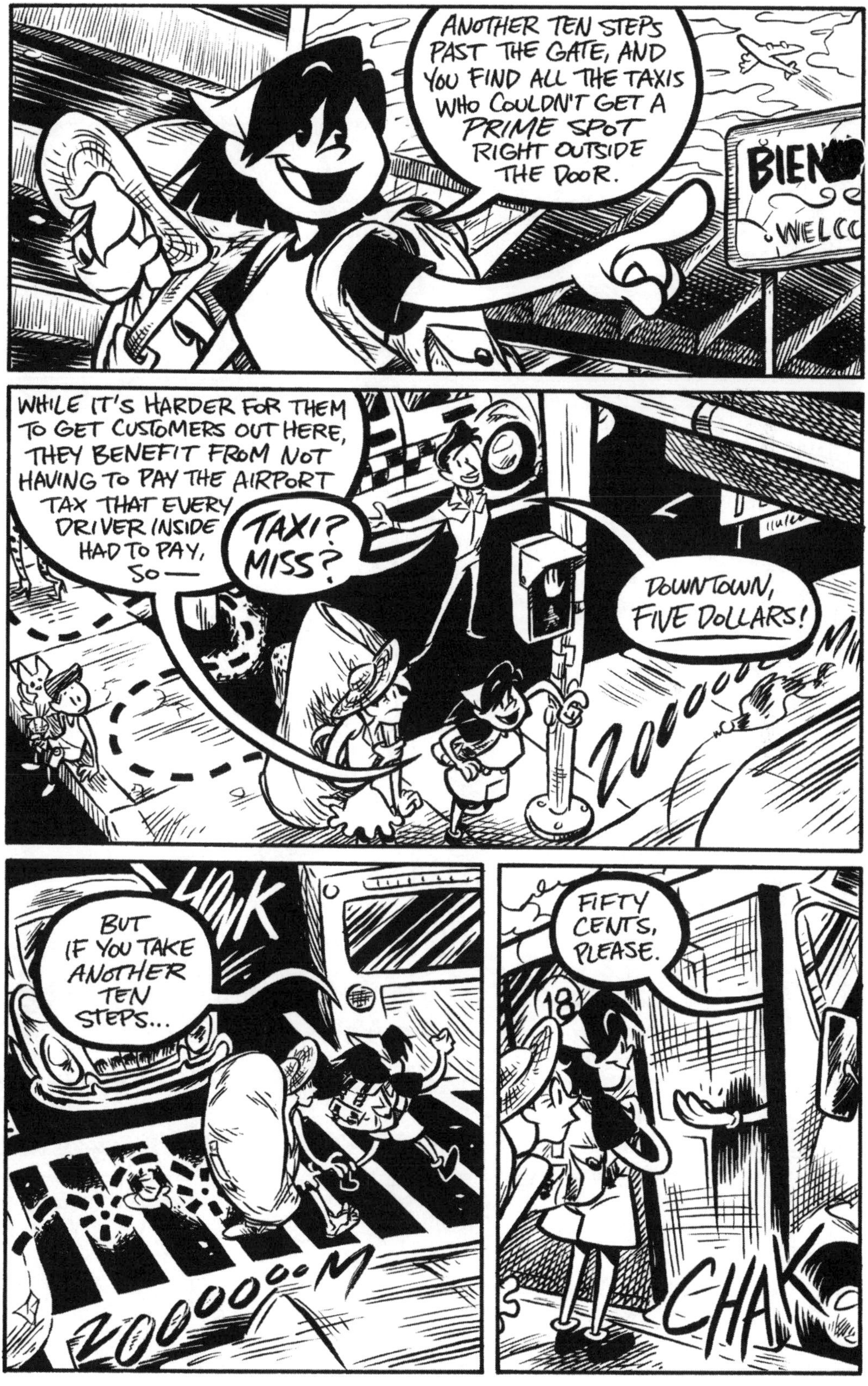
ANOTHER TEN STEPS PAST THE GATE, AND YOU FIND ALL THE TAXIS WHO COULDN'T GET A PRIME SPOT RIGHT OUTSIDE THE DOOR.
BIEN
WELC
WHILE IT'S HARDER FOR THEM TO GET CUSTOMERS OUT HERE, THEY BENEFIT FROM NOT HAVING TO PAY THE AIRPORT TAX THAT EVERY DRIVER INSIDE HAD TO PAY, SO—
TAXI? MISS?
DOWNTOWN, FIVE DOLLARS!
ZOOOOOOOM
HONK
BUT IF YOU TAKE ANOTHER TEN STEPS...
ZOOOOOOOM
FIFTY CENTS, PLEASE.
18
CHAK

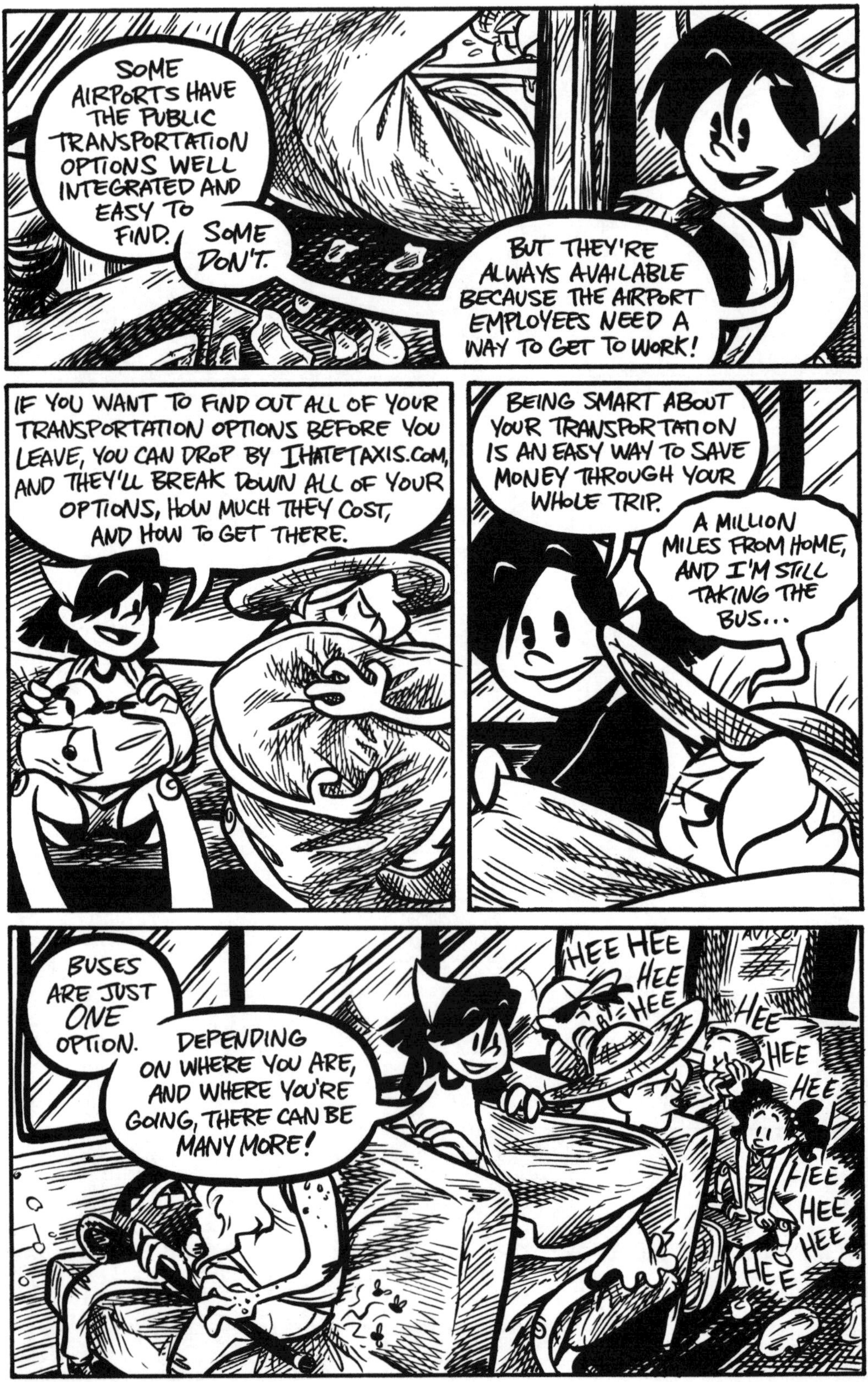
SOME AIRPORTS HAVE THE PUBLIC TRANSPORTATION OPTIONS WELL INTEGRATED AND EASY TO FIND.
SOME DON'T.
BUT THEY'RE ALWAYS AVAILABLE BECAUSE THE AIRPORT EMPLOYEES NEED A WAY TO GET TO WORK!
IF YOU WANT TO FIND OUT ALL OF YOUR TRANSPORTATION OPTIONS BEFORE YOU LEAVE, YOU CAN DROP BY IHATETAXIS.COM, AND THEY'LL BREAK DOWN ALL OF YOUR OPTIONS, HOW MUCH THEY COST, AND HOW TO GET THERE.
BEING SMART ABOUT YOUR TRANSPORTATION IS AN EASY WAY TO SAVE MONEY THROUGH YOUR WHOLE TRIP.
A MILLION MILES FROM HOME, AND I'M STILL TAKING THE BUS...
BUSES ARE JUST ONE OPTION.
DEPENDING ON WHERE YOU ARE, AND WHERE YOU'RE GOING, THERE CAN BE MANY MORE!
HEE HEE HEE HEE
HEE HEE HEE
HEE HEE HEE HEE

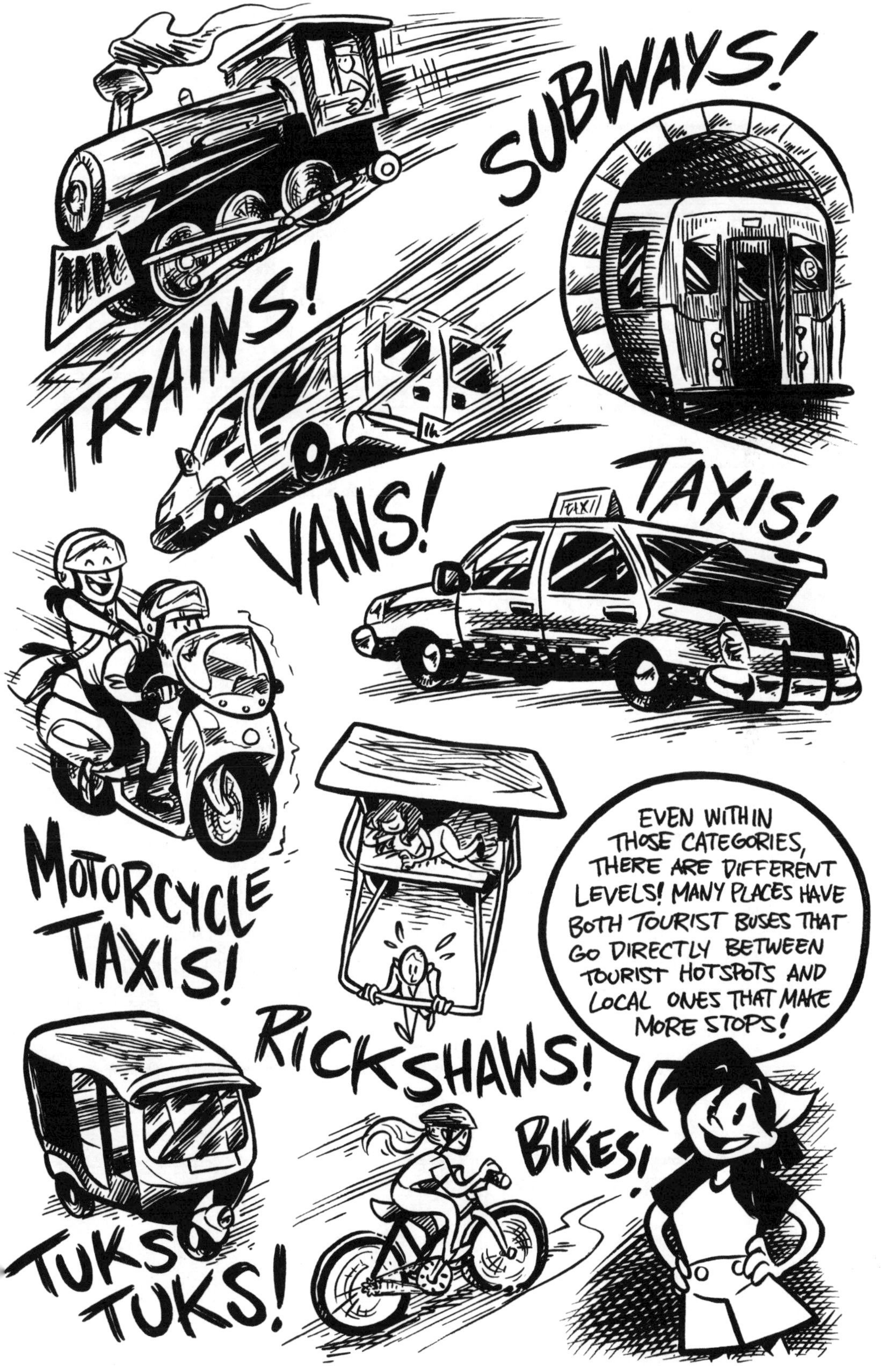
TRAINS!
SUBWAYS!
VANS!
TAXIS!
MOTORCYCLE TAXIS!
EVEN WITHIN THOSE CATEGORIES, THERE ARE DIFFERENT LEVELS! MANY PLACES HAVE BOTH TOURIST BUSES THAT GO DIRECTLY BETWEEN TOURIST HOTSPOTS AND LOCAL ONES THAT MAKE MORE STOPS!
RICKSHAWS!
TUKS TUKS!
BIKES!

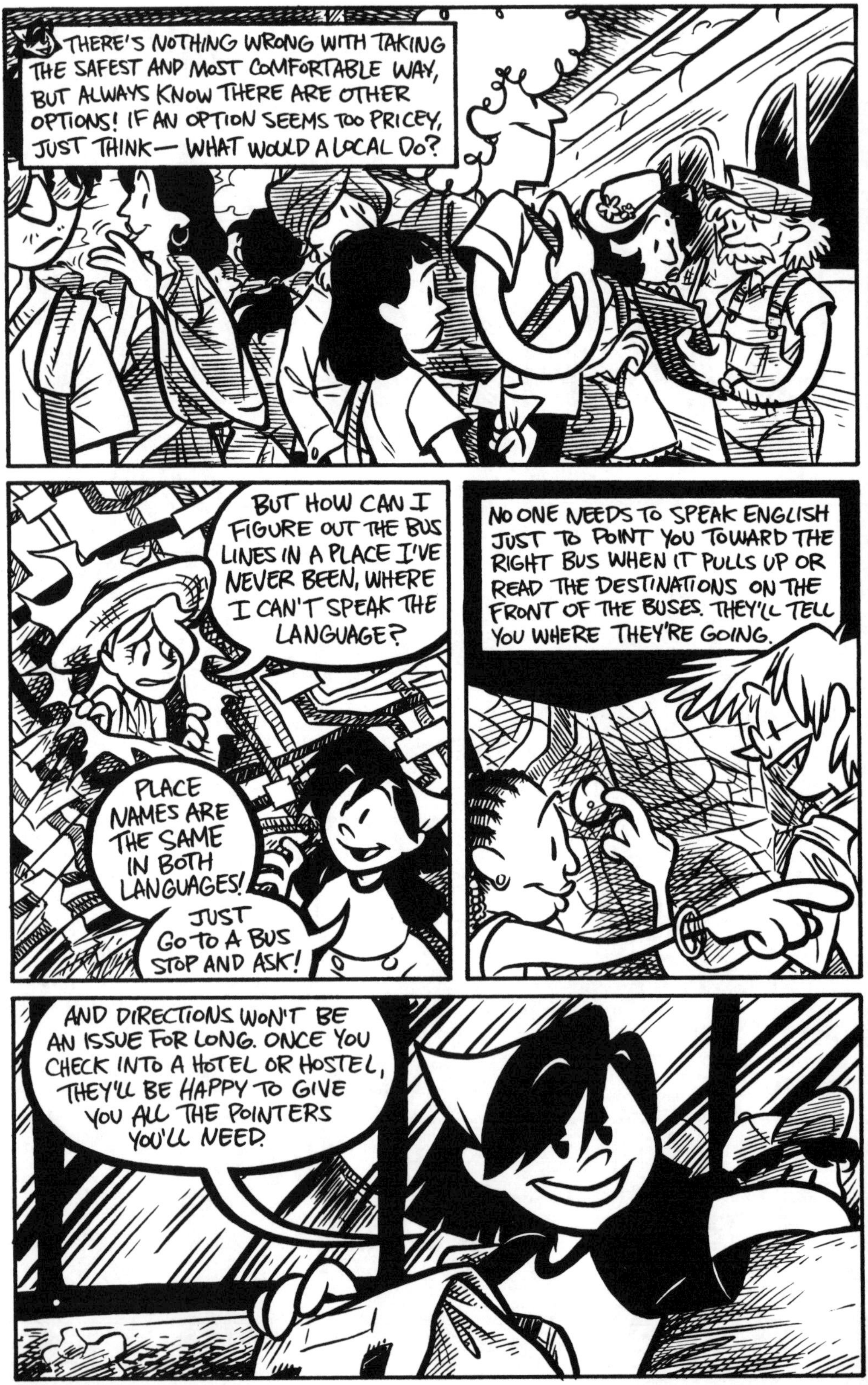
THERE'S NOTHING WRONG WITH TAKING THE SAFEST AND MOST COMFORTABLE WAY, BUT ALWAYS KNOW THERE ARE OTHER OPTIONS! IF AN OPTION SEEMS TOO PRICEY, JUST THINK— WHAT WOULD A LOCAL DO?
BUT HOW CAN I FIGURE OUT THE BUS LINES IN A PLACE I'VE NEVER BEEN, WHERE I CAN'T SPEAK THE LANGUAGE?
PLACE NAMES ARE THE SAME IN BOTH LANGUAGES!
JUST GO TO A BUS STOP AND ASK!
NO ONE NEEDS TO SPEAK ENGLISH JUST TO POINT YOU TOWARD THE RIGHT BUS WHEN IT PULLS UP OR READ THE DESTINATIONS ON THE FRONT OF THE BUSES. THEY'LL TELL YOU WHERE THEY'RE GOING.
AND DIRECTIONS WON'T BE AN ISSUE FOR LONG. ONCE YOU CHECK INTO A HOTEL OR HOSTEL, THEY'LL BE HAPPY TO GIVE YOU ALL THE POINTERS YOU'LL NEED.

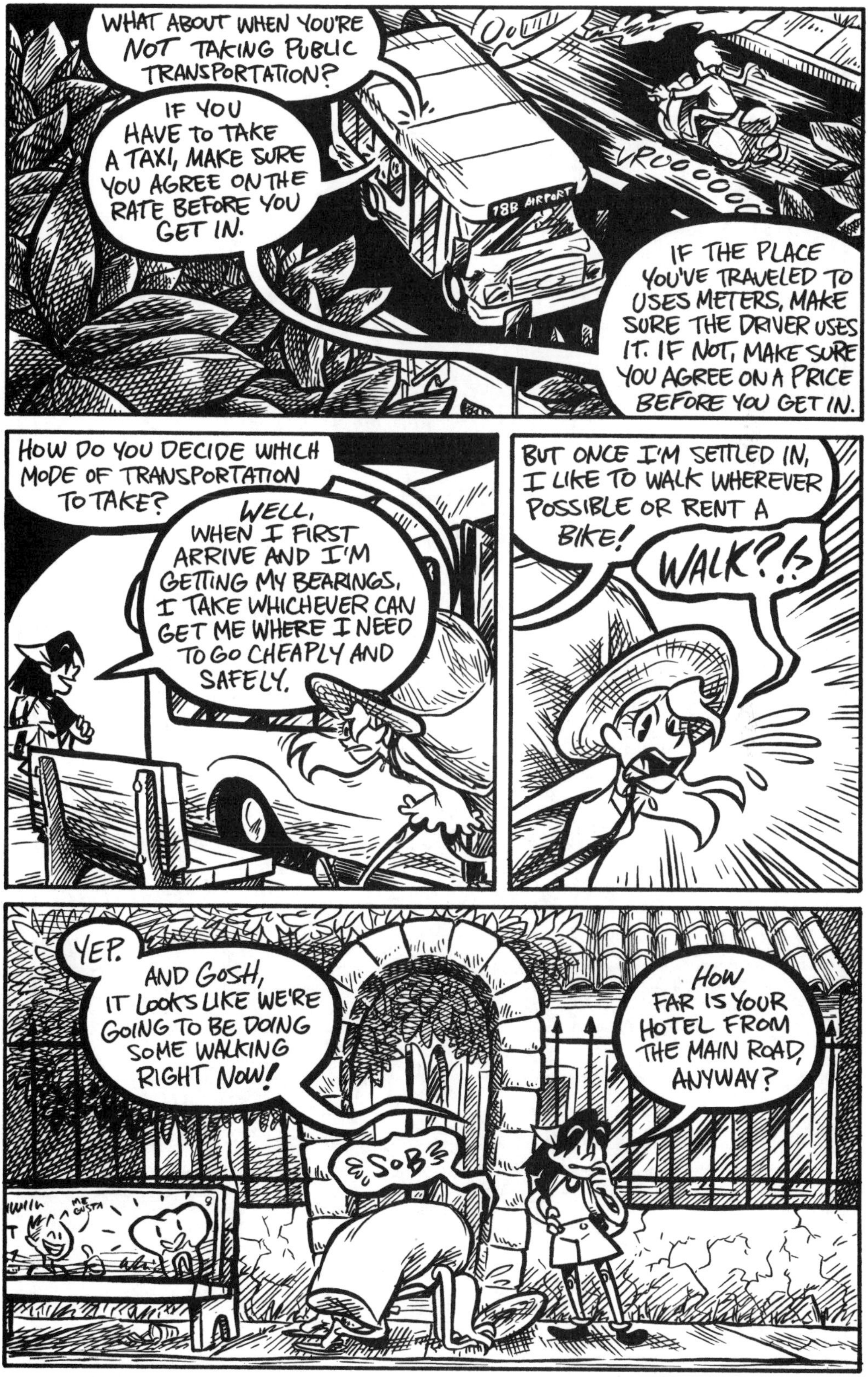
WHAT ABOUT WHEN YOU'RE NOT TAKING PUBLIC TRANSPORTATION?
IF YOU HAVE TO TAKE A TAXI, MAKE SURE YOU AGREE ON THE RATE BEFORE YOU GET IN.
18B AIRPORT
VROOOOOOO
IF THE PLACE YOU'VE TRAVELED TO USES METERS, MAKE SURE THE DRIVER USES IT. IF NOT, MAKE SURE YOU AGREE ON A PRICE BEFORE YOU GET IN.
HOW DO YOU DECIDE WHICH MODE OF TRANSPORTATION TO TAKE?
WELL, WHEN I FIRST ARRIVE AND I'M GETTING MY BEARINGS, I TAKE WHICHEVER CAN GET ME WHERE I NEED TO GO CHEAPLY AND SAFELY.
BUT ONCE I'M SETTLED IN, I LIKE TO WALK WHEREVER POSSIBLE OR RENT A BIKE!
WALK?!?
YEP.
AND GOSH, IT LOOKS LIKE WE'RE GOING TO BE DOING SOME WALKING RIGHT NOW!
HOW FAR IS YOUR HOTEL FROM THE MAIN ROAD, ANYWAY?
SOB
ME GUSTA

Chapter Five
Accommodations

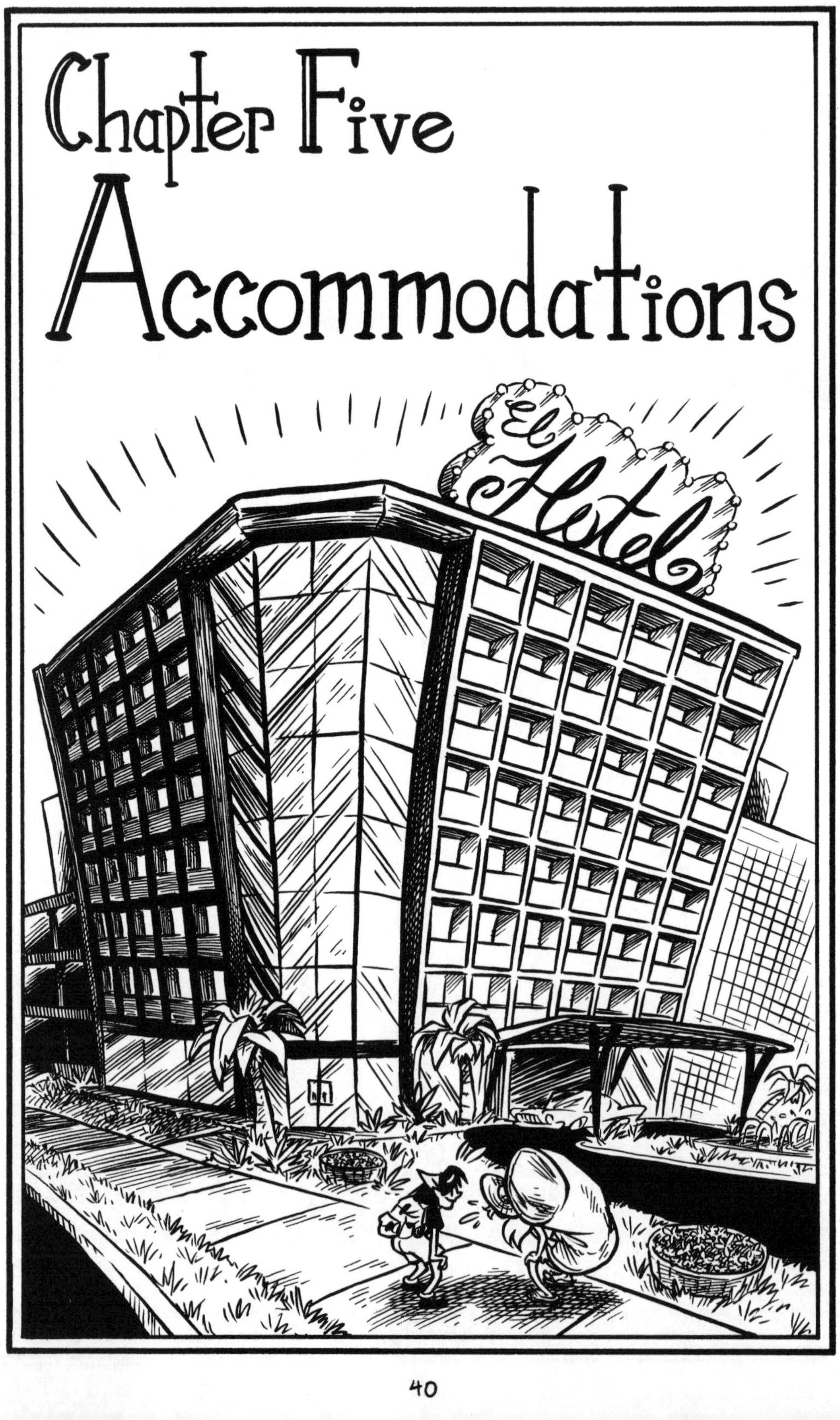
El Hotel

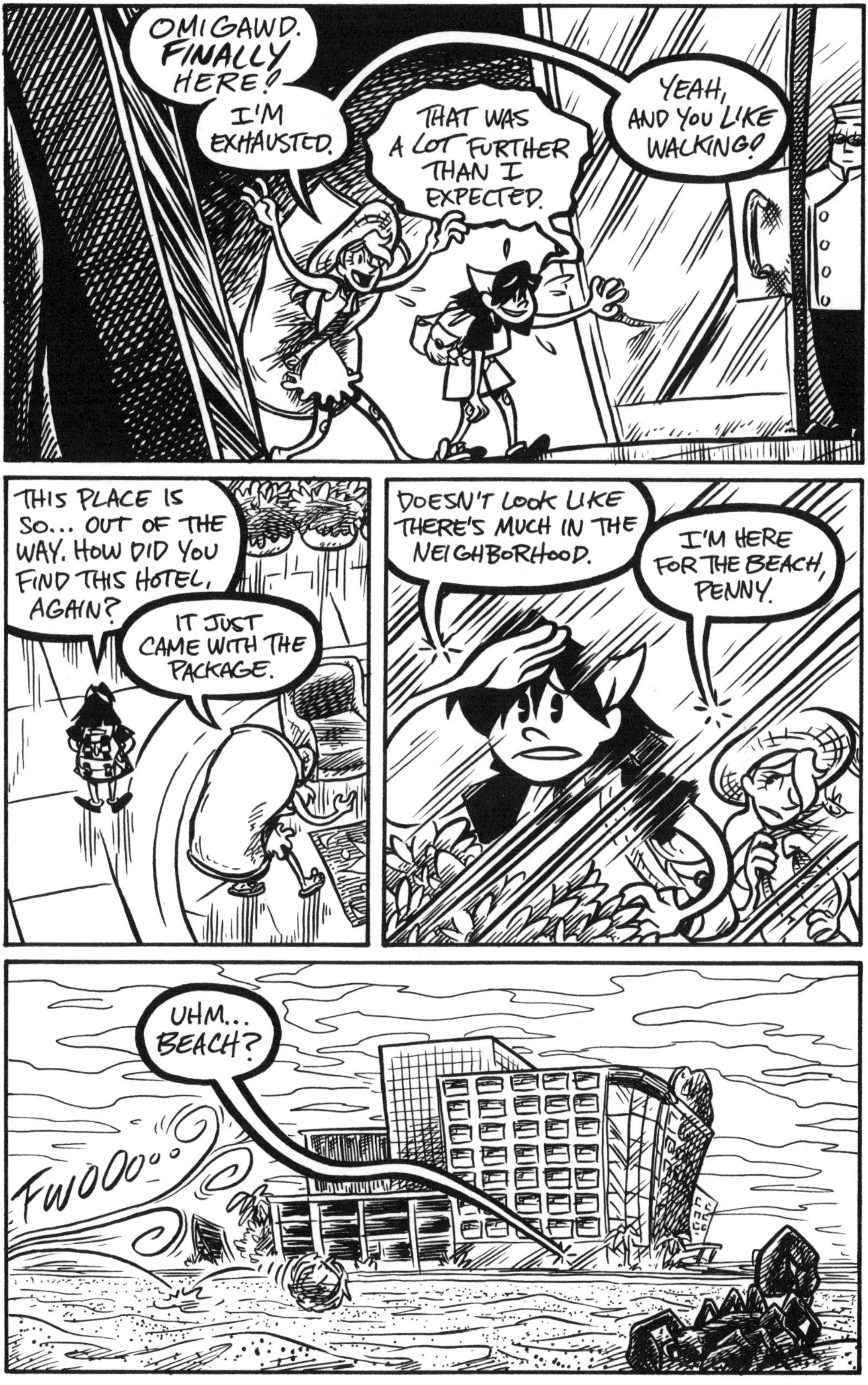
OMIGAWD. FINALLY HERE!
I'M EXHAUSTED.
THAT WAS A LOT FURTHER THAN I EXPECTED.
YEAH, AND YOU LIKE WALKING!
THIS PLACE IS SO... OUT OF THE WAY. HOW DID YOU FIND THIS HOTEL, AGAIN?
IT JUST CAME WITH THE PACKAGE.
DOESN'T LOOK LIKE THERE'S MUCH IN THE NEIGHBORHOOD.
I'M HERE FOR THE BEACH, PENNY.
UHM... BEACH?
FWOOOoo

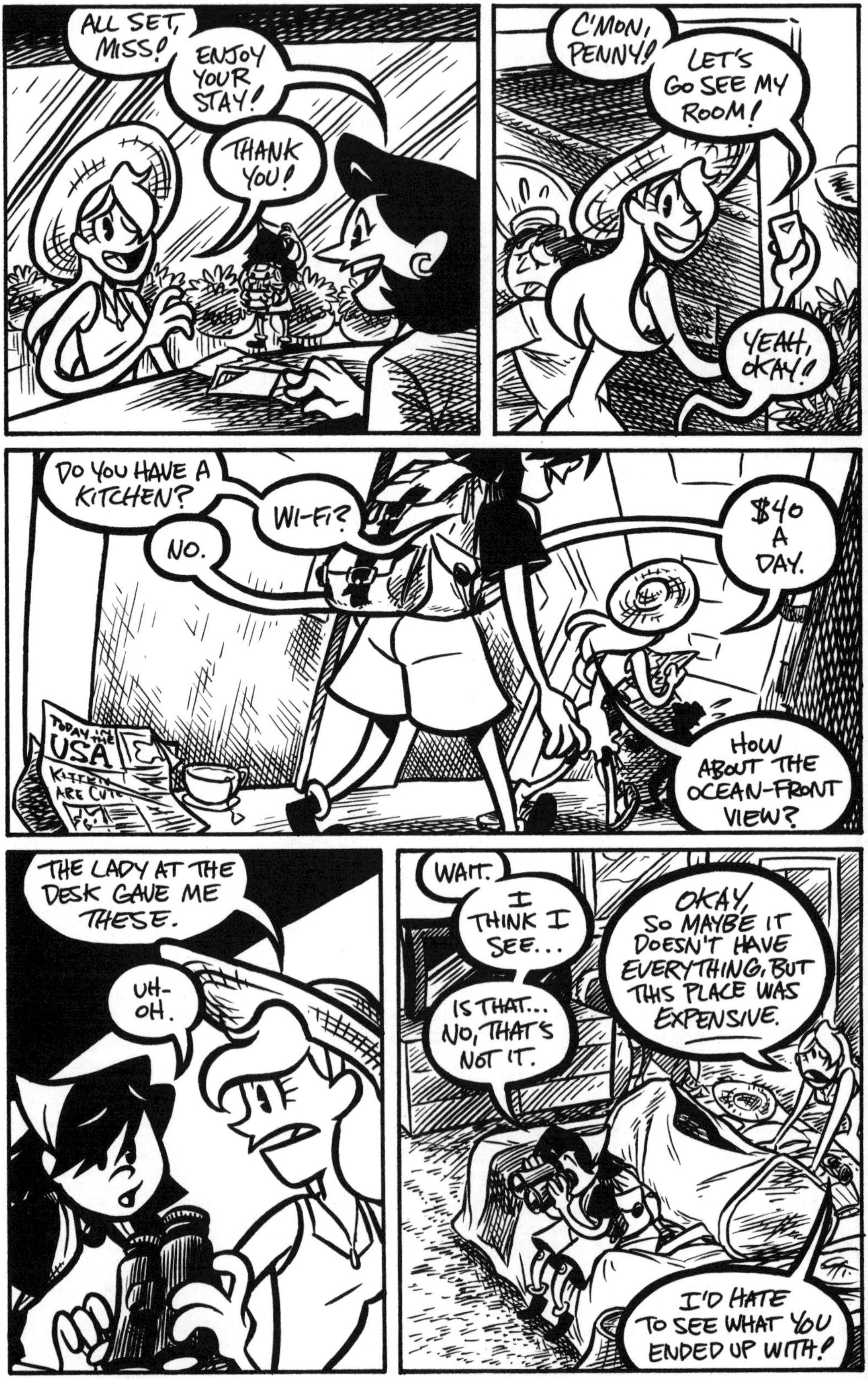
ALL SET, MISS!
ENJOY YOUR STAY!
THANK YOU!
C'MON, PENNY!
LET'S GO SEE MY ROOM!
YEAH, OKAY!
DO YOU HAVE A KITCHEN?
NO.
WI-FI?
$40 A DAY.
HOW ABOUT THE OCEAN-FRONT VIEW?
TODAY IN THE USA
KITTENS ARE CUTE
THE LADY AT THE DESK GAVE ME THESE.
UH-OH.
WAIT.
I THINK I SEE...
IS THAT... NO, THAT'S NOT IT.
OKAY, SO MAYBE IT DOESN'T HAVE EVERYTHING, BUT THIS PLACE WAS EXPENSIVE.
I'D HATE TO SEE WHAT YOU ENDED UP WITH!

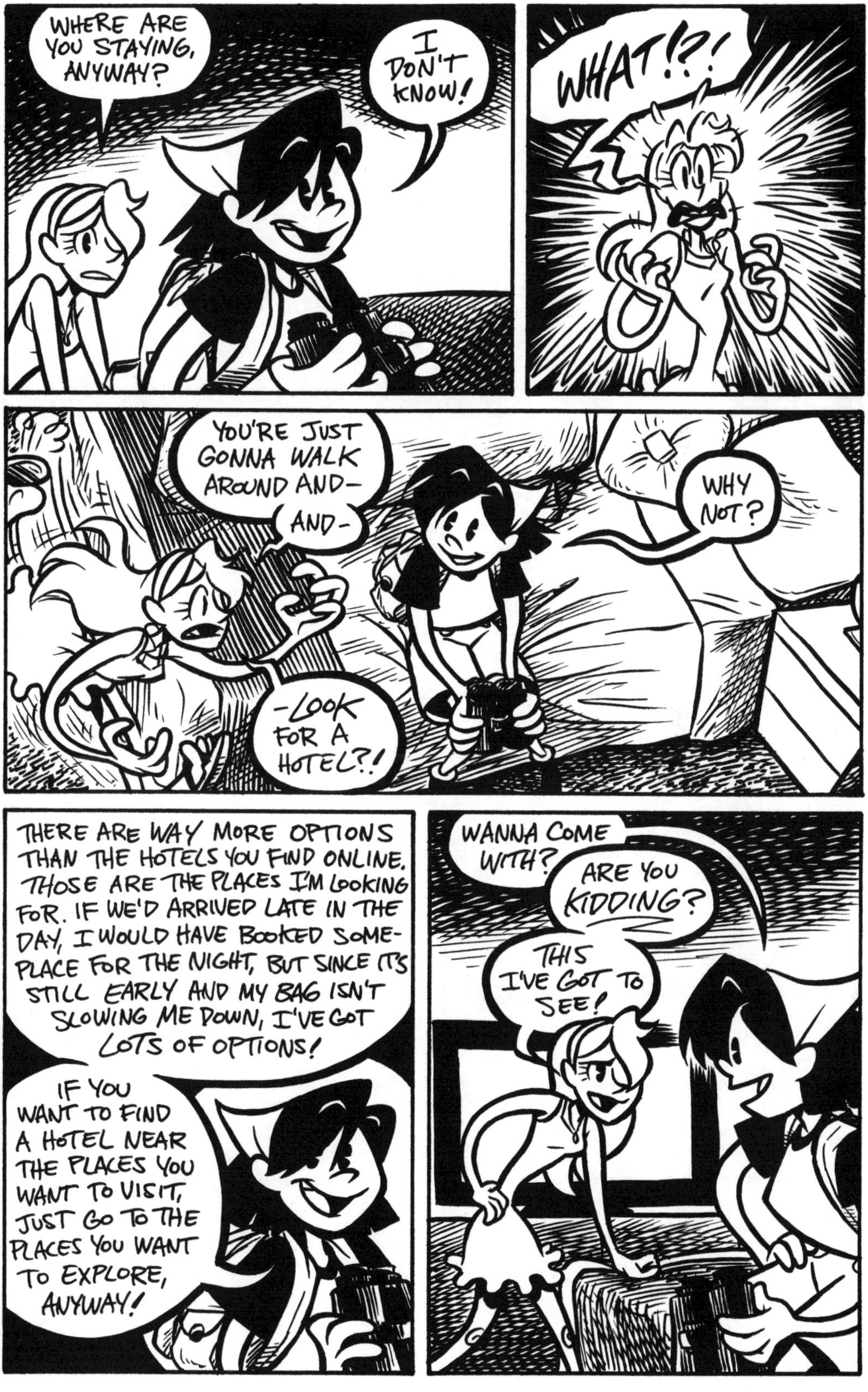
WHERE ARE YOU STAYING, ANYWAY?
I DON'T KNOW!
WHAT!?!
YOU'RE JUST GONNA WALK AROUND AND-
AND-
-LOOK FOR A HOTEL?!
WHY NOT?
THERE ARE WAY MORE OPTIONS THAN THE HOTELS YOU FIND ONLINE. THOSE ARE THE PLACES I'M LOOKING FOR. IF WE'D ARRIVED LATE IN THE DAY, I WOULD HAVE BOOKED SOME-PLACE FOR THE NIGHT, BUT SINCE IT'S STILL EARLY AND MY BAG ISN'T SLOWING ME DOWN, I'VE GOT LOTS OF OPTIONS!
IF YOU WANT TO FIND A HOTEL NEAR THE PLACES YOU WANT TO VISIT, JUST GO TO THE PLACES YOU WANT TO EXPLORE, ANYWAY!
WANNA COME WITH?
ARE YOU KIDDING?
THIS I'VE GOT TO SEE!

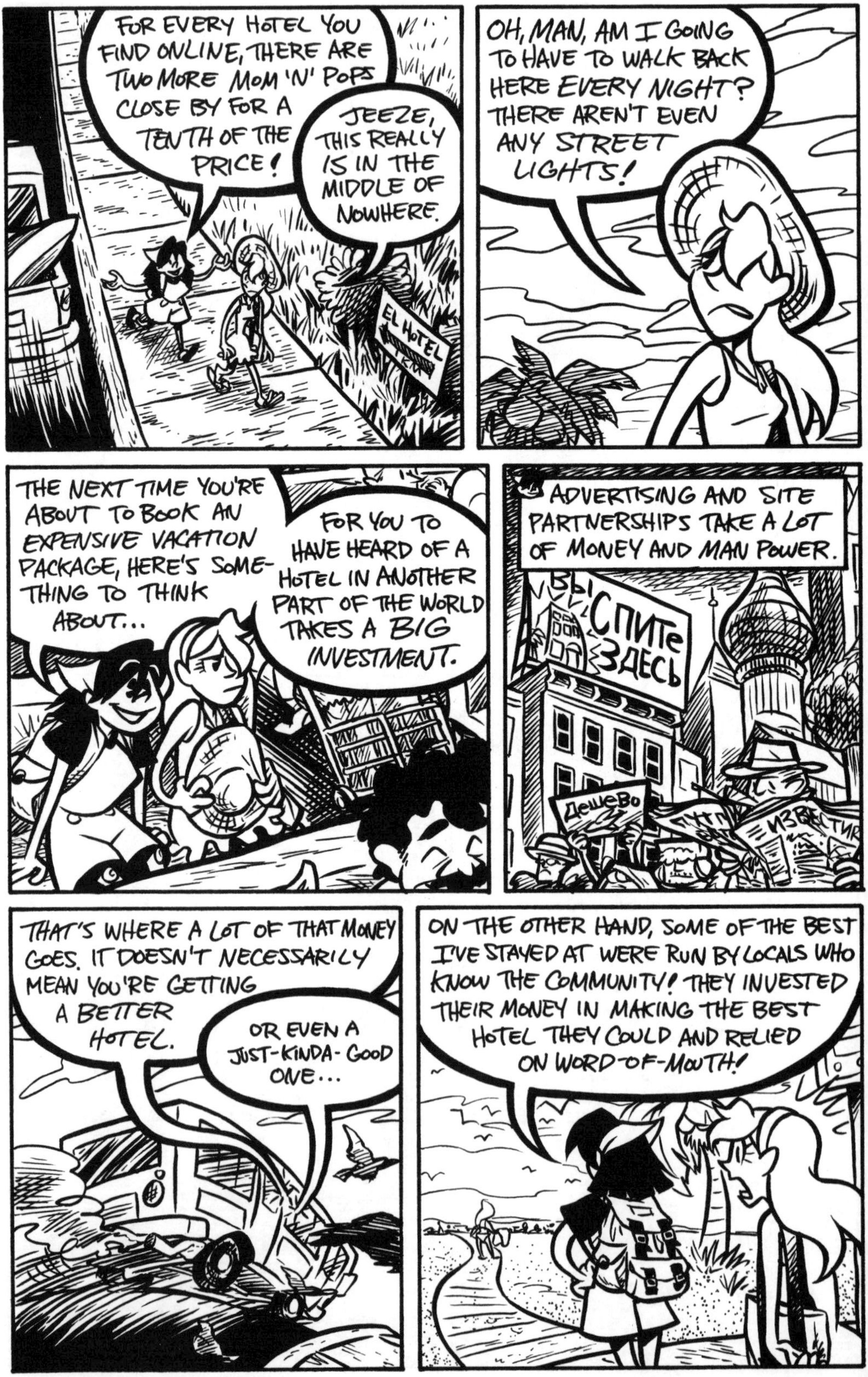
FOR EVERY HOTEL YOU FIND ONLINE, THERE ARE TWO MORE MOM 'N' POPS CLOSE BY FOR A TENTH OF THE PRICE!
JEEZE, THIS REALLY IS IN THE MIDDLE OF NOWHERE.
EL HOTEL
OH, MAN, AM I GOING TO HAVE TO WALK BACK HERE EVERY NIGHT? THERE AREN'T EVEN ANY STREET LIGHTS!
THE NEXT TIME YOU'RE ABOUT TO BOOK AN EXPENSIVE VACATION PACKAGE, HERE'S SOMETHING TO THINK ABOUT...
FOR YOU TO HAVE HEARD OF A HOTEL IN ANOTHER PART OF THE WORLD TAKES A BIG INVESTMENT.
ADVERTISING AND SITE PARTNERSHIPS TAKE A LOT OF MONEY AND MAN POWER.
СПИТЕ ЗДЕСЬ
ДешеВо
THAT'S WHERE A LOT OF THAT MONEY GOES. IT DOESN'T NECESSARILY MEAN YOU'RE GETTING A BETTER HOTEL.
OR EVEN A JUST-KINDA-GOOD ONE...
ON THE OTHER HAND, SOME OF THE BEST I'VE STAYED AT WERE RUN BY LOCALS WHO KNOW THE COMMUNITY! THEY INVESTED THEIR MONEY IN MAKING THE BEST HOTEL THEY COULD AND RELIED ON WORD-OF-MOUTH!

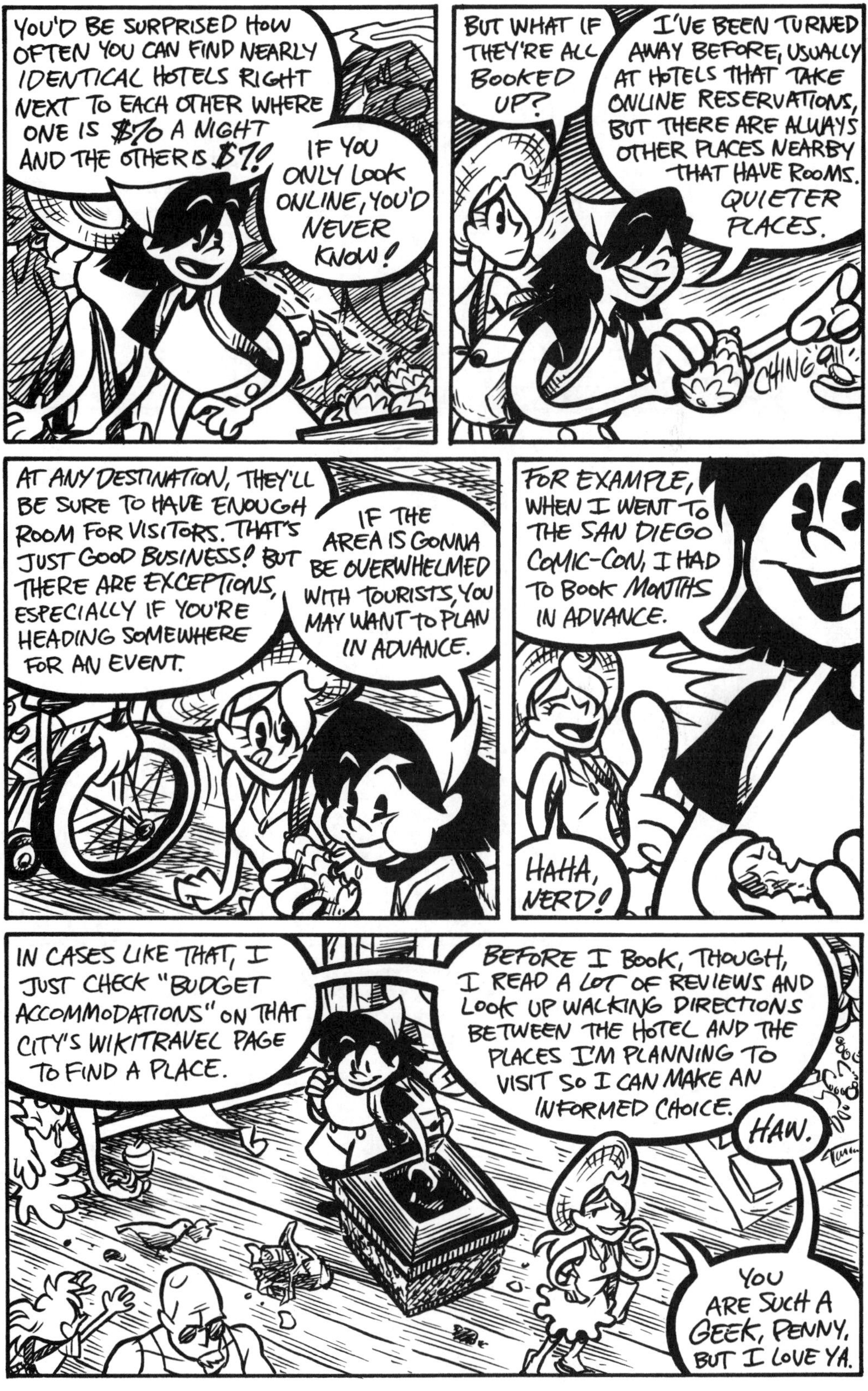
YOU'D BE SURPRISED HOW OFTEN YOU CAN FIND NEARLY IDENTICAL HOTELS RIGHT NEXT TO EACH OTHER WHERE ONE IS $70 A NIGHT AND THE OTHER IS $7!
IF YOU ONLY LOOK ONLINE, YOU'D NEVER KNOW!
BUT WHAT IF THEY'RE ALL BOOKED UP?
I'VE BEEN TURNED AWAY BEFORE, USUALLY AT HOTELS THAT TAKE ONLINE RESERVATIONS, BUT THERE ARE ALWAYS OTHER PLACES NEARBY THAT HAVE ROOMS. QUIETER PLACES.
CHING
AT ANY DESTINATION, THEY'LL BE SURE TO HAVE ENOUGH ROOM FOR VISITORS. THAT'S JUST GOOD BUSINESS! BUT THERE ARE EXCEPTIONS, ESPECIALLY IF YOU'RE HEADING SOMEWHERE FOR AN EVENT.
IF THE AREA IS GONNA BE OVERWHELMED WITH TOURISTS, YOU MAY WANT TO PLAN IN ADVANCE.
FOR EXAMPLE, WHEN I WENT TO THE SAN DIEGO COMIC-CON, I HAD TO BOOK MONTHS IN ADVANCE.
HAHA, NERD!
IN CASES LIKE THAT, I JUST CHECK "BUDGET ACCOMMODATIONS" ON THAT CITY'S WIKITRAVEL PAGE TO FIND A PLACE.
BEFORE I BOOK, THOUGH, I READ A LOT OF REVIEWS AND LOOK UP WALKING DIRECTIONS BETWEEN THE HOTEL AND THE PLACES I'M PLANNING TO VISIT SO I CAN MAKE AN INFORMED CHOICE.
HAW.
YOU ARE SUCH A GEEK, PENNY, BUT I LOVE YA.

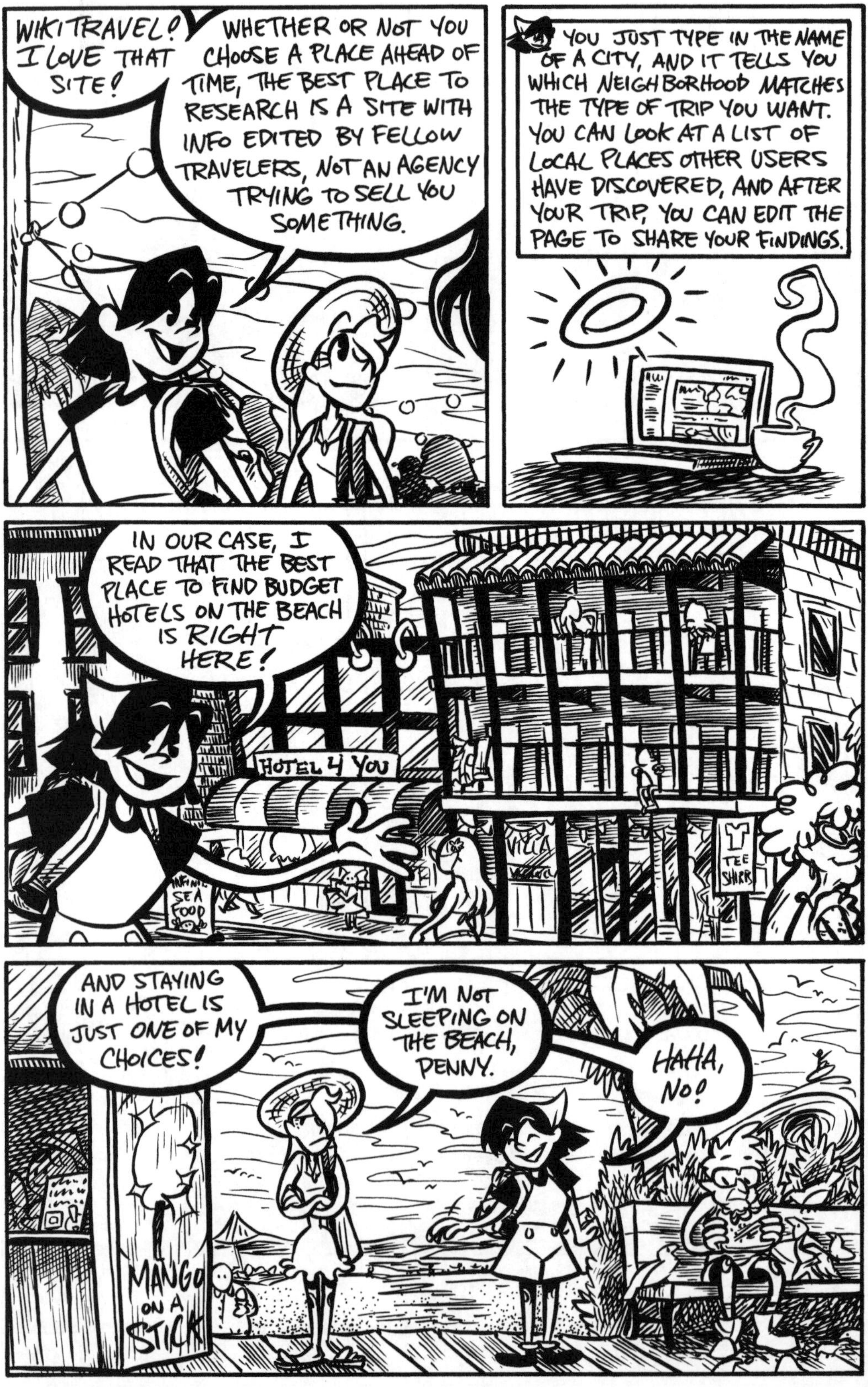
WIKITRAVEL! I LOVE THAT SITE!
WHETHER OR NOT YOU CHOOSE A PLACE AHEAD OF TIME, THE BEST PLACE TO RESEARCH IS A SITE WITH INFO EDITED BY FELLOW TRAVELERS, NOT AN AGENCY TRYING TO SELL YOU SOMETHING.
YOU JUST TYPE IN THE NAME OF A CITY, AND IT TELLS YOU WHICH NEIGHBORHOOD MATCHES THE TYPE OF TRIP YOU WANT. YOU CAN LOOK AT A LIST OF LOCAL PLACES OTHER USERS HAVE DISCOVERED, AND AFTER YOUR TRIP, YOU CAN EDIT THE PAGE TO SHARE YOUR FINDINGS.
IN OUR CASE, I READ THAT THE BEST PLACE TO FIND BUDGET HOTELS ON THE BEACH IS RIGHT HERE!
HOTEL 4 YOU
SEA FOOD
VILLA
TEE SHIRTS
AND STAYING IN A HOTEL IS JUST ONE OF MY CHOICES!
I'M NOT SLEEPING ON THE BEACH, PENNY.
HAHA, NO!
MANGO ON A STICK

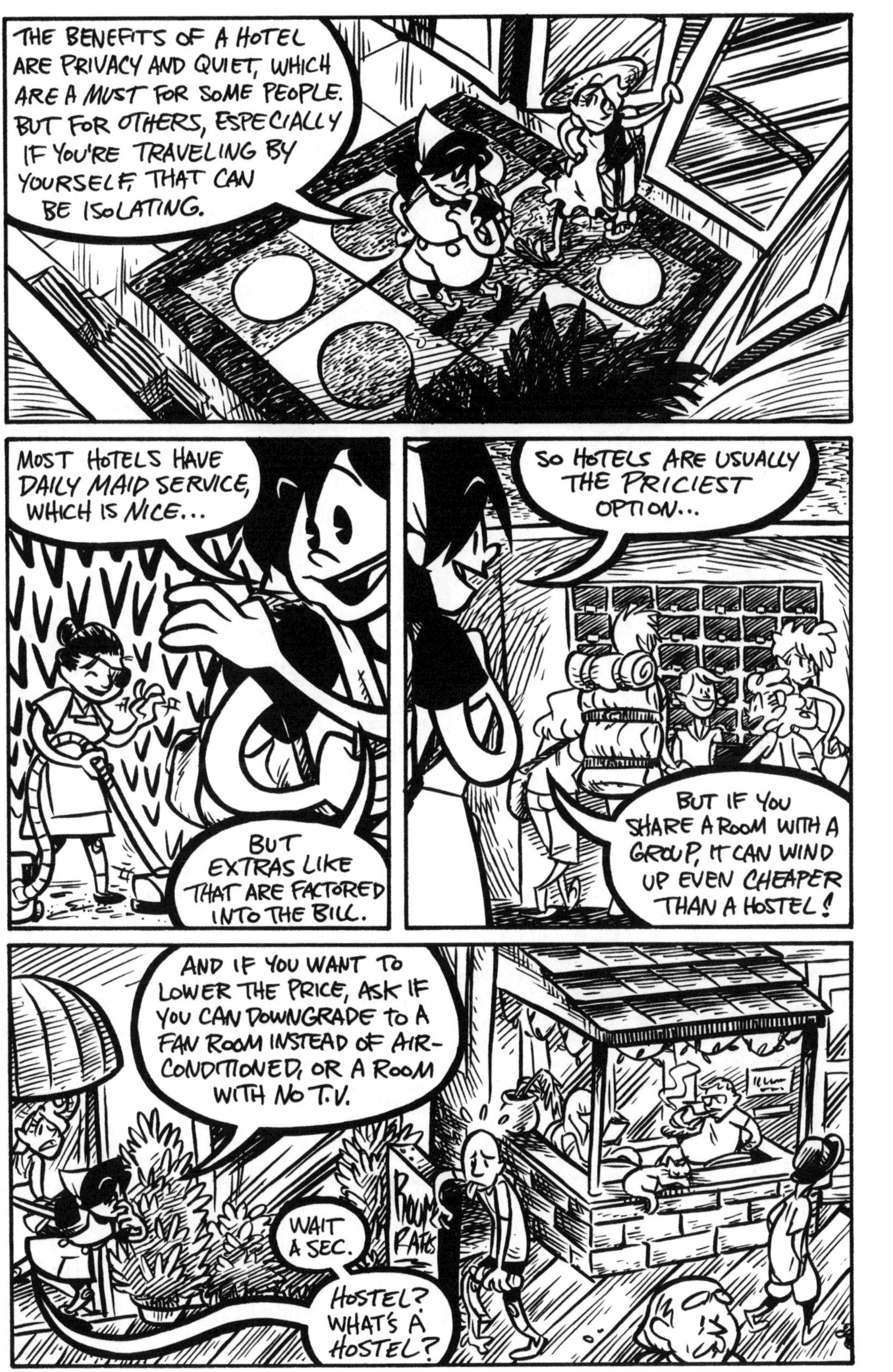
THE BENEFITS OF A HOTEL ARE PRIVACY AND QUIET, WHICH ARE A MUST FOR SOME PEOPLE. BUT FOR OTHERS, ESPECIALLY IF YOU'RE TRAVELING BY YOURSELF, THAT CAN BE ISOLATING.
MOST HOTELS HAVE DAILY MAID SERVICE, WHICH IS NICE...
BUT EXTRAS LIKE THAT ARE FACTORED INTO THE BILL.
SO HOTELS ARE USUALLY THE PRICIEST OPTION...
BUT IF YOU SHARE A ROOM WITH A GROUP, IT CAN WIND UP EVEN CHEAPER THAN A HOSTEL!
AND IF YOU WANT TO LOWER THE PRICE, ASK IF YOU CAN DOWNGRADE TO A FAN ROOM INSTEAD OF AIR-CONDITIONED, OR A ROOM WITH NO T.V.
ROOMS RATES
WAIT A SEC.
HOSTEL? WHAT'S A HOSTEL?

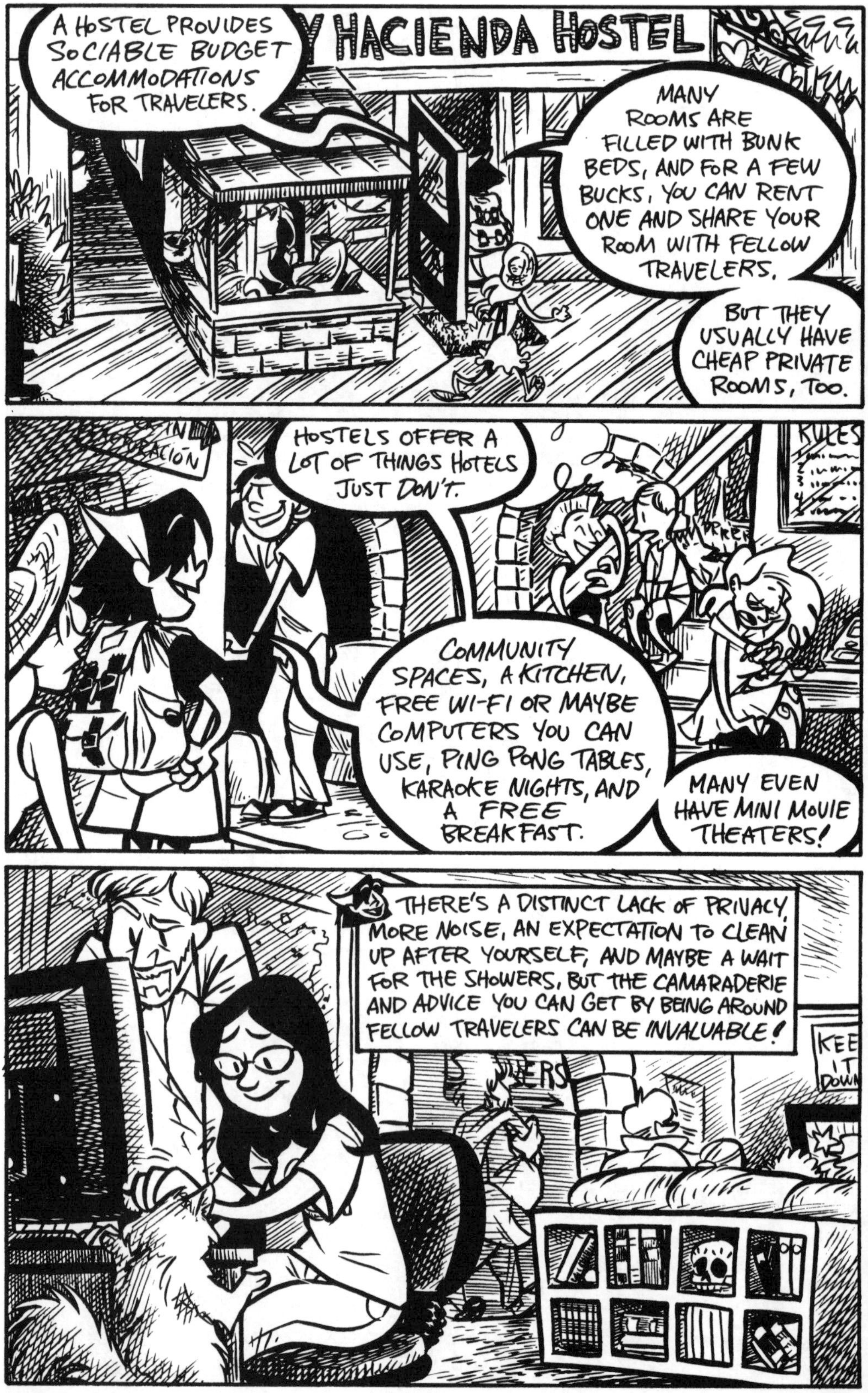
A HOSTEL PROVIDES SOCIABLE BUDGET ACCOMMODATIONS FOR TRAVELERS.
HACIENDA HOSTEL
MANY ROOMS ARE FILLED WITH BUNK BEDS, AND FOR A FEW BUCKS, YOU CAN RENT ONE AND SHARE YOUR ROOM WITH FELLOW TRAVELERS.
BUT THEY USUALLY HAVE CHEAP PRIVATE ROOMS, TOO.
HOSTELS OFFER A LOT OF THINGS HOTELS JUST DON'T.
COMMUNITY SPACES, A KITCHEN, FREE WI-FI OR MAYBE COMPUTERS YOU CAN USE, PING PONG TABLES, KARAOKE NIGHTS, AND A FREE BREAKFAST.
MANY EVEN HAVE MINI MOVIE THEATERS!
THERE'S A DISTINCT LACK OF PRIVACY, MORE NOISE, AN EXPECTATION TO CLEAN UP AFTER YOURSELF, AND MAYBE A WAIT FOR THE SHOWERS, BUT THE CAMARADERIE AND ADVICE YOU CAN GET BY BEING AROUND FELLOW TRAVELERS CAN BE INVALUABLE!

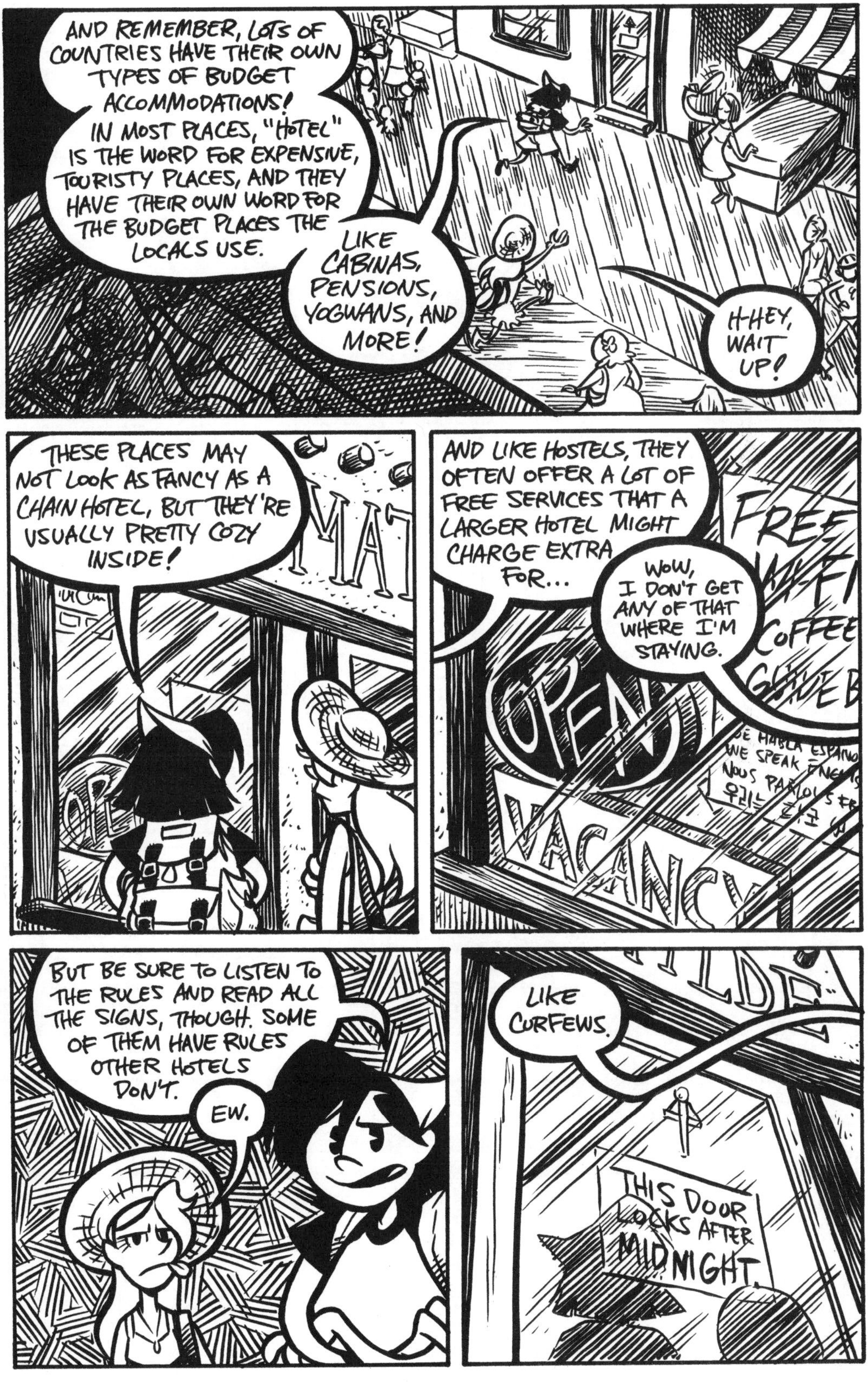
AND REMEMBER, LOTS OF COUNTRIES HAVE THEIR OWN TYPES OF BUDGET ACCOMMODATIONS! IN MOST PLACES, "HOTEL" IS THE WORD FOR EXPENSIVE, TOURISTY PLACES, AND THEY HAVE THEIR OWN WORD FOR THE BUDGET PLACES THE LOCALS USE.
LIKE CABINAS, PENSIONS, YOGWANS, AND MORE!
H-HEY, WAIT UP!
THESE PLACES MAY NOT LOOK AS FANCY AS A CHAIN HOTEL, BUT THEY'RE USUALLY PRETTY COZY INSIDE!
AND LIKE HOSTELS, THEY OFTEN OFFER A LOT OF FREE SERVICES THAT A LARGER HOTEL MIGHT CHARGE EXTRA FOR...
WOW, I DON'T GET ANY OF THAT WHERE I'M STAYING.
OPEN
VACANCY
BUT BE SURE TO LISTEN TO THE RULES AND READ ALL THE SIGNS, THOUGH. SOME OF THEM HAVE RULES OTHER HOTELS DON'T.
EW.
LIKE CURFEWS.
THIS DOOR LOCKS AFTER MIDNIGHT.

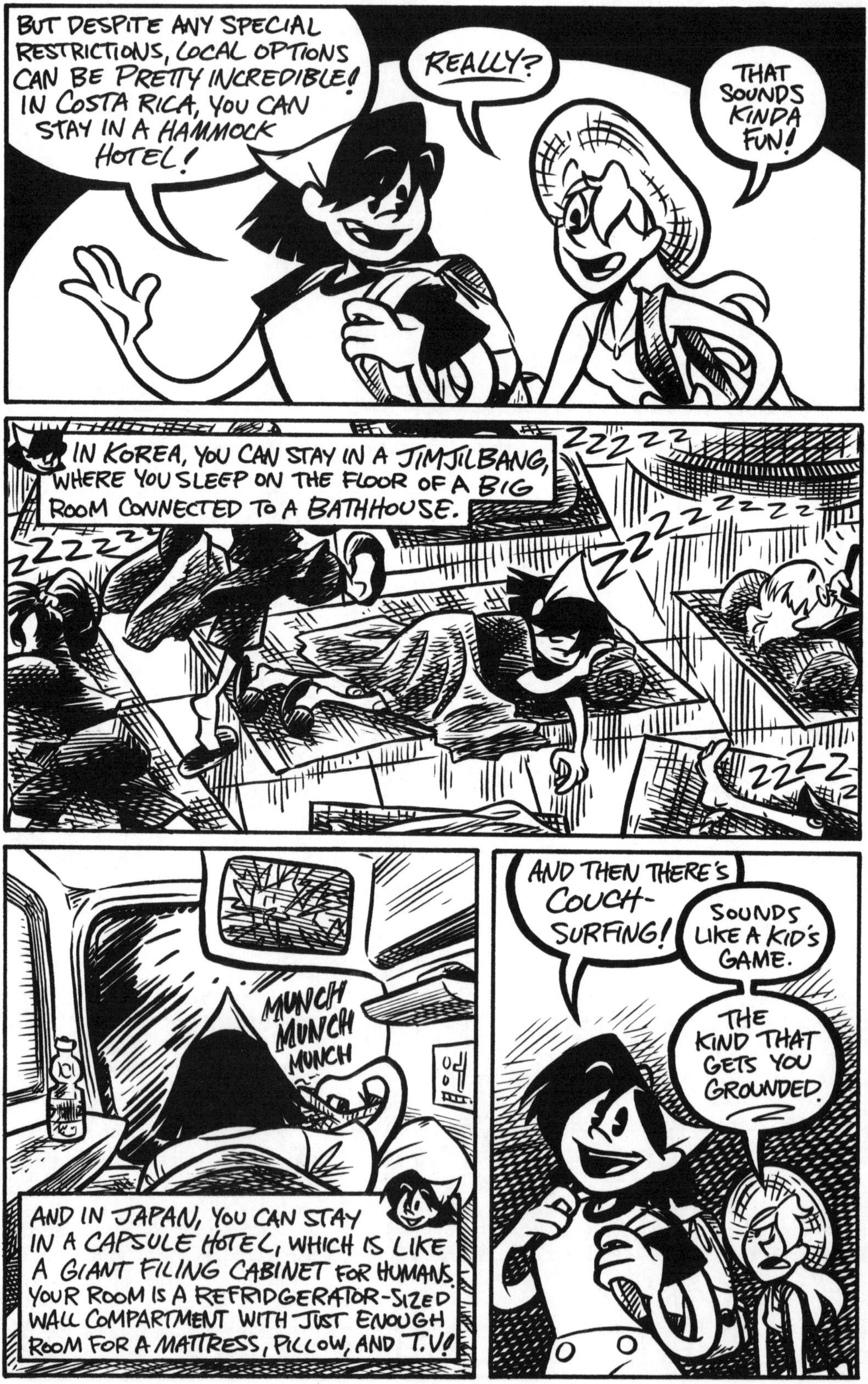
BUT DESPITE ANY SPECIAL RESTRICTIONS, LOCAL OPTIONS CAN BE PRETTY INCREDIBLE! IN COSTA RICA, YOU CAN STAY IN A HAMMOCK HOTEL!
REALLY?
THAT SOUNDS KINDA FUN!
IN KOREA, YOU CAN STAY IN A JIMJILBANG, WHERE YOU SLEEP ON THE FLOOR OF A BIG ROOM CONNECTED TO A BATHHOUSE.
ZZZZZ
MUNCH MUNCH MUNCH
AND IN JAPAN, YOU CAN STAY IN A CAPSULE HOTEL, WHICH IS LIKE A GIANT FILING CABINET FOR HUMANS. YOUR ROOM IS A REFRIDGERATOR-SIZED WALL COMPARTMENT WITH JUST ENOUGH ROOM FOR A MATTRESS, PILLOW, AND T.V!
AND THEN THERE'S COUCH-SURFING!
SOUNDS LIKE A KID'S GAME.
THE KIND THAT GETS YOU GROUNDED.

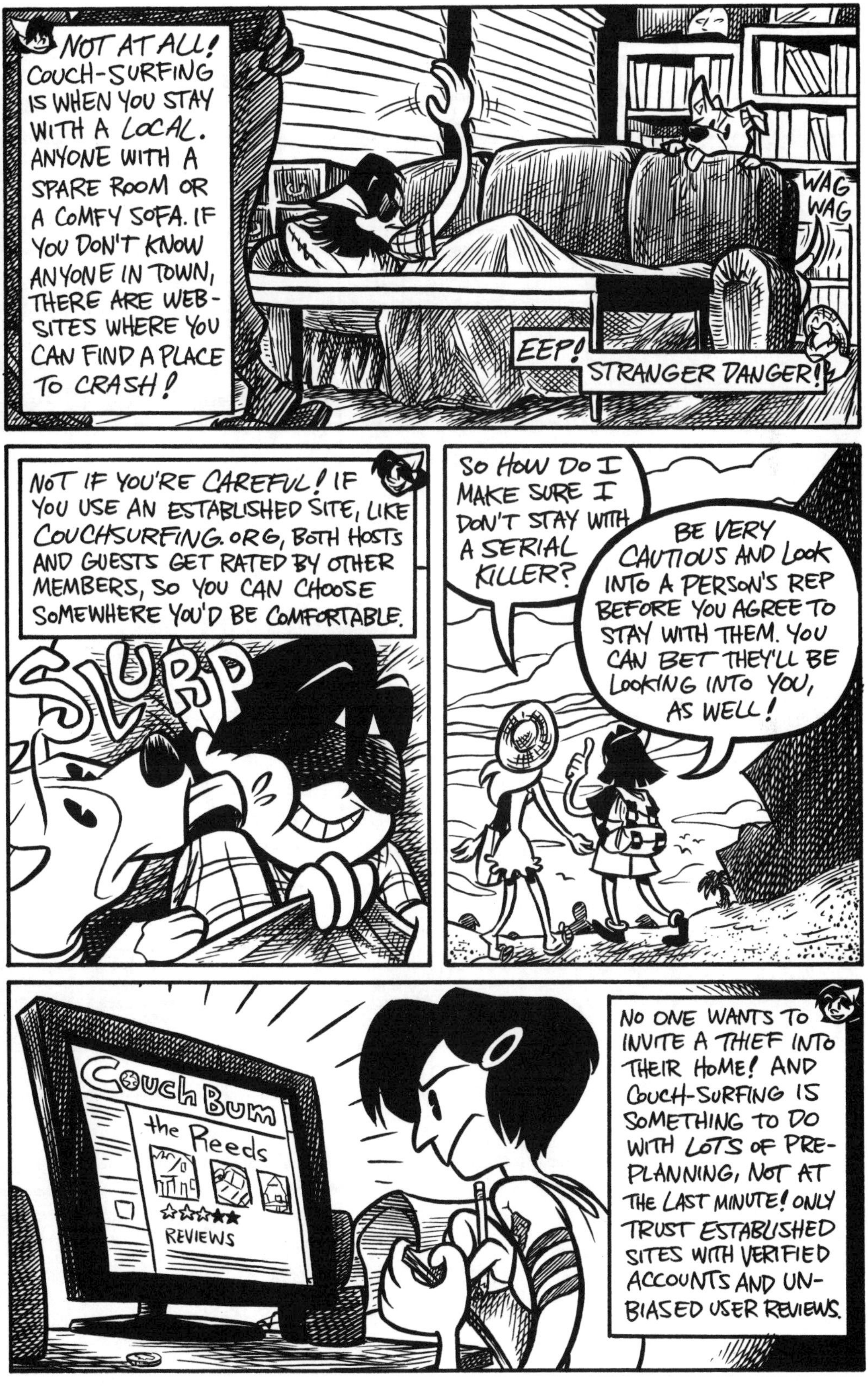
NOT AT ALL! COUCH-SURFING IS WHEN YOU STAY WITH A LOCAL. ANYONE WITH A SPARE ROOM OR A COMFY SOFA. IF YOU DON'T KNOW ANYONE IN TOWN, THERE ARE WEB-SITES WHERE YOU CAN FIND A PLACE TO CRASH!
WAG WAG
EEP!
STRANGER DANGER!
NOT IF YOU'RE CAREFUL! IF YOU USE AN ESTABLISHED SITE, LIKE COUCHSURFING.ORG, BOTH HOSTS AND GUESTS GET RATED BY OTHER MEMBERS, SO YOU CAN CHOOSE SOMEWHERE YOU'D BE COMFORTABLE.
SLURP
SO HOW DO I MAKE SURE I DON'T STAY WITH A SERIAL KILLER?
BE VERY CAUTIOUS AND LOOK INTO A PERSON'S REP BEFORE YOU AGREE TO STAY WITH THEM. YOU CAN BET THEY'LL BE LOOKING INTO YOU, AS WELL!
Couch Bum
the Reeds
REVIEWS
NO ONE WANTS TO INVITE A THIEF INTO THEIR HOME! AND COUCH-SURFING IS SOMETHING TO DO WITH LOTS OF PRE-PLANNING, NOT AT THE LAST MINUTE! ONLY TRUST ESTABLISHED SITES WITH VERIFIED ACCOUNTS AND UN-BIASED USER REVIEWS.

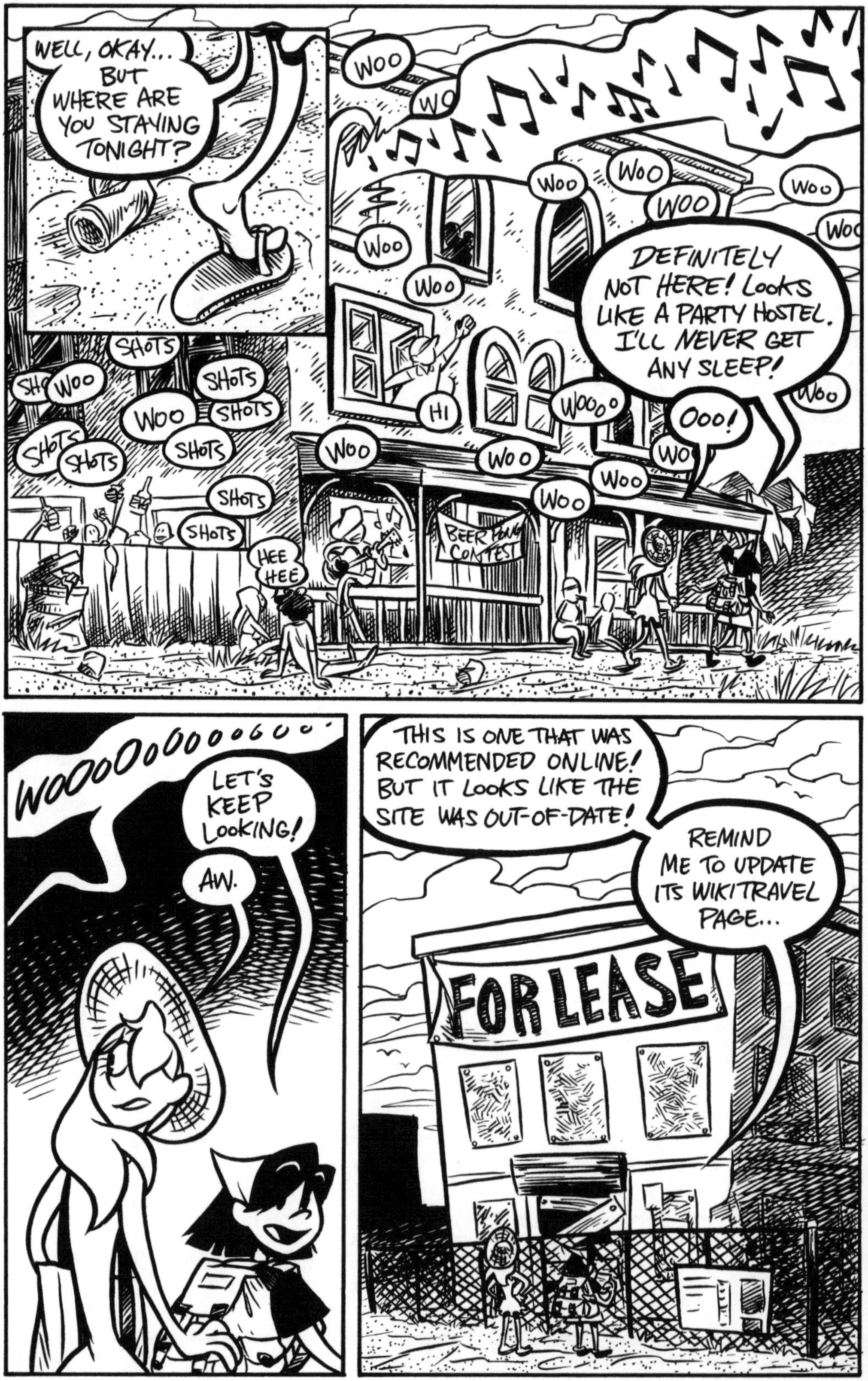
WELL, OKAY... BUT WHERE ARE YOU STAYING TONIGHT?
WOO
WOO
WOO
WOO
WOO
WOO
WOO
WOO
DEFINITELY NOT HERE! LOOKS LIKE A PARTY HOSTEL. I'LL NEVER GET ANY SLEEP!
SHOTS
WOO
SHOTS
WOO
SHOTS
SHOTS
SHOTS
SHOTS
SHOTS
SHOTS
HI
WOOOO
OOO!
WOO
WOO
WOO
WOO
WOO
WOO
BEER PONG CONTEST
HEE HEE
WOOOOOOOOOOOOO...
LET'S KEEP LOOKING!
AW.
THIS IS ONE THAT WAS RECOMMENDED ONLINE! BUT IT LOOKS LIKE THE SITE WAS OUT-OF-DATE!
REMIND ME TO UPDATE ITS WIKITRAVEL PAGE...
FOR LEASE

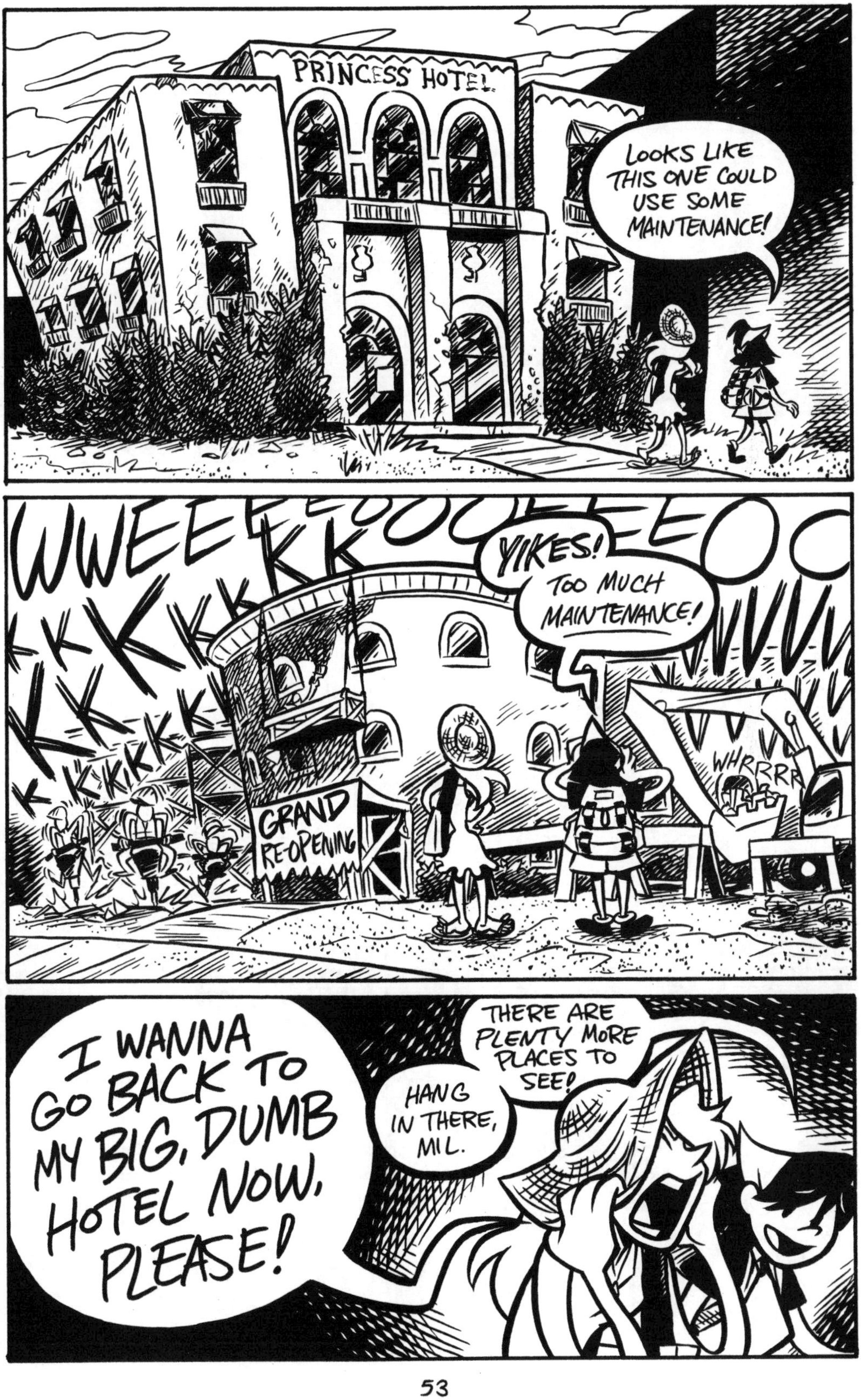
PRINCESS HOTEL
LOOKS LIKE THIS ONE COULD USE SOME MAINTENANCE!
YIKES! TOO MUCH MAINTENANCE!
GRAND RE-OPENING
WHRRRR
I WANNA GO BACK TO MY BIG, DUMB HOTEL NOW, PLEASE!
HANG IN THERE, MIL.
THERE ARE PLENTY MORE PLACES TO SEE!

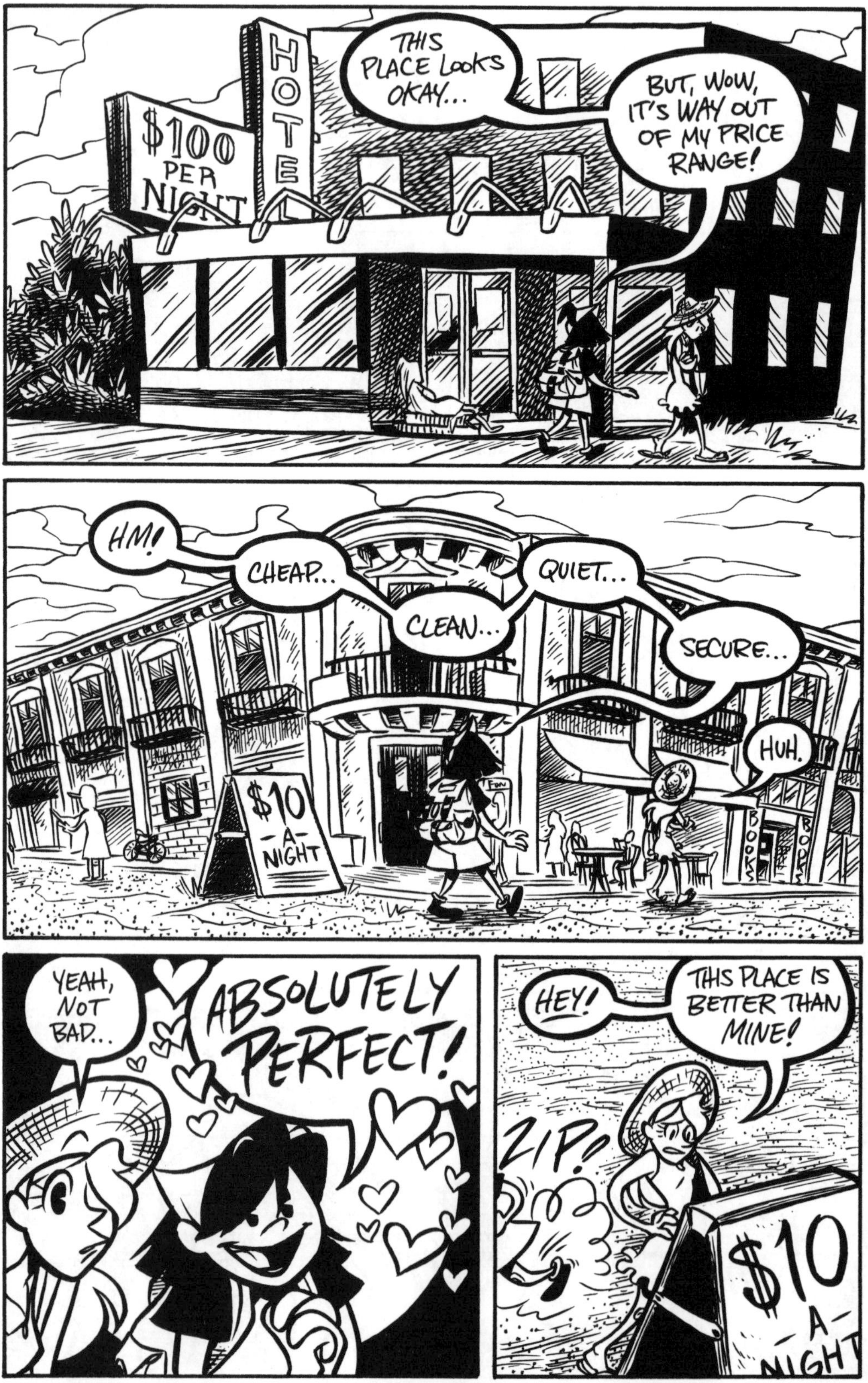
$100 PER NIGHT
HOTE
THIS PLACE LOOKS OKAY...
BUT, WOW, IT'S WAY OUT OF MY PRICE RANGE!
HM!
CHEAP...
CLEAN...
QUIET...
SECURE...
HUH.
$10 -A- NIGHT
BOOKS
YEAH, NOT BAD...
ABSOLUTELY PERFECT!
HEY!
THIS PLACE IS BETTER THAN MINE!
ZIP!
$10 A NIGHT

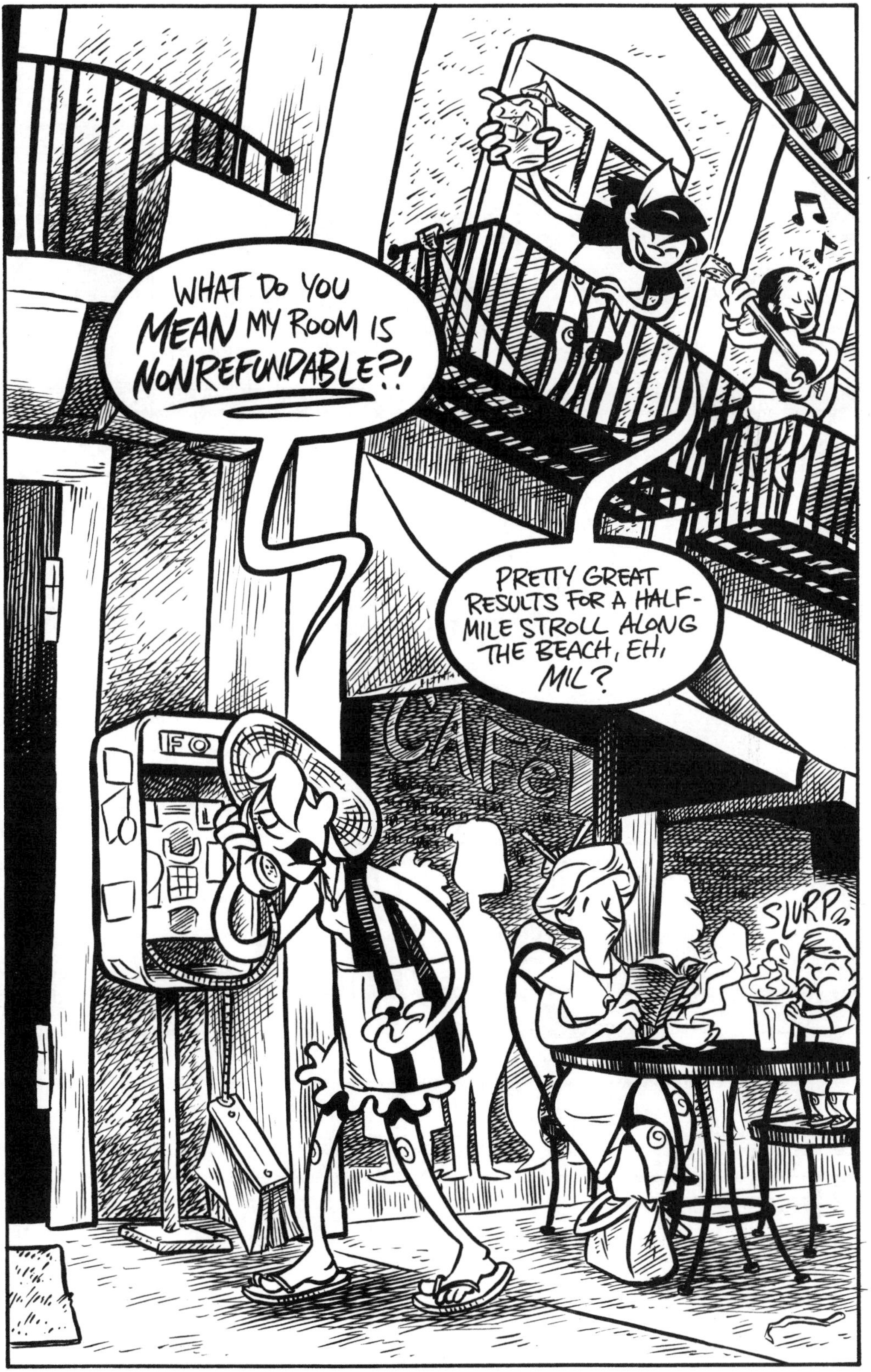
WHAT DO YOU MEAN MY ROOM IS NONREFUNDABLE?!
PRETTY GREAT RESULTS FOR A HALF-MILE STROLL ALONG THE BEACH, EH, MIL?
CAFÉ
SLURP

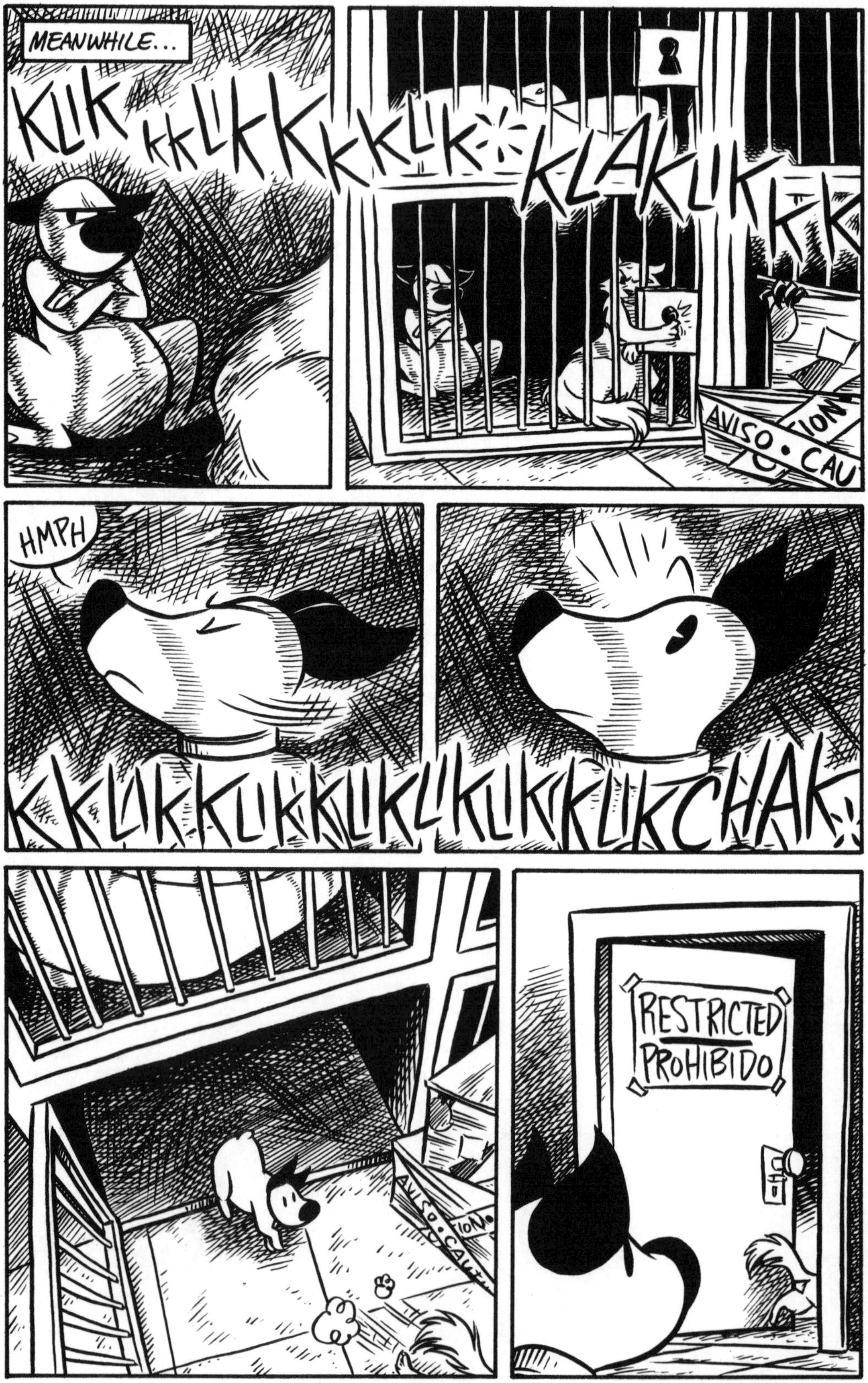
MEANWHILE...
KLIK KKLIK KKKLIK
KLAKLIK KK
AVISO • CAU
HMPH
KKLIKKLIKKLIKKLIKKLIKKLIKKLIKCHAK
AVISO • CAU
RESTRICTED
PROHIBIDO

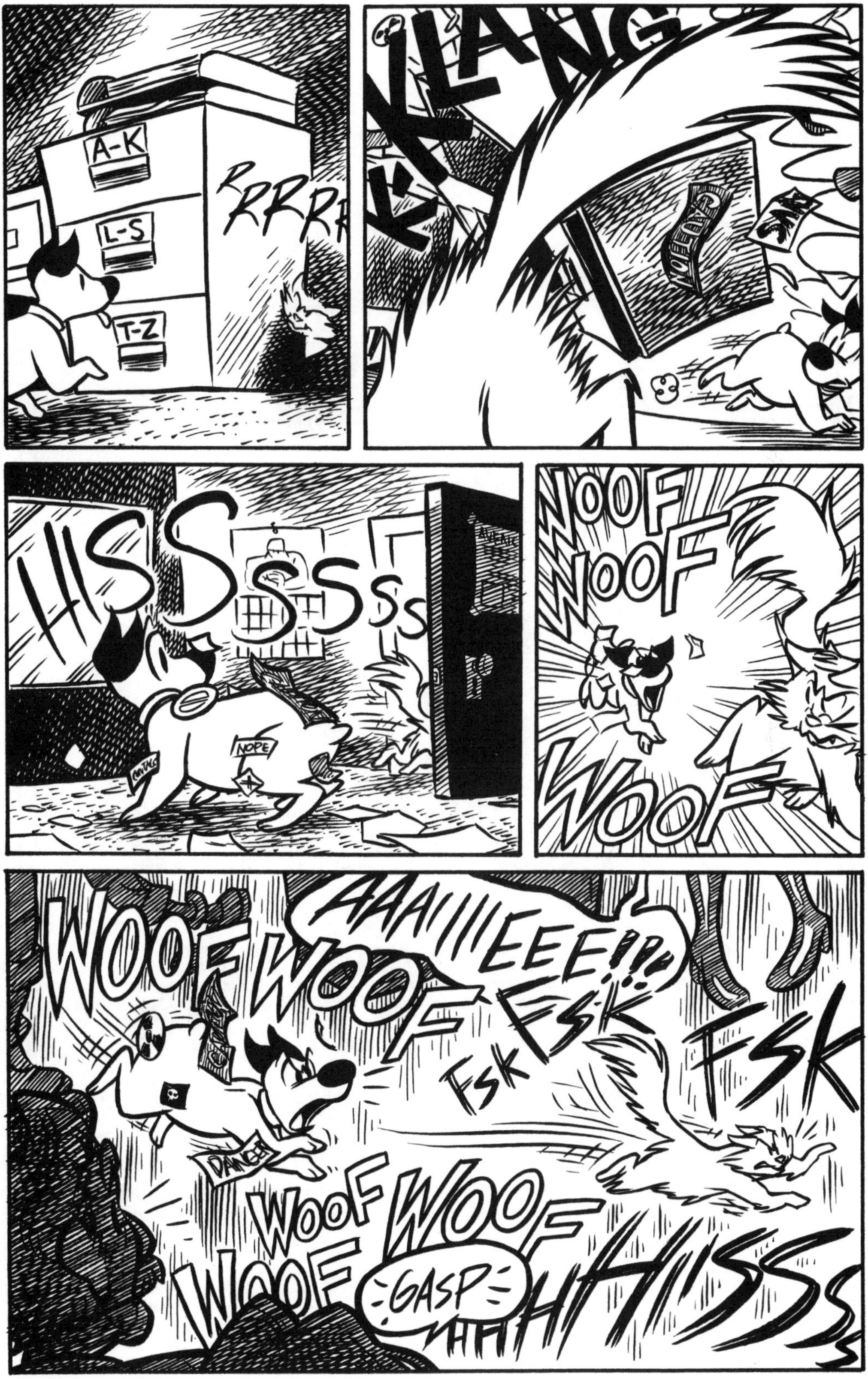
A-K
L-S
T-Z
RRRRRR
KLANG
CAUTION
HISSSSSS
NOPE
WOOF
WOOF
WOOF
WOOF WOOF
AAA!!!EEE!!!
FSK FSK
FSK
FSK
DANGER
WOOF WOOF
WOOF
GASP
HHHISSS

Chapter Six

Food

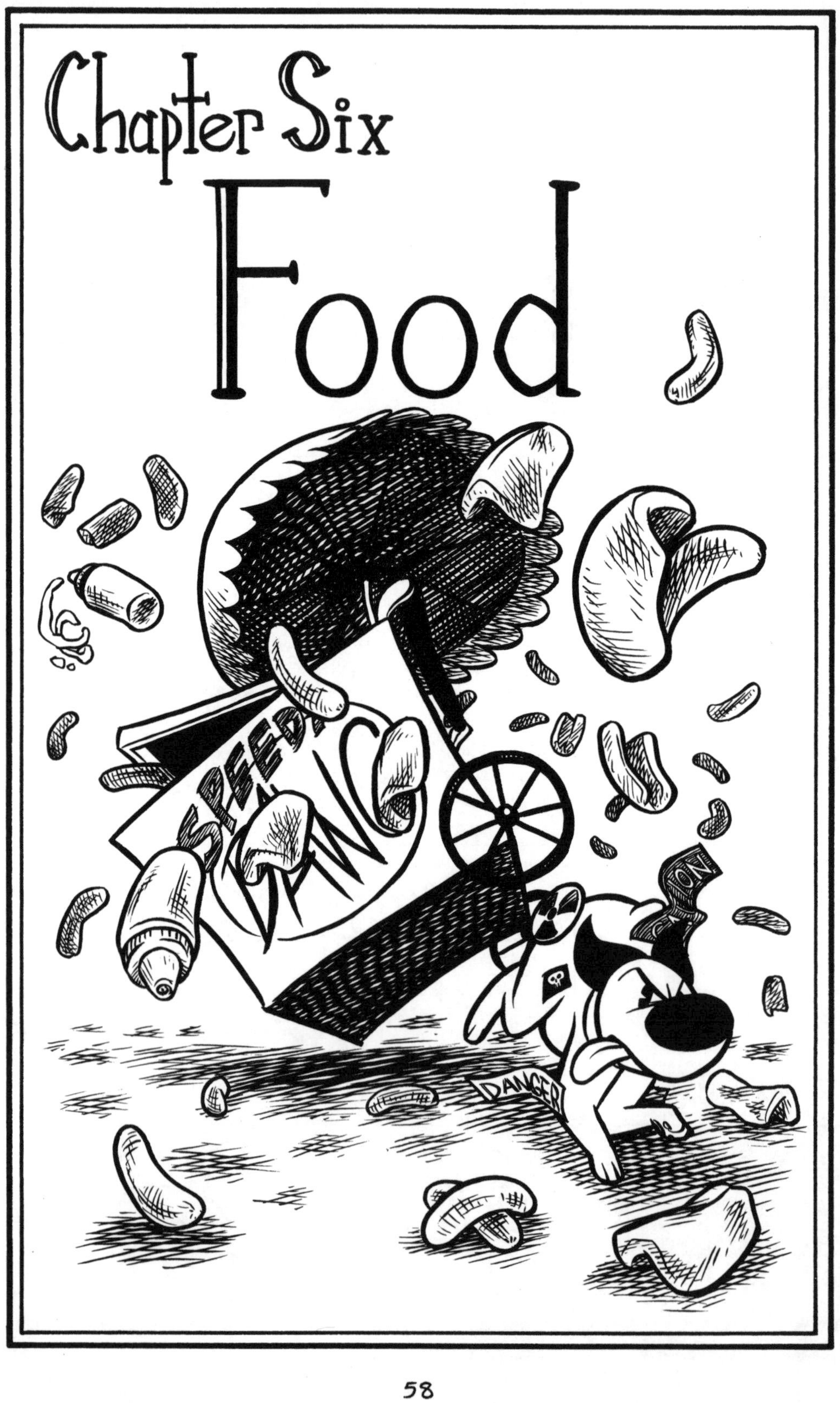
DANGER

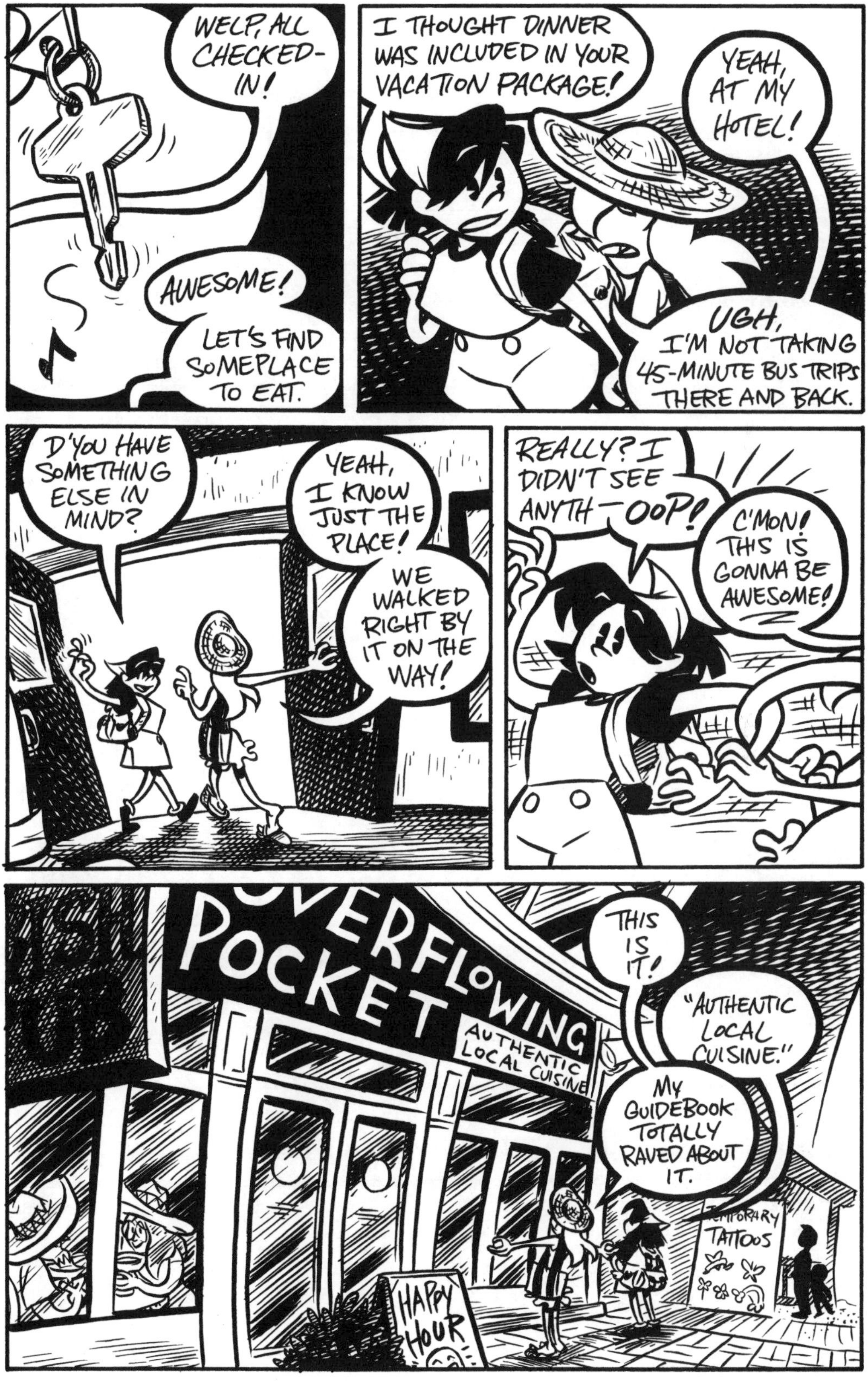
WELP, ALL CHECKED-IN!
AWESOME!
LET'S FIND SOMEPLACE TO EAT.
I THOUGHT DINNER WAS INCLUDED IN YOUR VACATION PACKAGE!
YEAH, AT MY HOTEL!
UGH, I'M NOT TAKING 45-MINUTE BUS TRIPS THERE AND BACK.
D'YOU HAVE SOMETHING ELSE IN MIND?
YEAH, I KNOW JUST THE PLACE!
WE WALKED RIGHT BY IT ON THE WAY!
REALLY? I DIDN'T SEE ANYTH—OOP!
C'MON! THIS IS GONNA BE AWESOME!
OVERFLOWING POCKET
AUTHENTIC LOCAL CUISINE
THIS IS IT!
"AUTHENTIC LOCAL CUISINE."
MY GUIDEBOOK TOTALLY RAVED ABOUT IT.
HAPPY HOUR
TEMPORARY TATTOOS

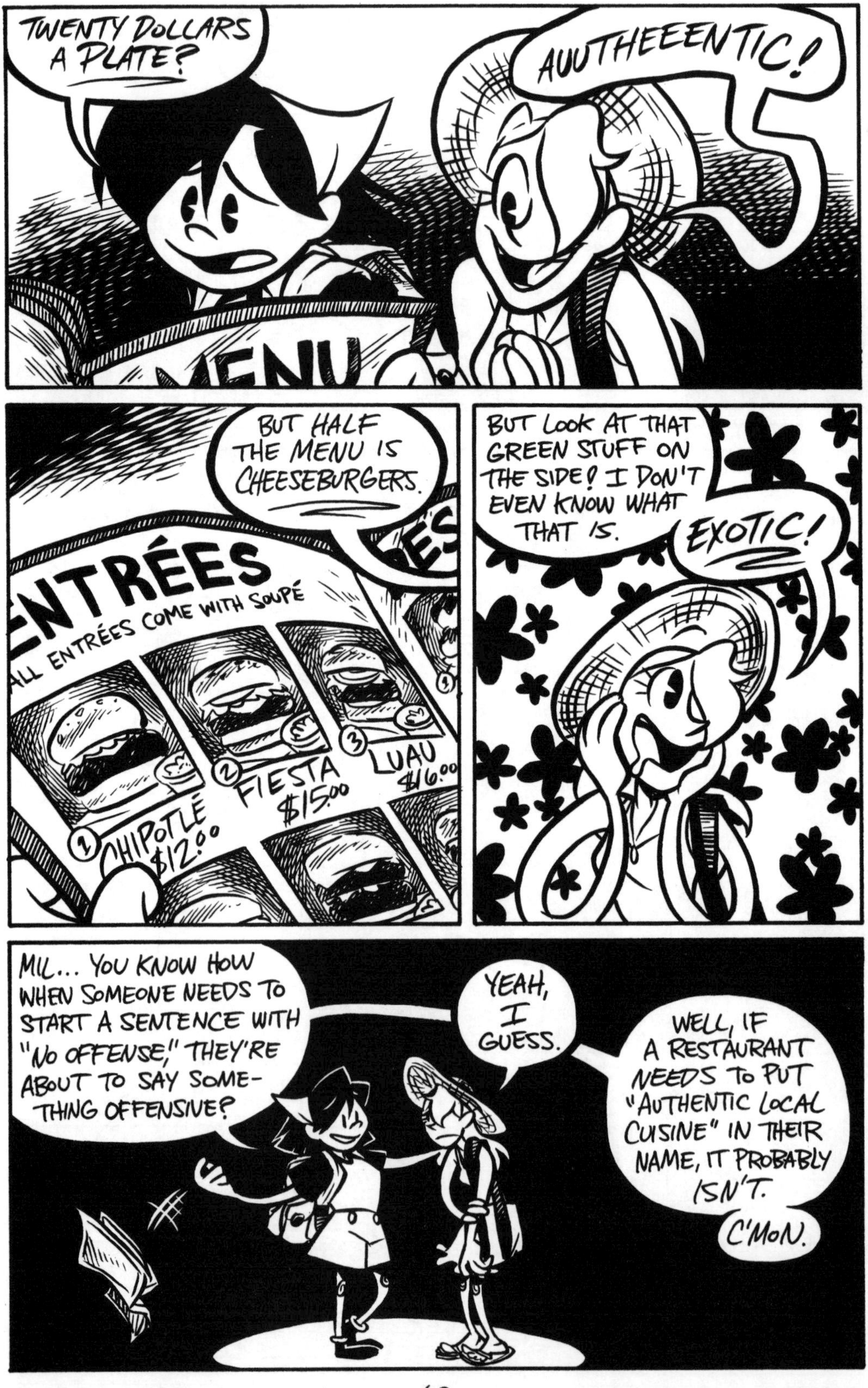

TWENTY DOLLARS A PLATE?
AUUTHEEENTIC!
MENU
BUT HALF THE MENU IS CHEESEBURGERS.
ENTRÉES
ALL ENTRÉES COME WITH SOUPÉ
1 CHIPOTLE $12.00
2 FIESTA $15.00
3 LUAU $16.00
BUT LOOK AT THAT GREEN STUFF ON THE SIDE! I DON'T EVEN KNOW WHAT THAT IS.
EXOTIC!
MIL... YOU KNOW HOW WHEN SOMEONE NEEDS TO START A SENTENCE WITH "NO OFFENSE," THEY'RE ABOUT TO SAY SOMETHING OFFENSIVE?
YEAH, I GUESS.
WELL, IF A RESTAURANT NEEDS TO PUT "AUTHENTIC LOCAL CUISINE" IN THEIR NAME, IT PROBABLY ISN'T.
C'MON.

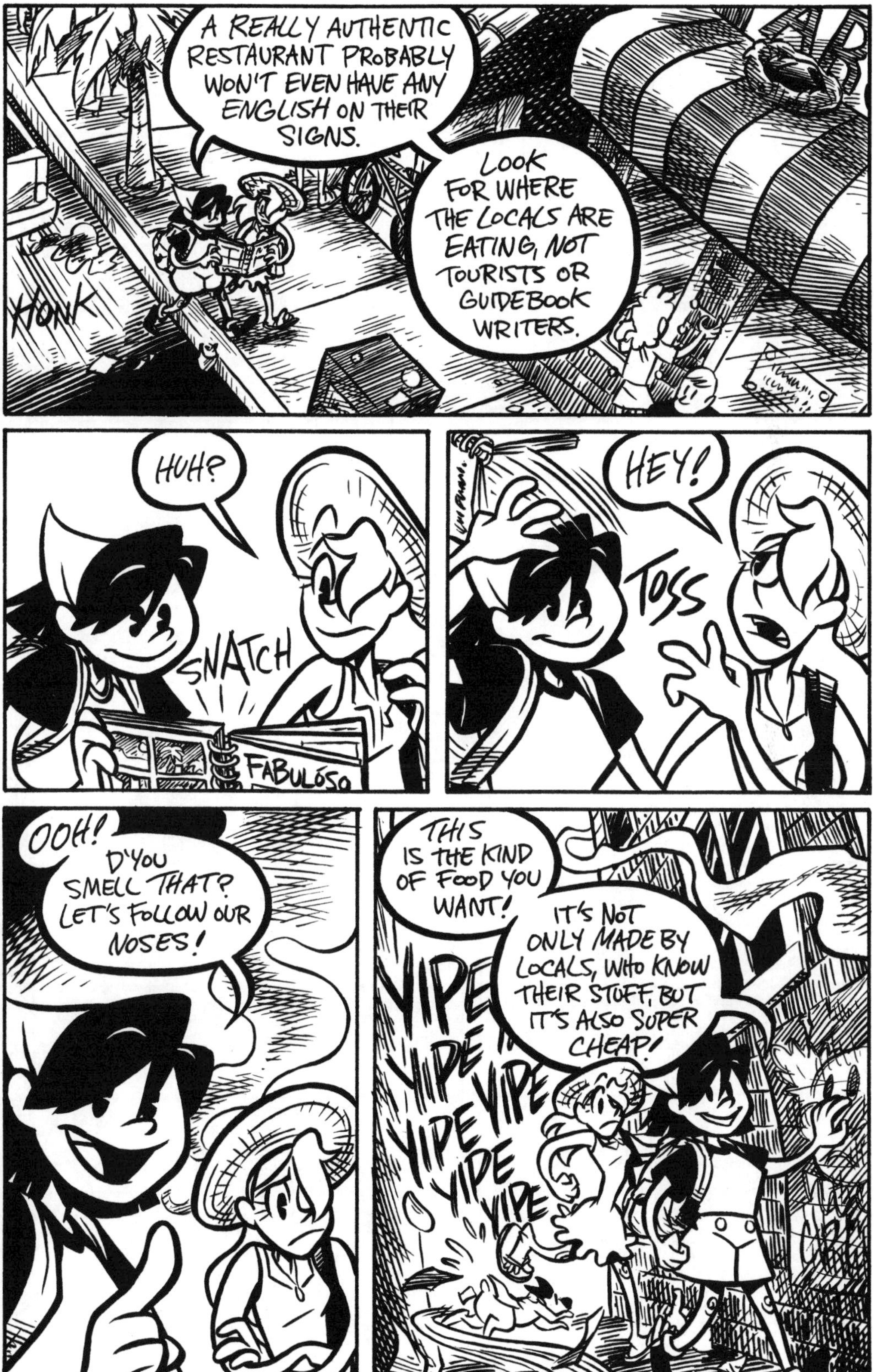
A REALLY AUTHENTIC RESTAURANT PROBABLY WON'T EVEN HAVE ANY ENGLISH ON THEIR SIGNS.
LOOK FOR WHERE THE LOCALS ARE EATING, NOT TOURISTS OR GUIDEBOOK WRITERS.
HONK
HUH?
SNATCH
FABULÓSO
HEY!
TOSS
OOH! D'YOU SMELL THAT? LET'S FOLLOW OUR NOSES!
THIS IS THE KIND OF FOOD YOU WANT!
IT'S NOT ONLY MADE BY LOCALS, WHO KNOW THEIR STUFF, BUT IT'S ALSO SUPER CHEAP!
YIPE YIPE YIPE YIPE YIPE YIPE YIPE

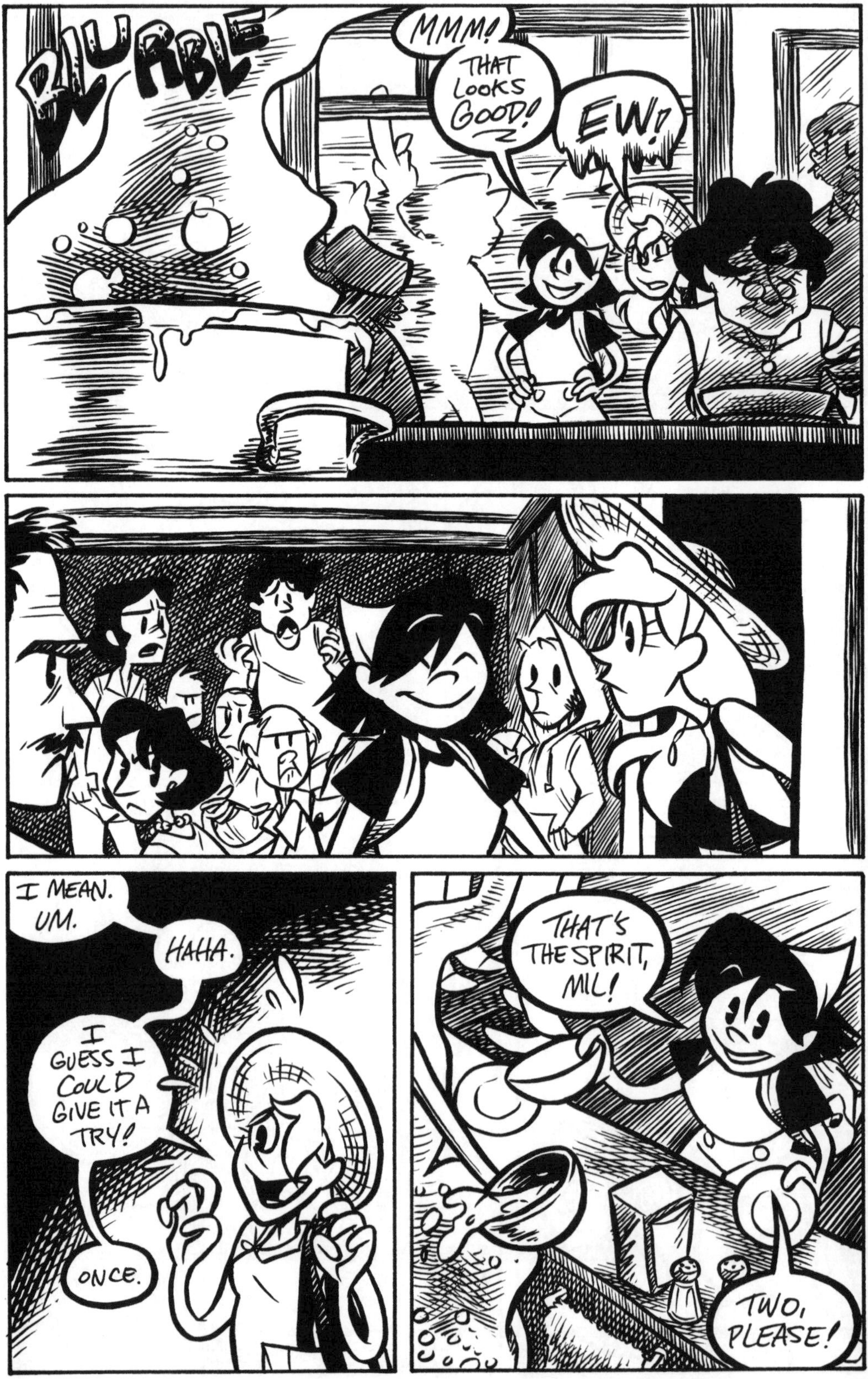
BLURBLE
MMM!
THAT LOOKS GOOD!
EW!
I MEAN. UM.
HAHA.
I GUESS I COULD GIVE IT A TRY!
ONCE.
THAT'S THE SPIRIT, MIL!
TWO, PLEASE!

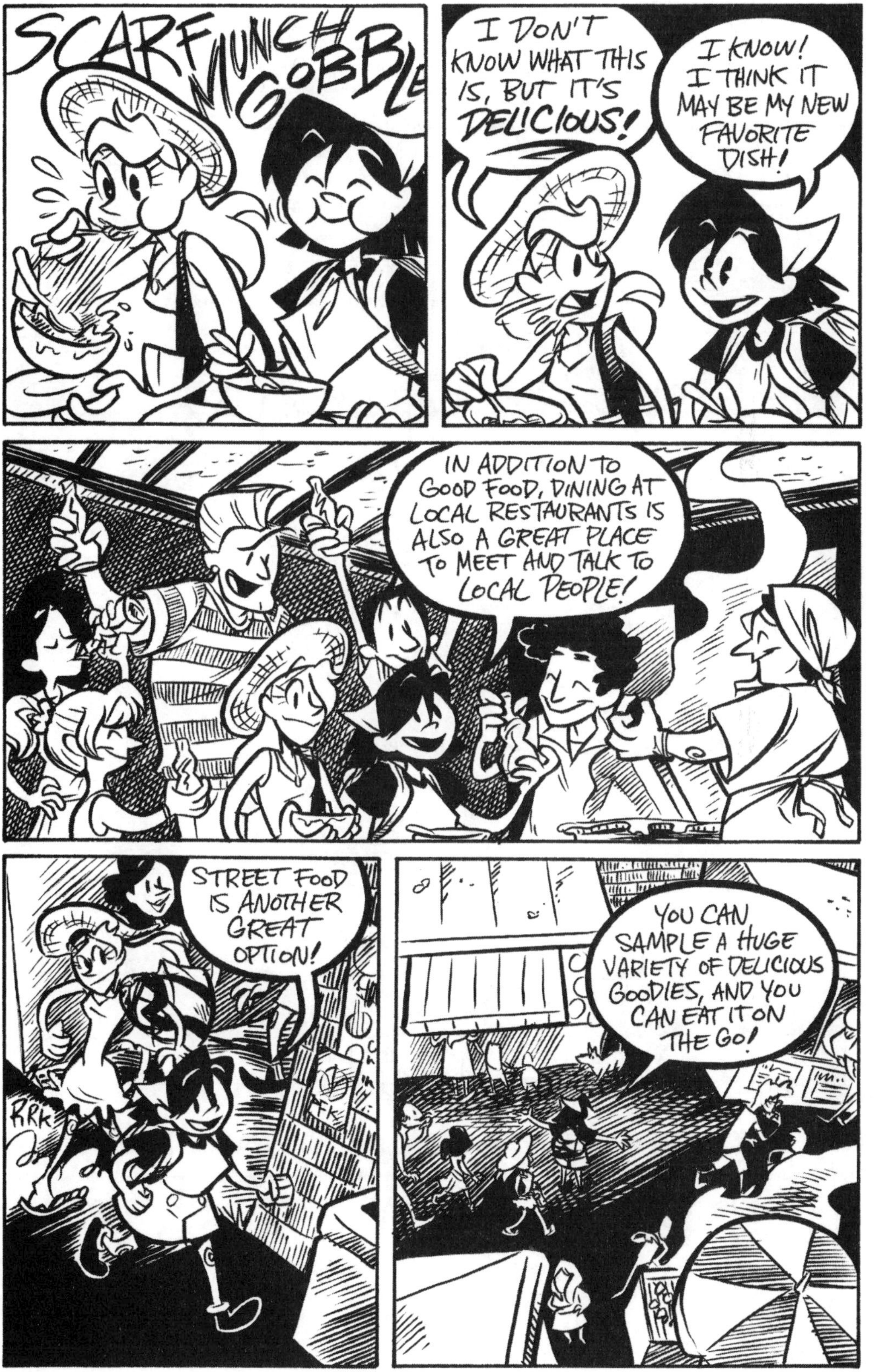
SCARF MUNCH GOBBLE
I DON'T KNOW WHAT THIS IS, BUT IT'S DELICIOUS!
I KNOW! I THINK IT MAY BE MY NEW FAVORITE DISH!
IN ADDITION TO GOOD FOOD, DINING AT LOCAL RESTAURANTS IS ALSO A GREAT PLACE TO MEET AND TALK TO LOCAL PEOPLE!
STREET FOOD IS ANOTHER GREAT OPTION!
RRK
YOU CAN SAMPLE A HUGE VARIETY OF DELICIOUS GOODIES, AND YOU CAN EAT IT ON THE GO!

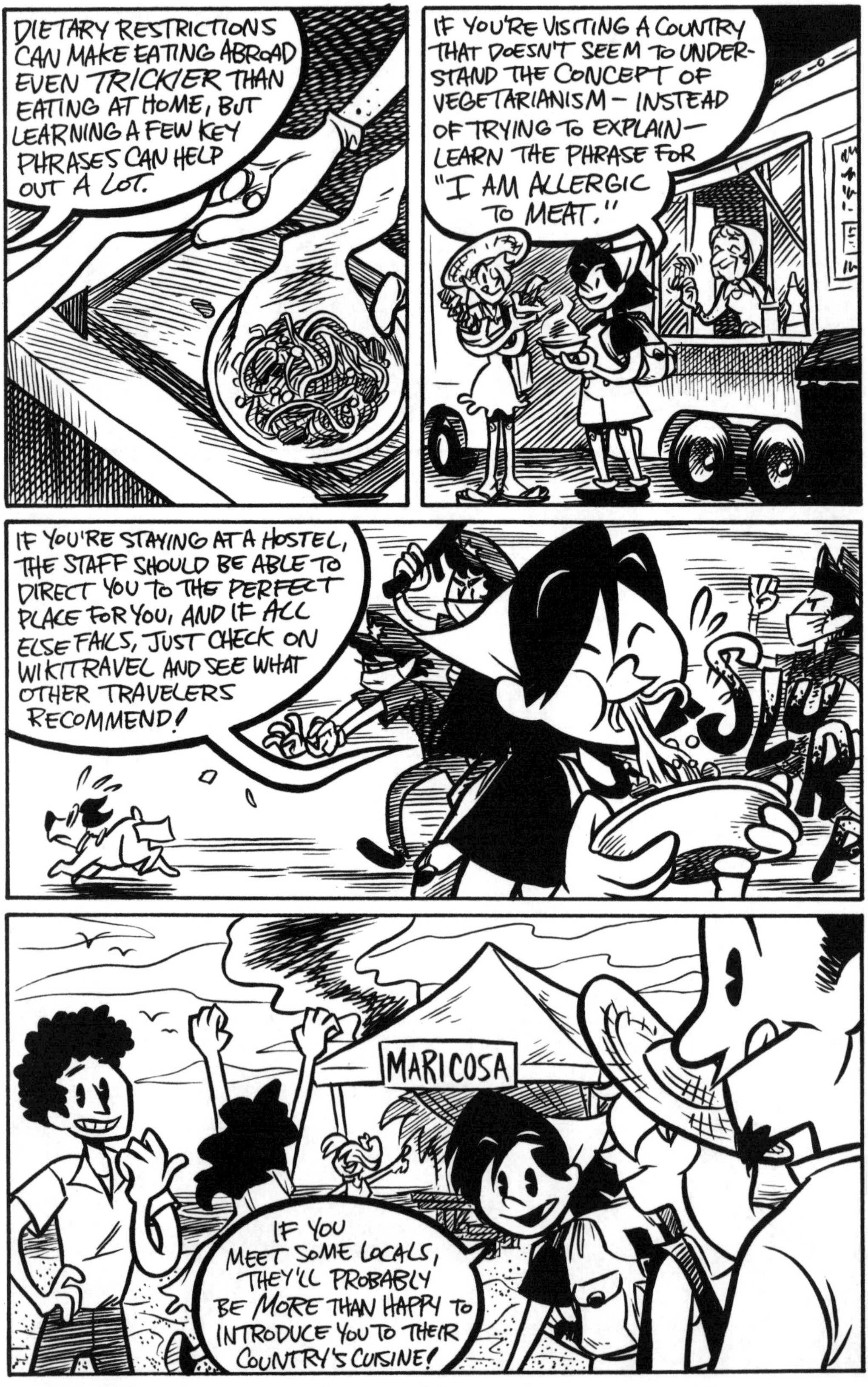
DIETARY RESTRICTIONS CAN MAKE EATING ABROAD EVEN TRICKIER THAN EATING AT HOME, BUT LEARNING A FEW KEY PHRASES CAN HELP OUT A LOT.
IF YOU'RE VISITING A COUNTRY THAT DOESN'T SEEM TO UNDERSTAND THE CONCEPT OF VEGETARIANISM — INSTEAD OF TRYING TO EXPLAIN — LEARN THE PHRASE FOR "I AM ALLERGIC TO MEAT."
IF YOU'RE STAYING AT A HOSTEL, THE STAFF SHOULD BE ABLE TO DIRECT YOU TO THE PERFECT PLACE FOR YOU, AND IF ALL ELSE FAILS, JUST CHECK ON WIKITRAVEL AND SEE WHAT OTHER TRAVELERS RECOMMEND!
MARICOSA
IF YOU MEET SOME LOCALS, THEY'LL PROBABLY BE MORE THAN HAPPY TO INTRODUCE YOU TO THEIR COUNTRY'S CUISINE!

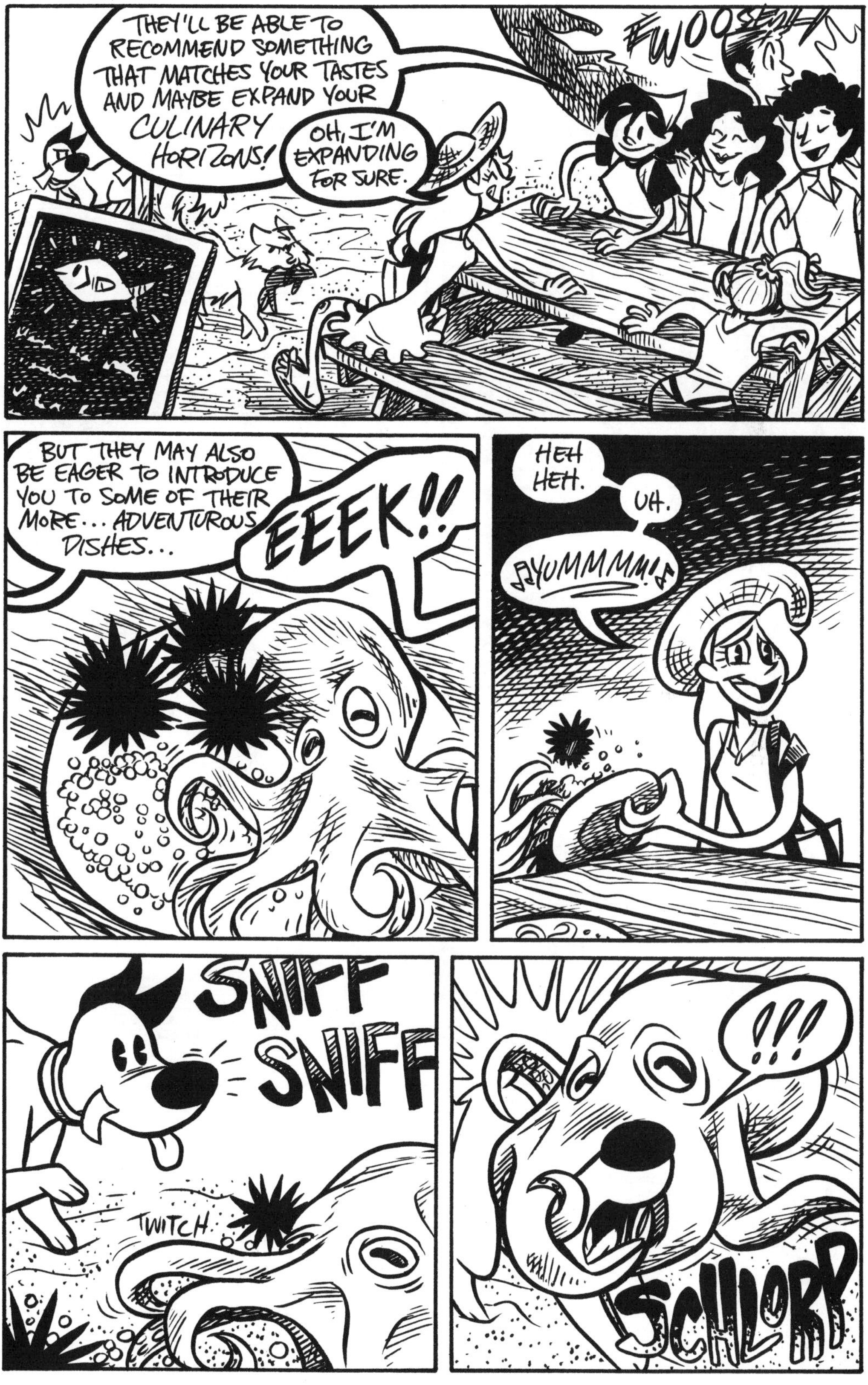
THEY'LL BE ABLE TO RECOMMEND SOMETHING THAT MATCHES YOUR TASTES AND MAYBE EXPAND YOUR CULINARY HORIZONS!
OH, I'M EXPANDING FOR SURE.
FWOOSH!!
BUT THEY MAY ALSO BE EAGER TO INTRODUCE YOU TO SOME OF THEIR MORE... ADVENTUROUS DISHES...
EEEK!!
HEH HEH.
UH.
♫YUMMMM!♫
SNIFF
SNIFF
TWITCH
!!!
SCHLORP

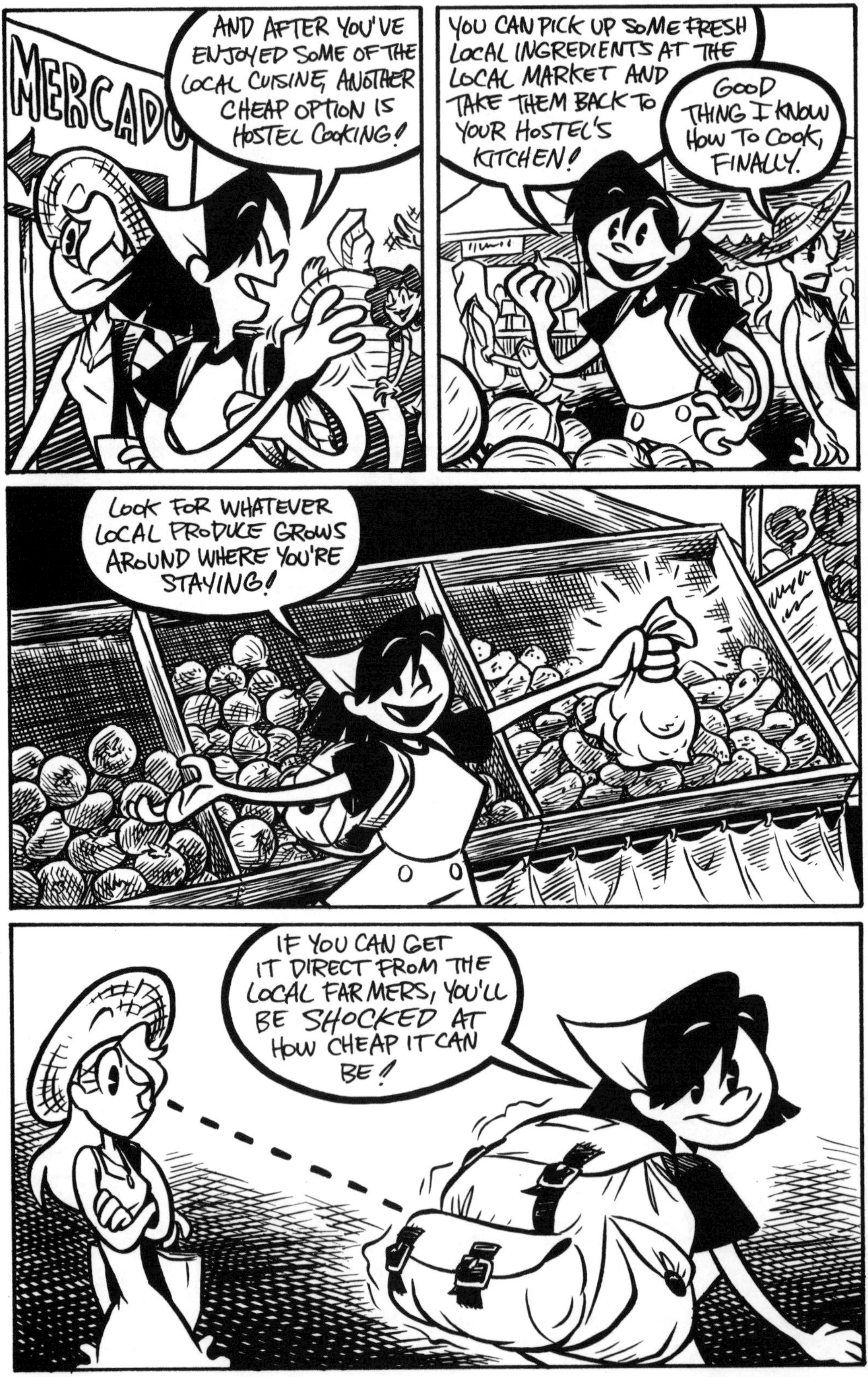
MERCADO
AND AFTER YOU'VE ENJOYED SOME OF THE LOCAL CUISINE, ANOTHER CHEAP OPTION IS HOSTEL COOKING!
YOU CAN PICK UP SOME FRESH LOCAL INGREDIENTS AT THE LOCAL MARKET AND TAKE THEM BACK TO YOUR HOSTEL'S KITCHEN!
GOOD THING I KNOW HOW TO COOK, FINALLY.
LOOK FOR WHATEVER LOCAL PRODUCE GROWS AROUND WHERE YOU'RE STAYING!
IF YOU CAN GET IT DIRECT FROM THE LOCAL FARMERS, YOU'LL BE SHOCKED AT HOW CHEAP IT CAN BE!

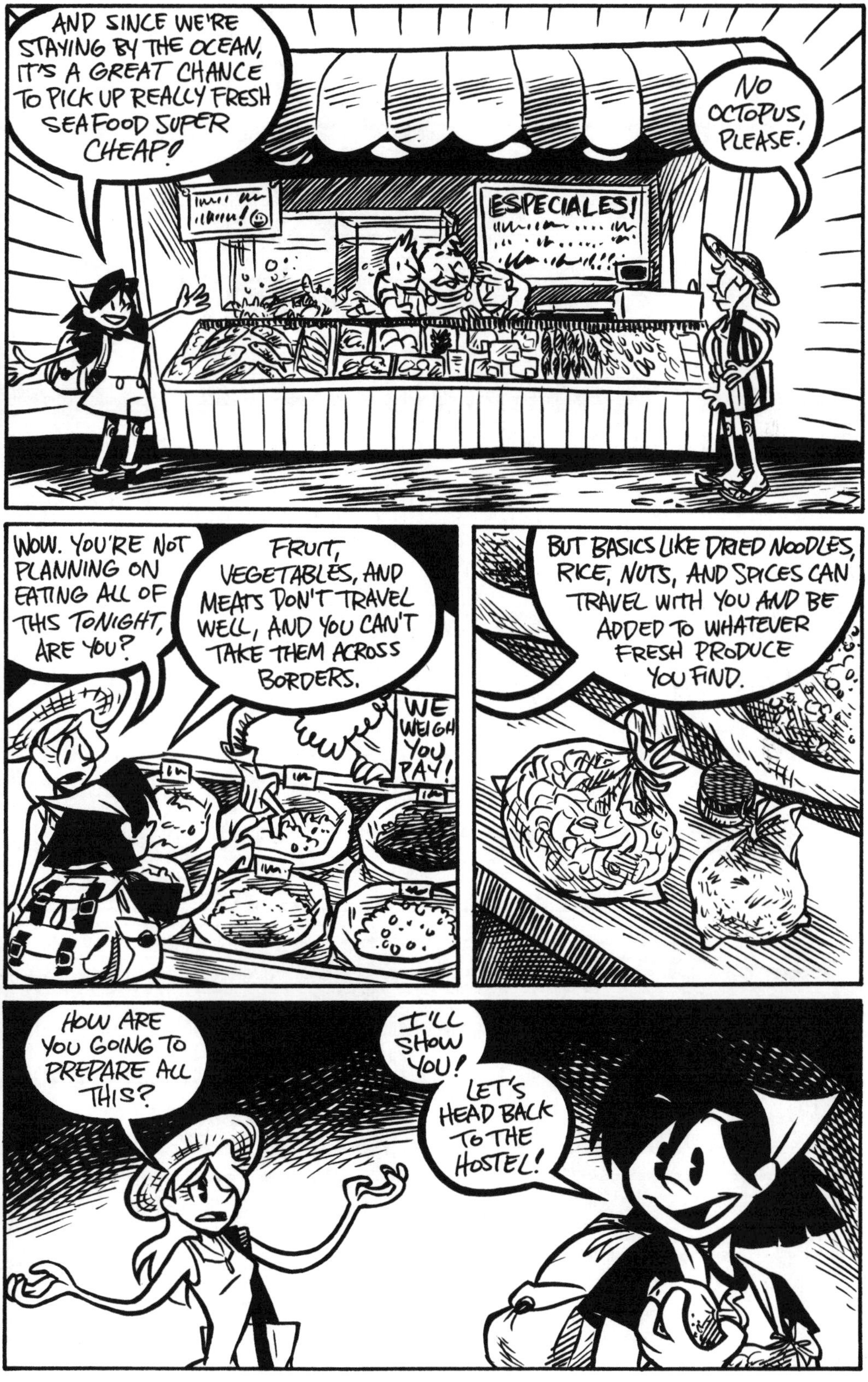
AND SINCE WE'RE STAYING BY THE OCEAN, IT'S A GREAT CHANCE TO PICK UP REALLY FRESH SEAFOOD SUPER CHEAP!
ESPECIALES!
NO OCTOPUS, PLEASE.
WOW. YOU'RE NOT PLANNING ON EATING ALL OF THIS TONIGHT, ARE YOU?
FRUIT, VEGETABLES, AND MEATS DON'T TRAVEL WELL, AND YOU CAN'T TAKE THEM ACROSS BORDERS.
WE WEIGH YOU PAY!
BUT BASICS LIKE DRIED NOODLES, RICE, NUTS, AND SPICES CAN TRAVEL WITH YOU AND BE ADDED TO WHATEVER FRESH PRODUCE YOU FIND.
HOW ARE YOU GOING TO PREPARE ALL THIS?
I'LL SHOW YOU!
LET'S HEAD BACK TO THE HOSTEL!

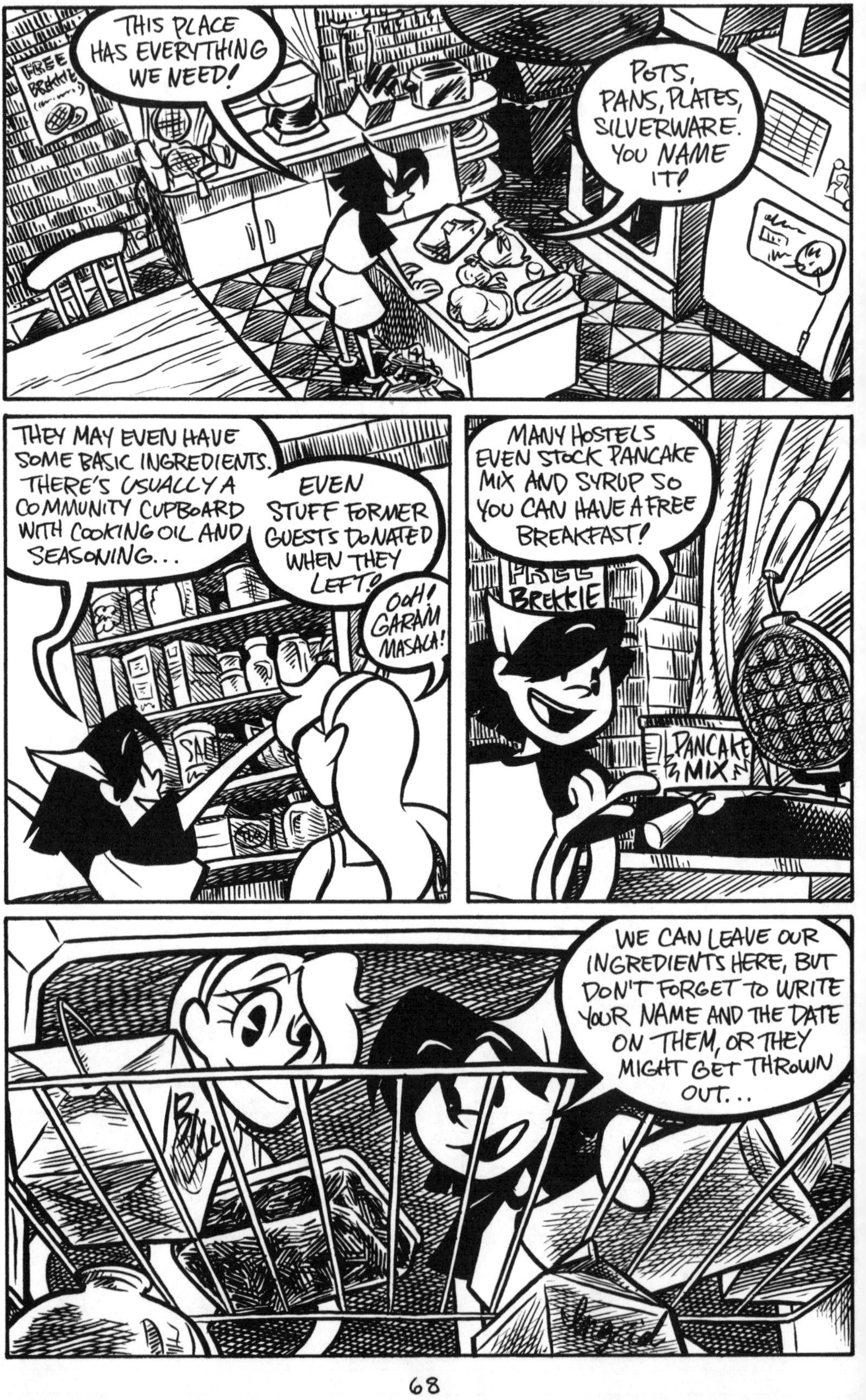
FREE BREKKIE
THIS PLACE HAS EVERYTHING WE NEED!
POTS, PANS, PLATES, SILVERWARE. YOU NAME IT!
THEY MAY EVEN HAVE SOME BASIC INGREDIENTS. THERE'S USUALLY A COMMUNITY CUPBOARD WITH COOKING OIL AND SEASONING...
EVEN STUFF FORMER GUESTS DONATED WHEN THEY LEFT!
OOH! GARAM MASALA!
MANY HOSTELS EVEN STOCK PANCAKE MIX AND SYRUP SO YOU CAN HAVE A FREE BREAKFAST!
FREE BREKKIE
PANCAKE MIX
WE CAN LEAVE OUR INGREDIENTS HERE, BUT DON'T FORGET TO WRITE YOUR NAME AND THE DATE ON THEM, OR THEY MIGHT GET THROWN OUT...

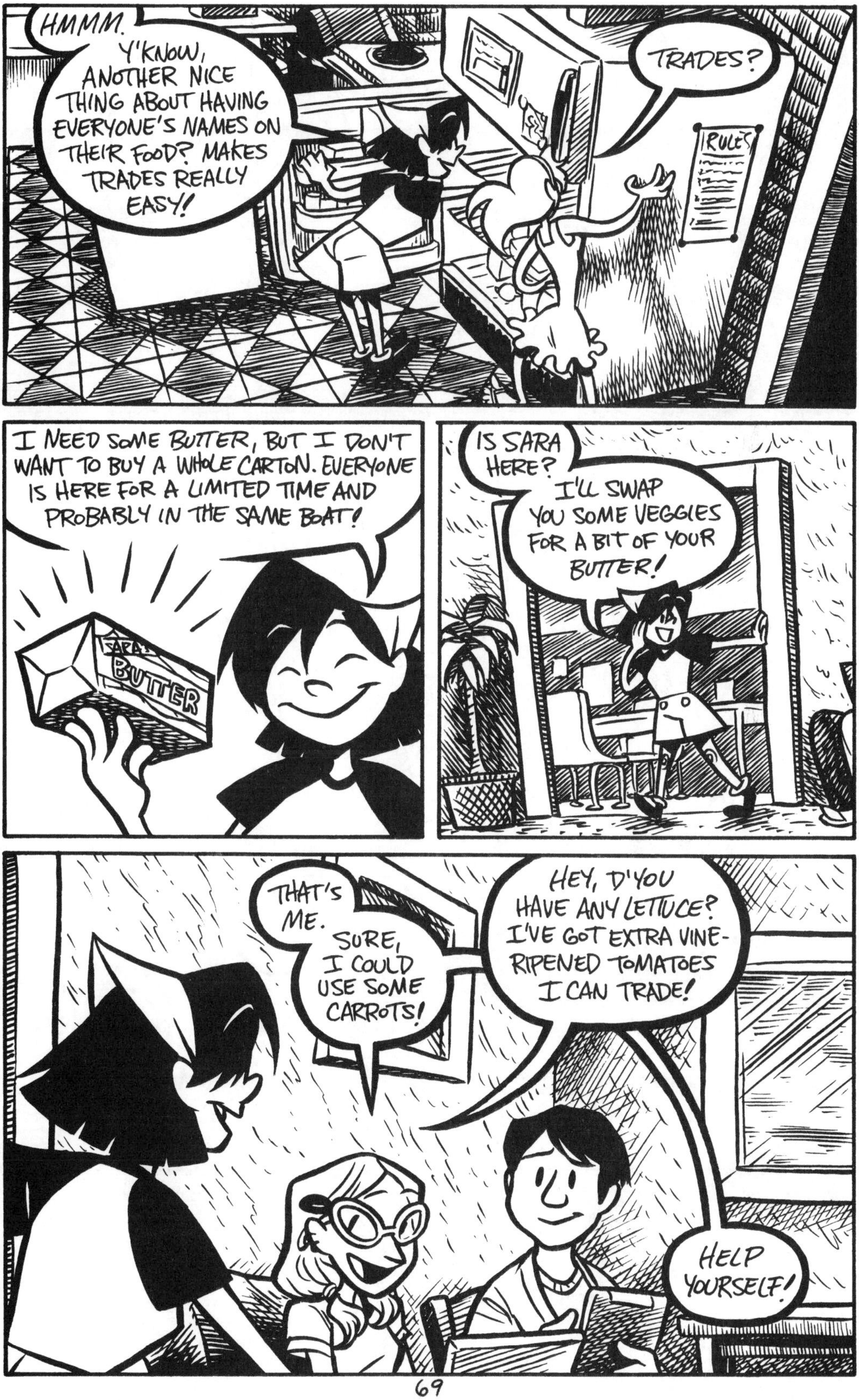
HMMM.
Y'KNOW, ANOTHER NICE THING ABOUT HAVING EVERYONE'S NAMES ON THEIR FOOD? MAKES TRADES REALLY EASY!
TRADES?
I NEED SOME BUTTER, BUT I DON'T WANT TO BUY A WHOLE CARTON. EVERYONE IS HERE FOR A LIMITED TIME AND PROBABLY IN THE SAME BOAT!
SARA'S BUTTER
IS SARA HERE?
I'LL SWAP YOU SOME VEGGIES FOR A BIT OF YOUR BUTTER!
THAT'S ME.
SURE, I COULD USE SOME CARROTS!
HEY, D'YOU HAVE ANY LETTUCE? I'VE GOT EXTRA VINE-RIPENED TOMATOES I CAN TRADE!
HELP YOURSELF!

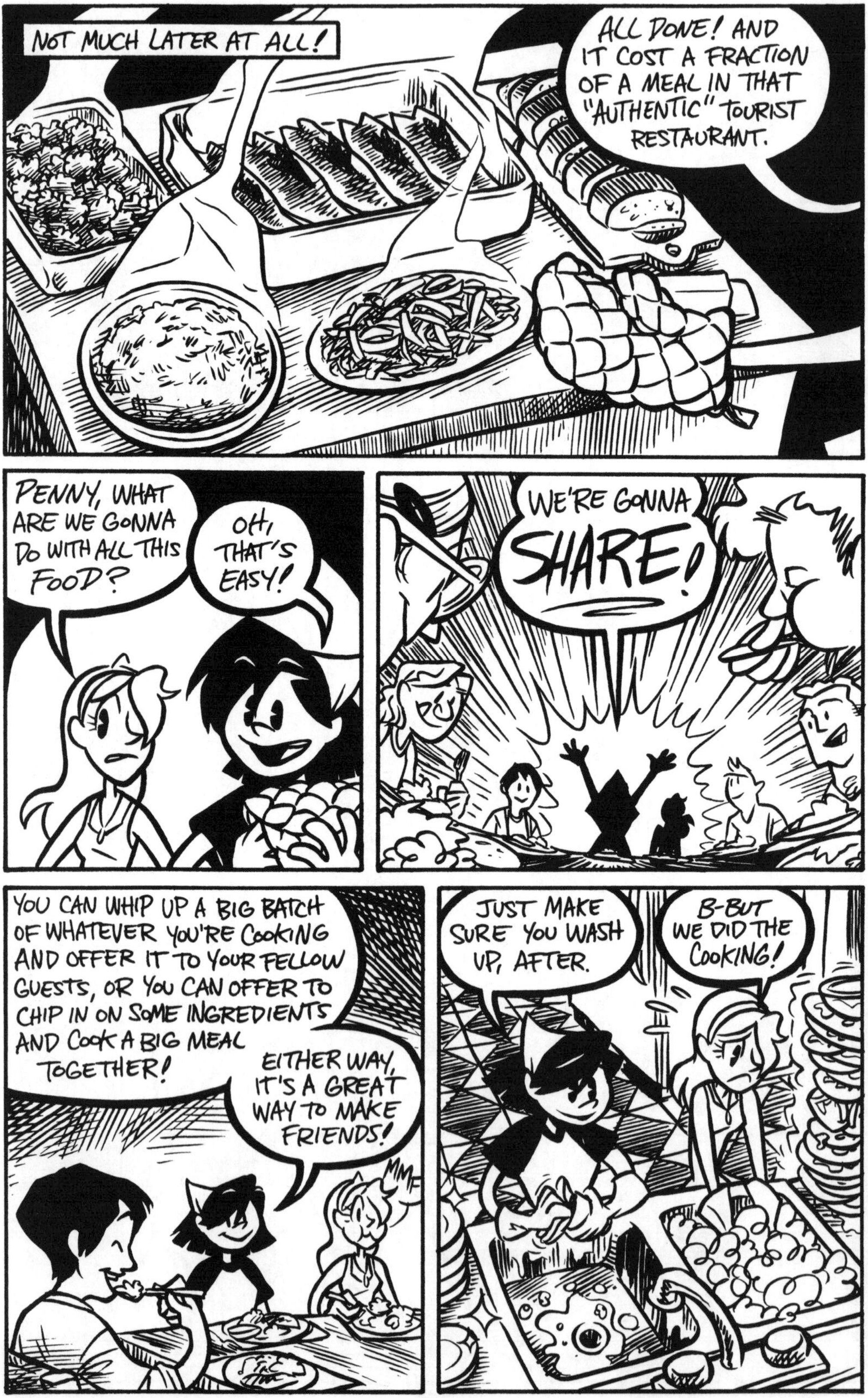
NOT MUCH LATER AT ALL!
ALL DONE! AND IT COST A FRACTION OF A MEAL IN THAT "AUTHENTIC" TOURIST RESTAURANT.
PENNY, WHAT ARE WE GONNA DO WITH ALL THIS FOOD?
OH, THAT'S EASY!
WE'RE GONNA SHARE!
YOU CAN WHIP UP A BIG BATCH OF WHATEVER YOU'RE COOKING AND OFFER IT TO YOUR FELLOW GUESTS, OR YOU CAN OFFER TO CHIP IN ON SOME INGREDIENTS AND COOK A BIG MEAL TOGETHER!
EITHER WAY, IT'S A GREAT WAY TO MAKE FRIENDS!
MM
JUST MAKE SURE YOU WASH UP, AFTER.
B-BUT WE DID THE COOKING!

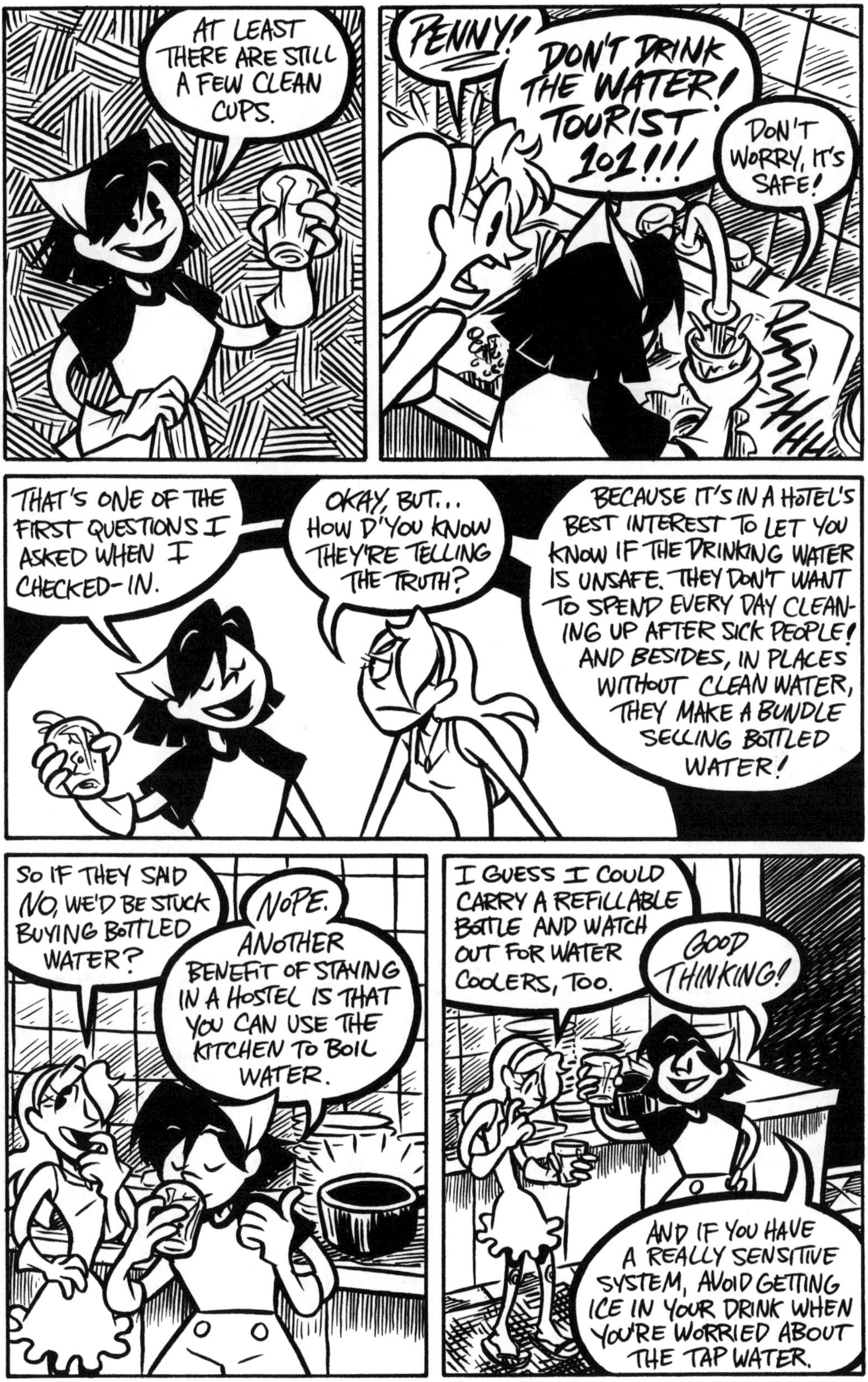
AT LEAST THERE ARE STILL A FEW CLEAN CUPS.
PENNY!
DON'T DRINK THE WATER! TOURIST 101!!!
DON'T WORRY, IT'S SAFE!
PSSSHHHH
THAT'S ONE OF THE FIRST QUESTIONS I ASKED WHEN I CHECKED-IN.
OKAY, BUT... HOW D'YOU KNOW THEY'RE TELLING THE TRUTH?
BECAUSE IT'S IN A HOTEL'S BEST INTEREST TO LET YOU KNOW IF THE DRINKING WATER IS UNSAFE. THEY DON'T WANT TO SPEND EVERY DAY CLEANING UP AFTER SICK PEOPLE! AND BESIDES, IN PLACES WITHOUT CLEAN WATER, THEY MAKE A BUNDLE SELLING BOTTLED WATER!
SO IF THEY SAID NO, WE'D BE STUCK BUYING BOTTLED WATER?
NOPE.
ANOTHER BENEFIT OF STAYING IN A HOSTEL IS THAT YOU CAN USE THE KITCHEN TO BOIL WATER.
I GUESS I COULD CARRY A REFILLABLE BOTTLE AND WATCH OUT FOR WATER COOLERS, TOO.
GOOD THINKING!
AND IF YOU HAVE A REALLY SENSITIVE SYSTEM, AVOID GETTING ICE IN YOUR DRINK WHEN YOU'RE WORRIED ABOUT THE TAP WATER.

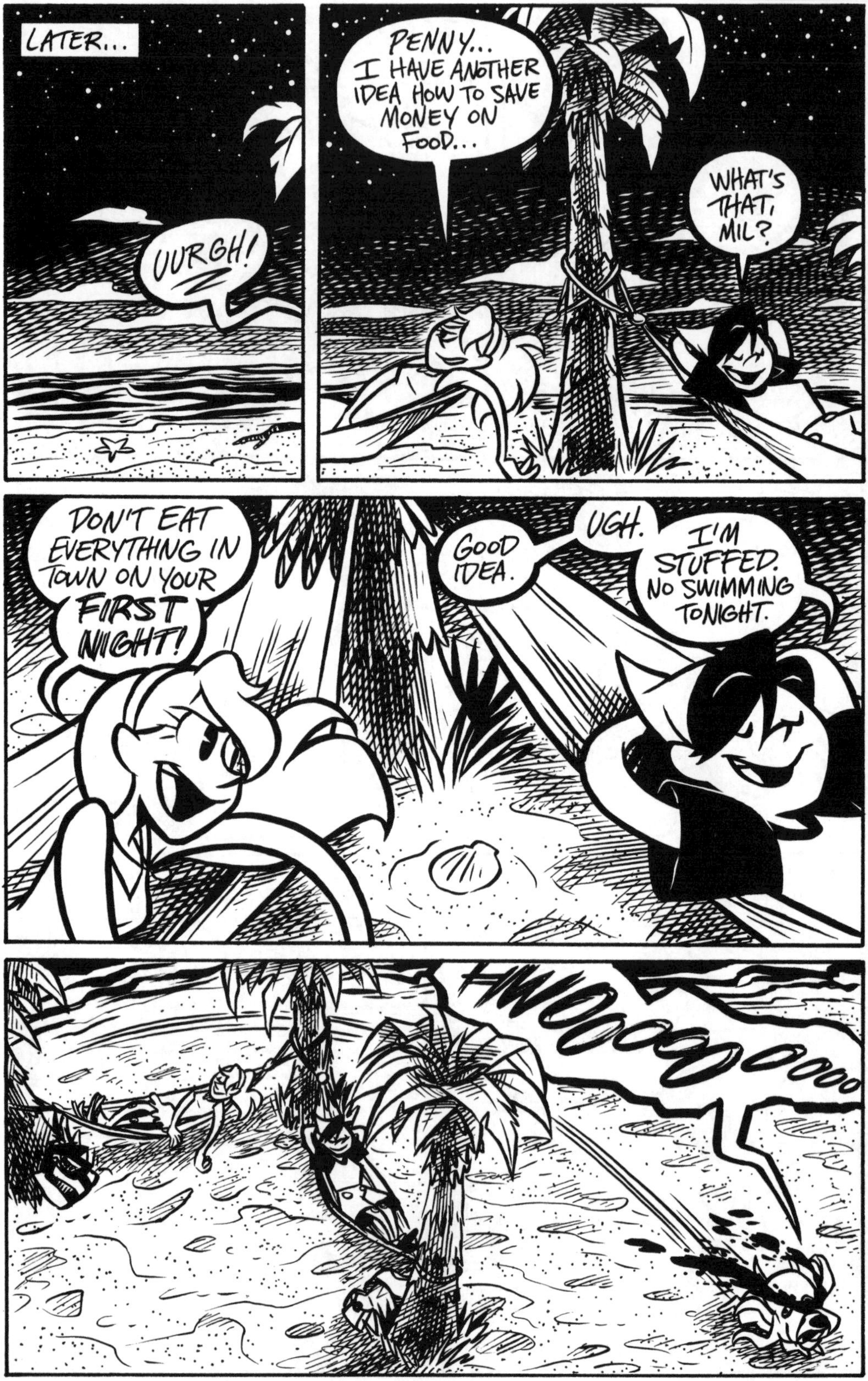
LATER...
UURGH!
PENNY... I HAVE ANOTHER IDEA HOW TO SAVE MONEY ON FOOD...
WHAT'S THAT, MIL?
DON'T EAT EVERYTHING IN TOWN ON YOUR FIRST NIGHT!
GOOD IDEA.
UGH.
I'M STUFFED. NO SWIMMING TONIGHT.
HWOOOOOOOOOO

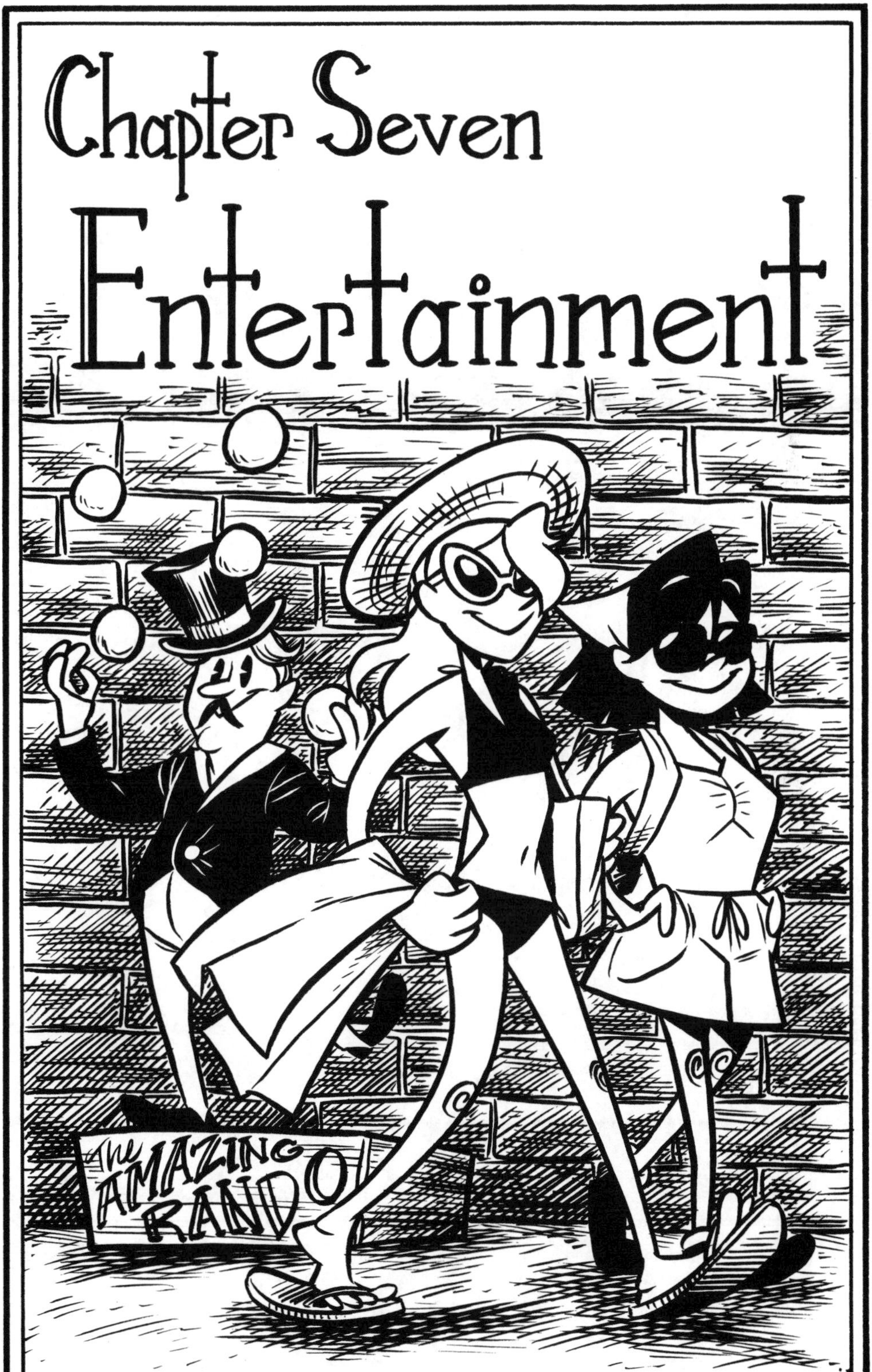
Chapter Seven
Entertainment
The AMAZING RANDO

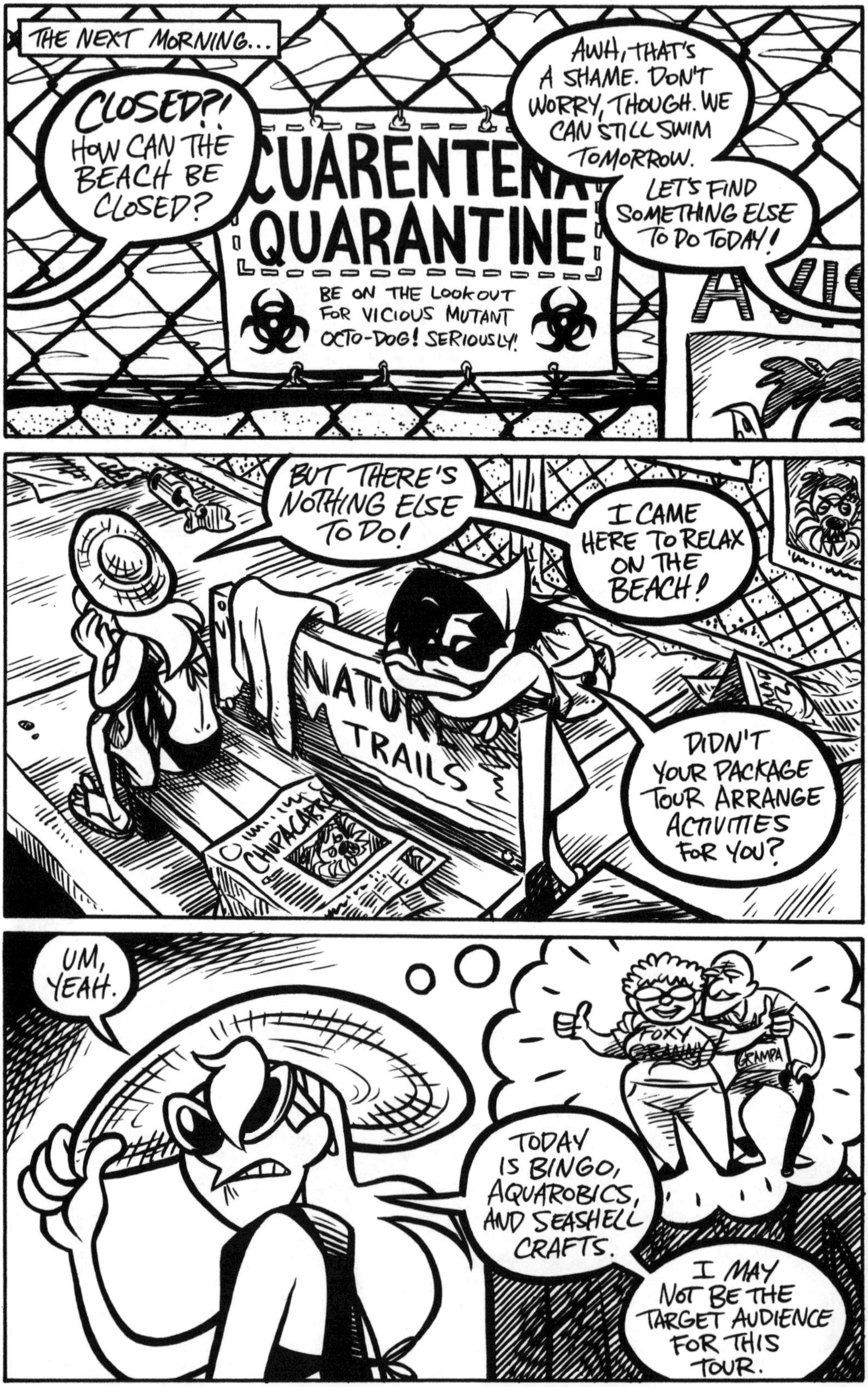
THE NEXT MORNING...
CLOSED?! HOW CAN THE BEACH BE CLOSED?
CUARENTENA
QUARANTINE
BE ON THE LOOKOUT FOR VICIOUS MUTANT OCTO-DOG! SERIOUSLY!
AWH, THAT'S A SHAME. DON'T WORRY, THOUGH. WE CAN STILL SWIM TOMORROW.
LET'S FIND SOMETHING ELSE TO DO TODAY!
BUT THERE'S NOTHING ELSE TO DO!
I CAME HERE TO RELAX ON THE BEACH!
NATURE TRAILS
DIDN'T YOUR PACKAGE TOUR ARRANGE ACTIVITIES FOR YOU?
UM, YEAH.
FOXY GRANNY
GRAMPA
TODAY IS BINGO, AQUAROBICS, AND SEASHELL CRAFTS.
I MAY NOT BE THE TARGET AUDIENCE FOR THIS TOUR.

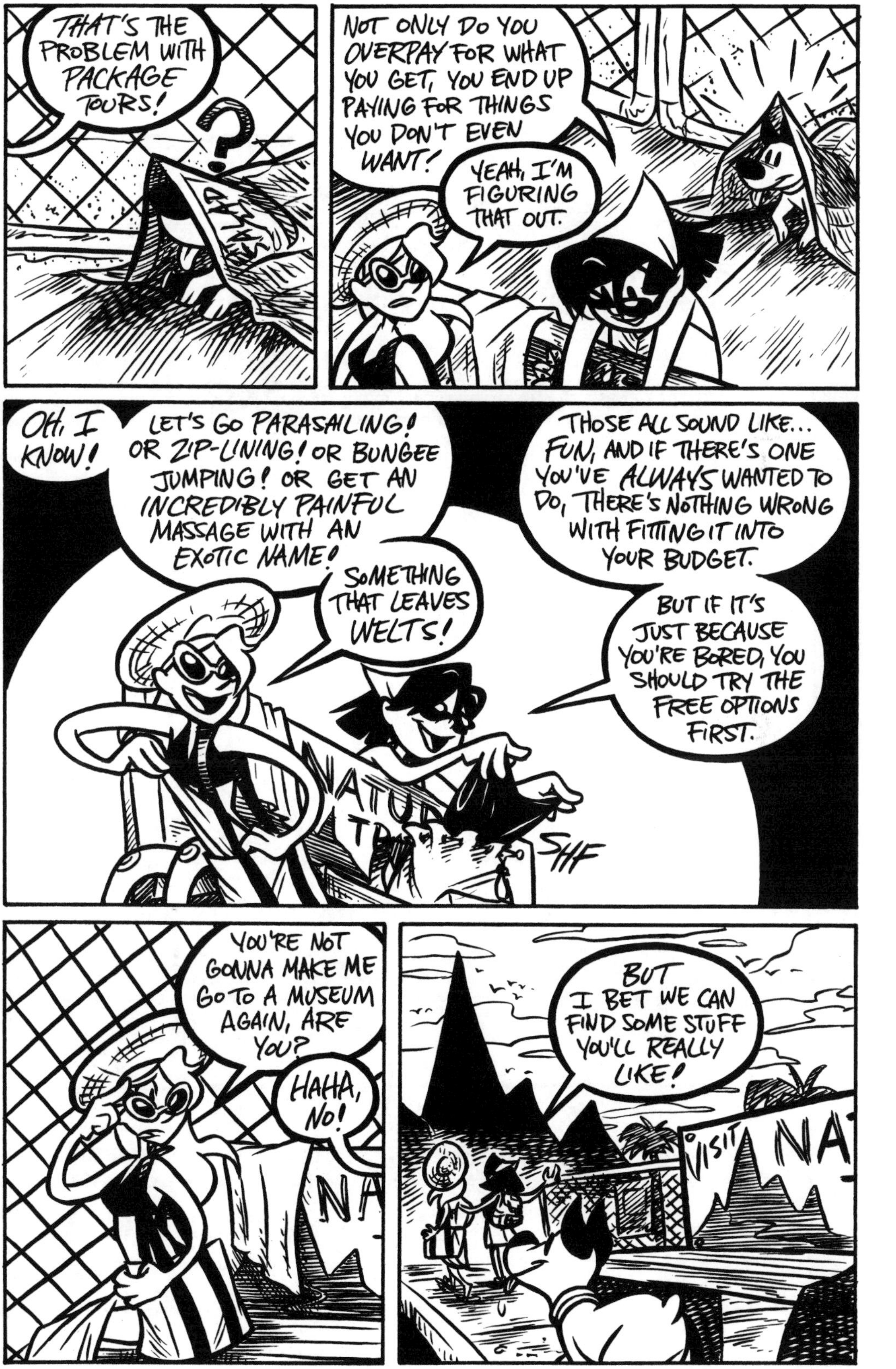
THAT'S THE PROBLEM WITH PACKAGE TOURS!
?
NOT ONLY DO YOU OVERPAY FOR WHAT YOU GET, YOU END UP PAYING FOR THINGS YOU DON'T EVEN WANT!
YEAH, I'M FIGURING THAT OUT.
OH, I KNOW!
LET'S GO PARASAILING! OR ZIP-LINING! OR BUNGEE JUMPING! OR GET AN INCREDIBLY PAINFUL MASSAGE WITH AN EXOTIC NAME!
SOMETHING THAT LEAVES WELTS!
THOSE ALL SOUND LIKE... FUN, AND IF THERE'S ONE YOU'VE ALWAYS WANTED TO DO, THERE'S NOTHING WRONG WITH FITTING IT INTO YOUR BUDGET.
BUT IF IT'S JUST BECAUSE YOU'RE BORED, YOU SHOULD TRY THE FREE OPTIONS FIRST.
SHF
YOU'RE NOT GONNA MAKE ME GO TO A MUSEUM AGAIN, ARE YOU?
HAHA, NO!
BUT I BET WE CAN FIND SOME STUFF YOU'LL REALLY LIKE!
VISIT NA

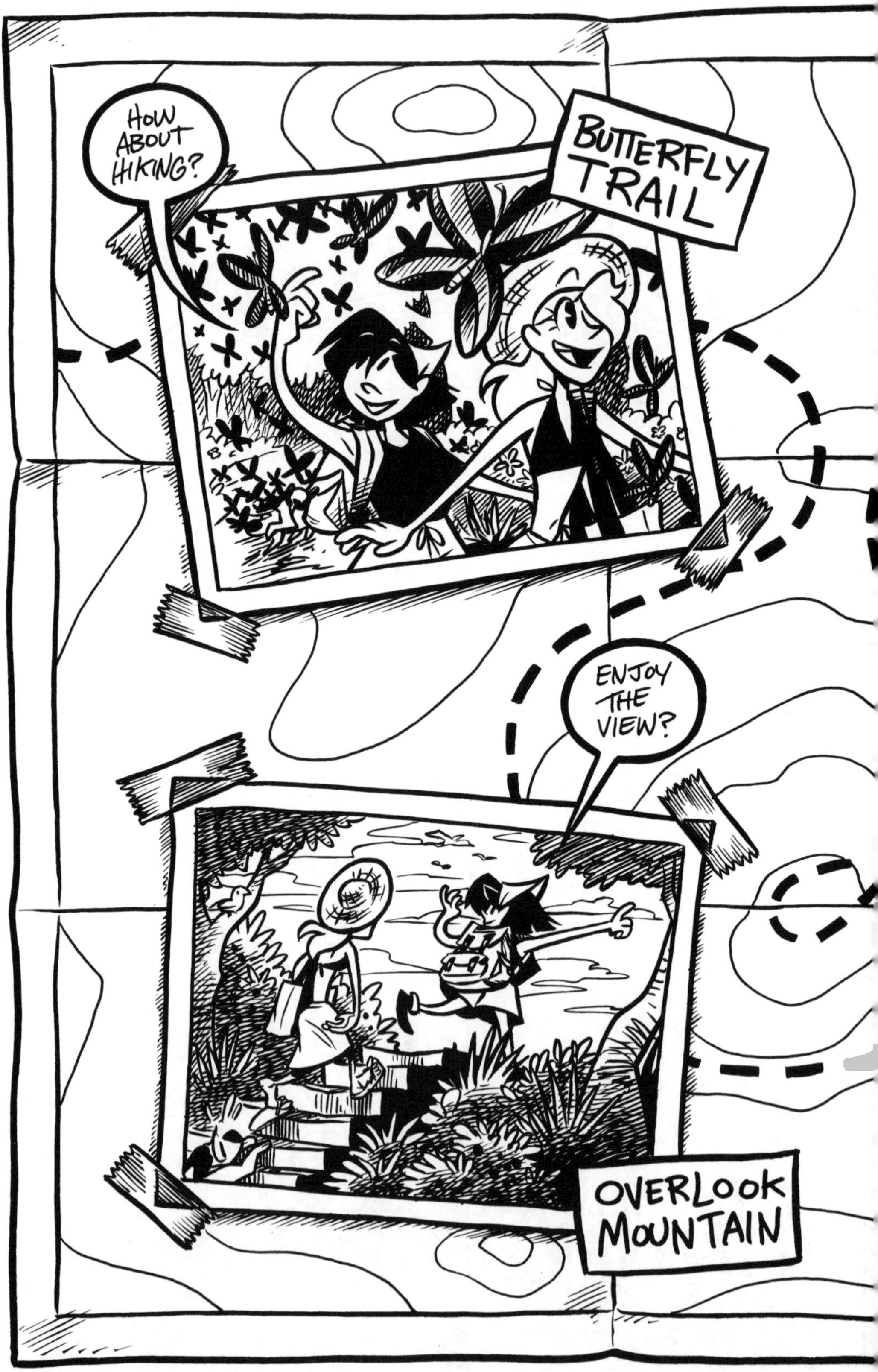
HOW ABOUT HIKING?
BUTTERFLY TRAIL
ENJOY THE VIEW?
OVERLOOK MOUNTAIN

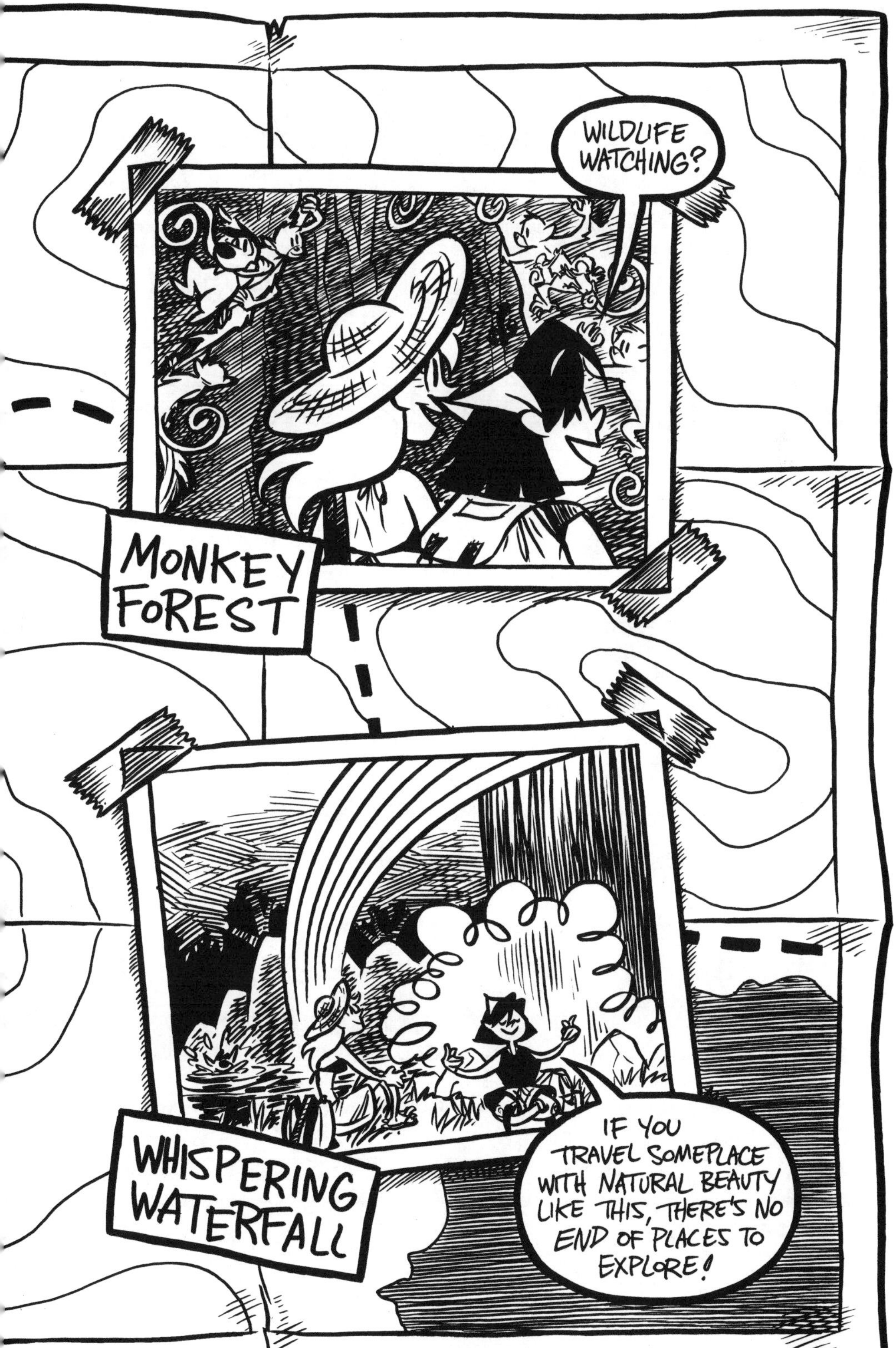
WILDLIFE WATCHING?
MONKEY FOREST
WHISPERING WATERFALL
IF YOU TRAVEL SOMEPLACE WITH NATURAL BEAUTY LIKE THIS, THERE'S NO END OF PLACES TO EXPLORE!

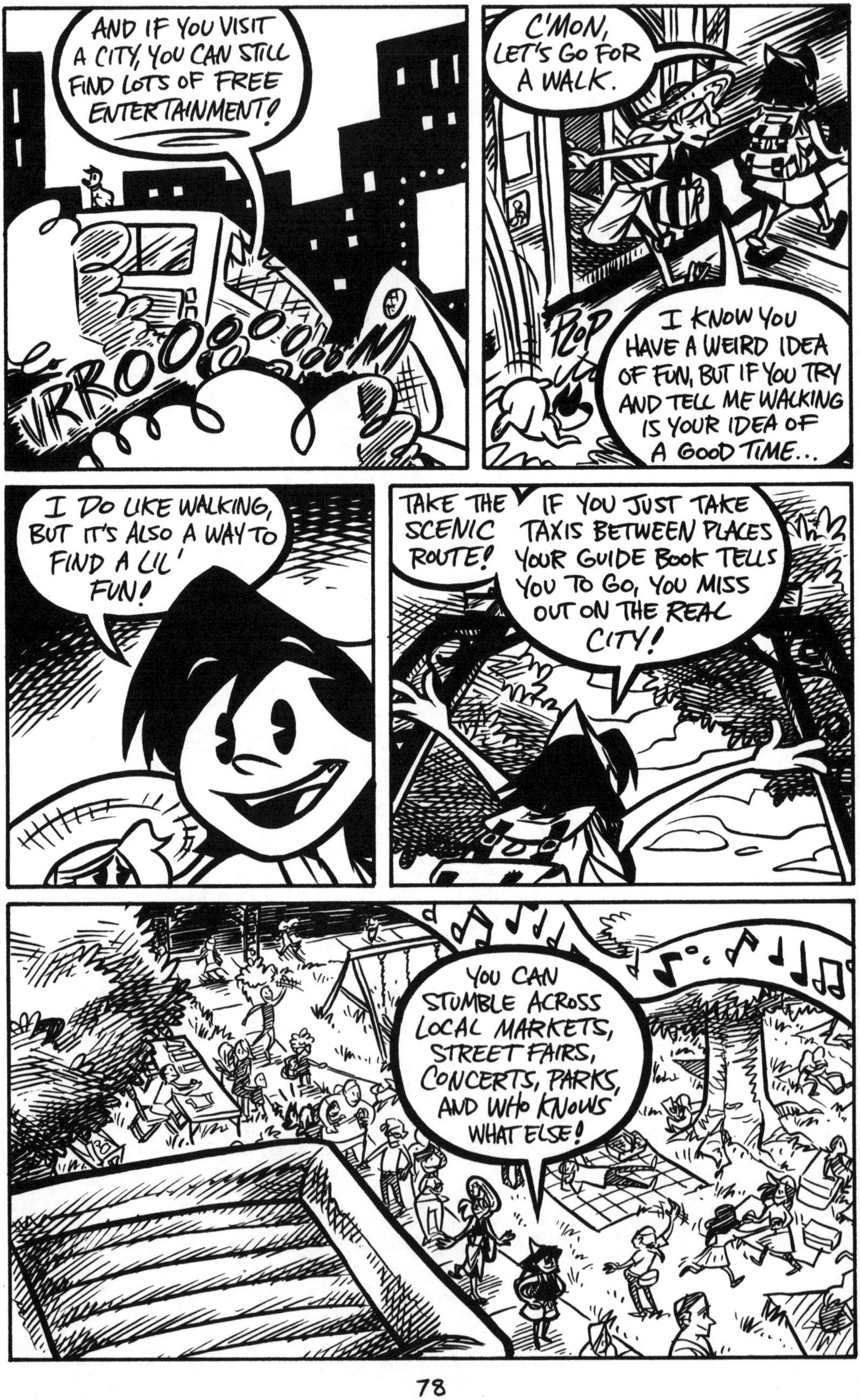
AND IF YOU VISIT A CITY, YOU CAN STILL FIND LOTS OF FREE ENTERTAINMENT!
VRROOOOOOOOM
C'MON, LET'S GO FOR A WALK.
PLOP
I KNOW YOU HAVE A WEIRD IDEA OF FUN, BUT IF YOU TRY AND TELL ME WALKING IS YOUR IDEA OF A GOOD TIME...
I DO LIKE WALKING, BUT IT'S ALSO A WAY TO FIND A LIL' FUN!
TAKE THE SCENIC ROUTE!
IF YOU JUST TAKE TAXIS BETWEEN PLACES YOUR GUIDE BOOK TELLS YOU TO GO, YOU MISS OUT ON THE REAL CITY!
YOU CAN STUMBLE ACROSS LOCAL MARKETS, STREET FAIRS, CONCERTS, PARKS, AND WHO KNOWS WHAT ELSE!

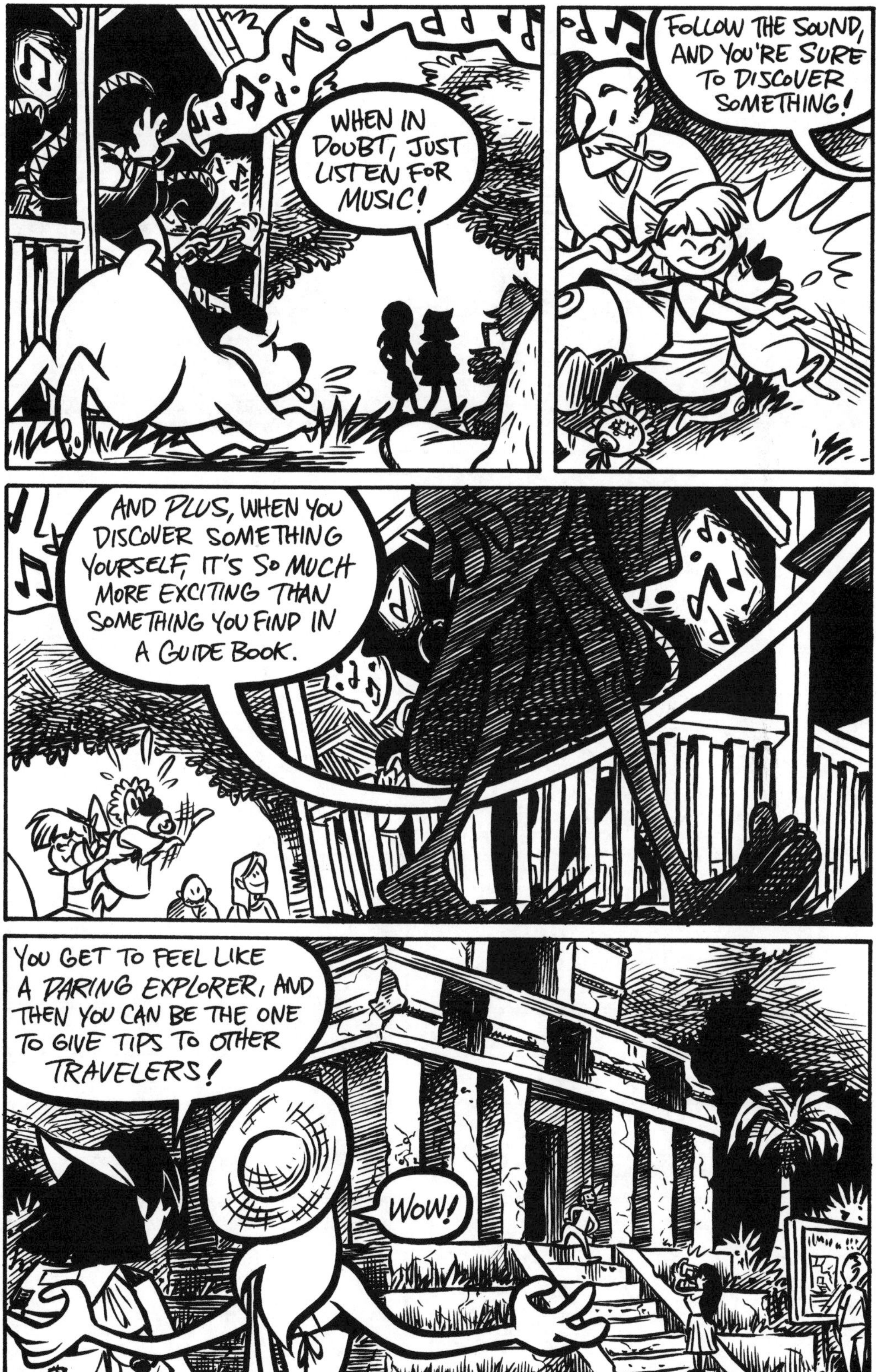
WHEN IN DOUBT, JUST LISTEN FOR MUSIC!
FOLLOW THE SOUND, AND YOU'RE SURE TO DISCOVER SOMETHING!
AND PLUS, WHEN YOU DISCOVER SOMETHING YOURSELF, IT'S SO MUCH MORE EXCITING THAN SOMETHING YOU FIND IN A GUIDE BOOK.
YOU GET TO FEEL LIKE A DARING EXPLORER, AND THEN YOU CAN BE THE ONE TO GIVE TIPS TO OTHER TRAVELERS!
WOW!

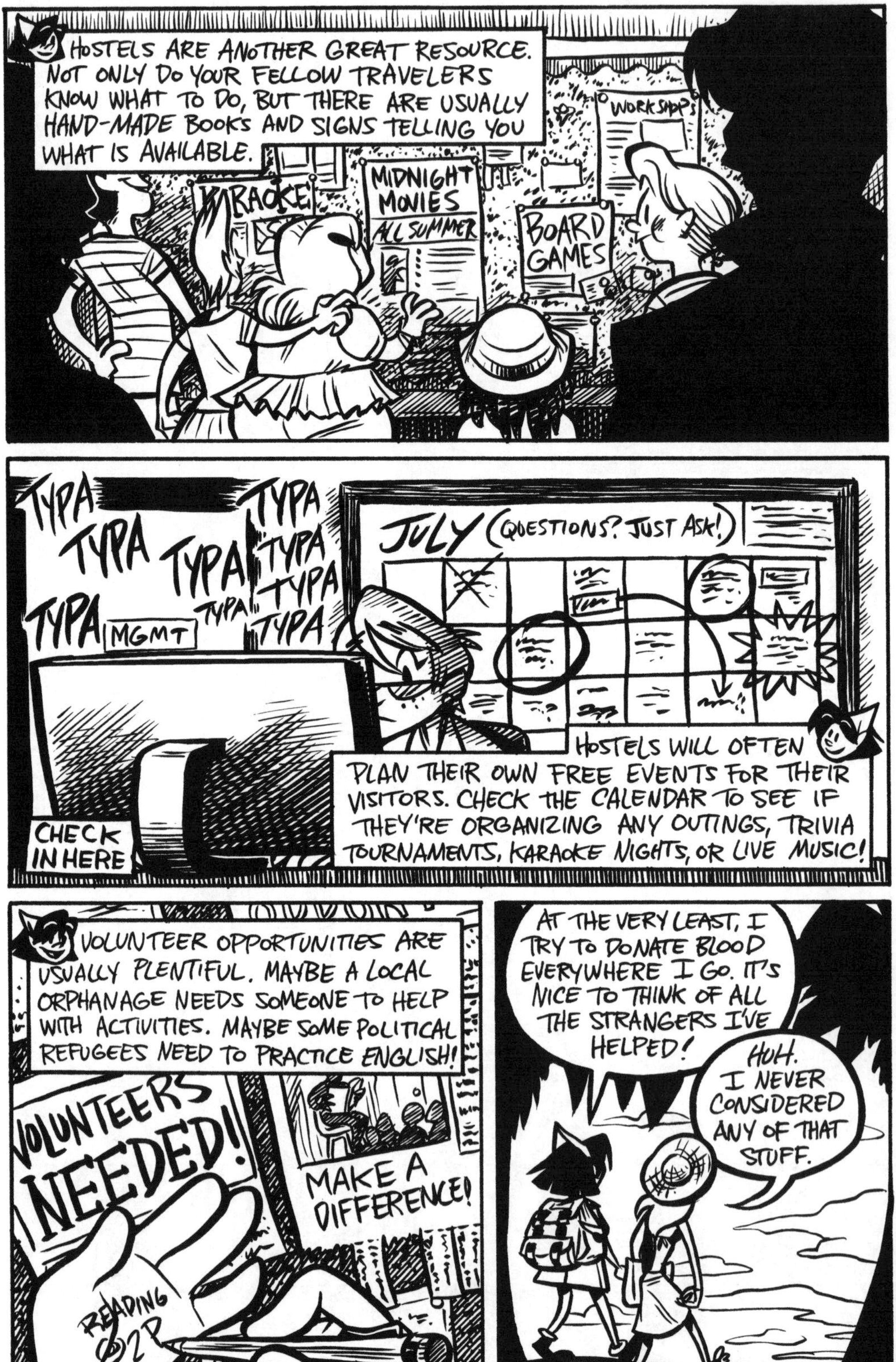
HOSTELS ARE ANOTHER GREAT RESOURCE. NOT ONLY DO YOUR FELLOW TRAVELERS KNOW WHAT TO DO, BUT THERE ARE USUALLY HAND-MADE BOOKS AND SIGNS TELLING YOU WHAT IS AVAILABLE.
MIDNIGHT MOVIES
ALL SUMMER
BOARD GAMES
TYPA TYPA TYPA TYPA TYPA TYPA TYPA TYPA TYPA
MGMT
JULY (QUESTIONS? JUST ASK!)
HOSTELS WILL OFTEN PLAN THEIR OWN FREE EVENTS FOR THEIR VISITORS. CHECK THE CALENDAR TO SEE IF THEY'RE ORGANIZING ANY OUTINGS, TRIVIA TOURNAMENTS, KARAOKE NIGHTS, OR LIVE MUSIC!
CHECK IN HERE
VOLUNTEER OPPORTUNITIES ARE USUALLY PLENTIFUL. MAYBE A LOCAL ORPHANAGE NEEDS SOMEONE TO HELP WITH ACTIVITIES. MAYBE SOME POLITICAL REFUGEES NEED TO PRACTICE ENGLISH!
VOLUNTEERS NEEDED!
MAKE A DIFFERENCE!
READING @2P
AT THE VERY LEAST, I TRY TO DONATE BLOOD EVERYWHERE I GO. IT'S NICE TO THINK OF ALL THE STRANGERS I'VE HELPED!
HUH. I NEVER CONSIDERED ANY OF THAT STUFF.

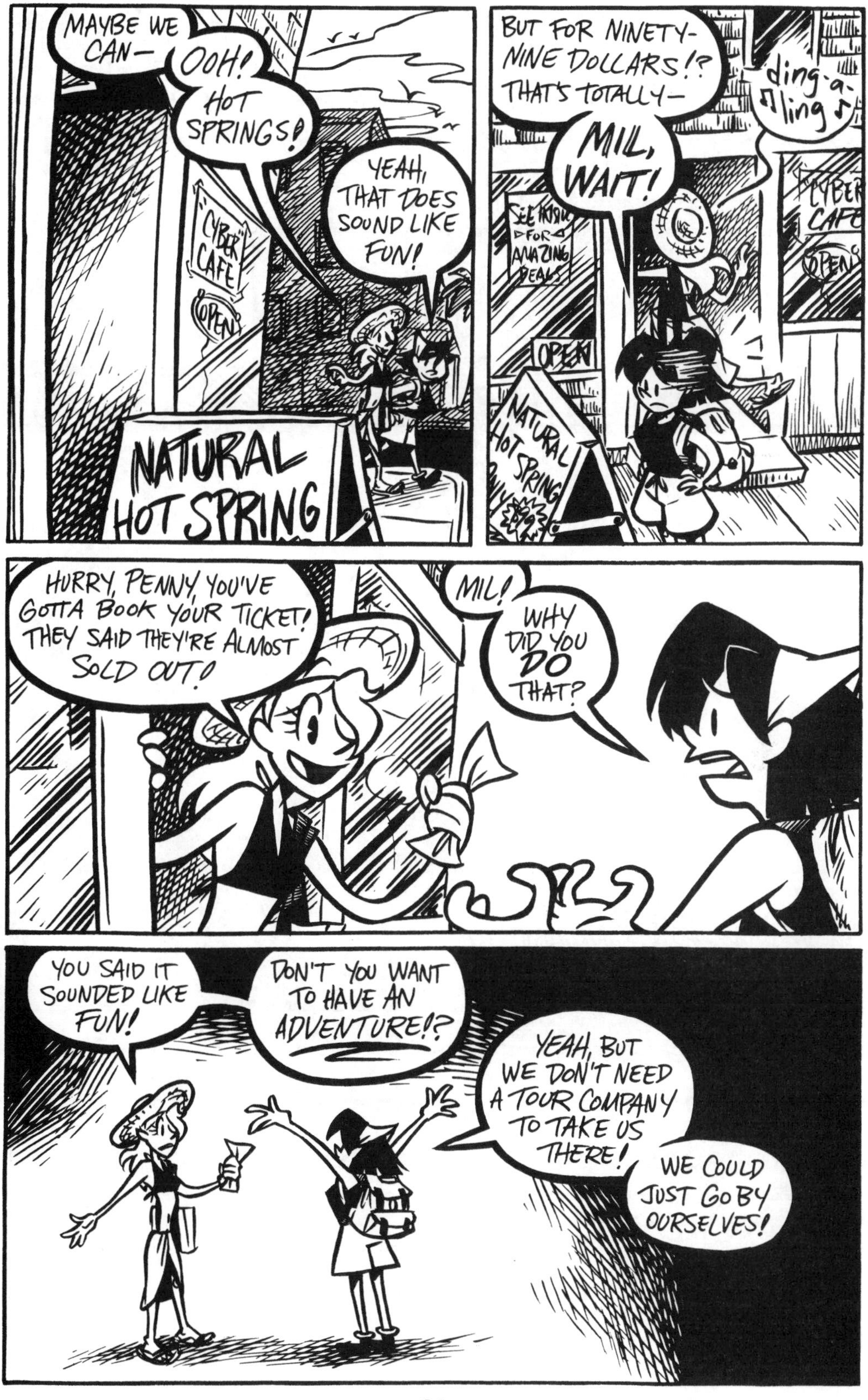
MAYBE WE CAN—
OOH! HOT SPRINGS!
CYBER CAFE
OPEN
YEAH, THAT DOES SOUND LIKE FUN!
NATURAL HOT SPRING
BUT FOR NINETY-NINE DOLLARS!? THAT'S TOTALLY—
ding-a-ling
MIL, WAIT!
OPEN
NATURAL HOT SPRING
HURRY, PENNY, YOU'VE GOTTA BOOK YOUR TICKET! THEY SAID THEY'RE ALMOST SOLD OUT!
MIL!
WHY DID YOU DO THAT?
YOU SAID IT SOUNDED LIKE FUN!
DON'T YOU WANT TO HAVE AN ADVENTURE!?
YEAH, BUT WE DON'T NEED A TOUR COMPANY TO TAKE US THERE!
WE COULD JUST GO BY OURSELVES!

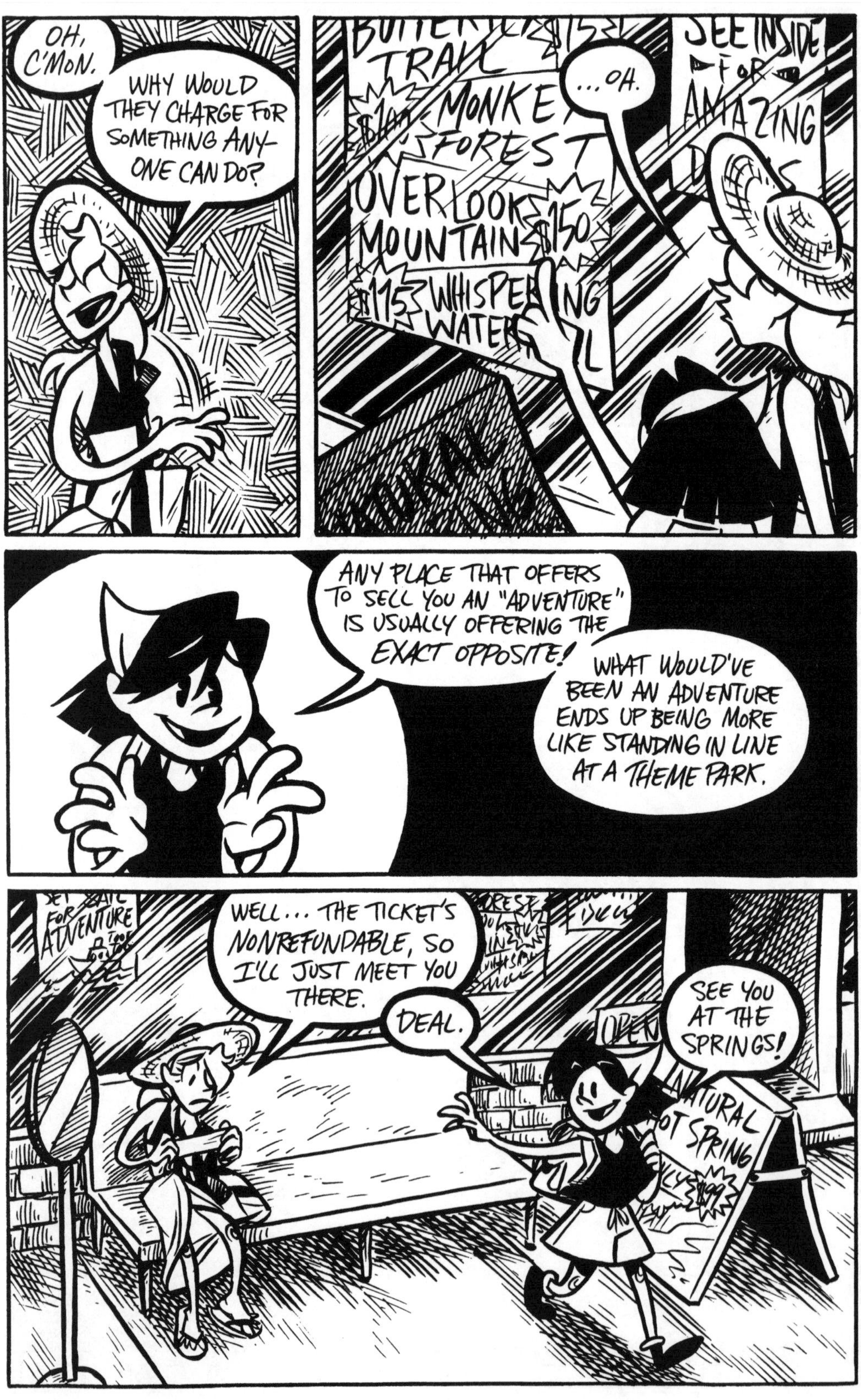

OH, C'MON.
WHY WOULD THEY CHARGE FOR SOMETHING ANYONE CAN DO?
MONKEY FOREST
OVERLOOK MOUNTAIN $150
$115 WHISPERING WATERFALL
SEE INSIDE FOR AMAZING
...OH.
ANY PLACE THAT OFFERS TO SELL YOU AN "ADVENTURE" IS USUALLY OFFERING THE EXACT OPPOSITE!
WHAT WOULD'VE BEEN AN ADVENTURE ENDS UP BEING MORE LIKE STANDING IN LINE AT A THEME PARK.
FOR ADVENTURE
WELL... THE TICKET'S NONREFUNDABLE, SO I'LL JUST MEET YOU THERE.
DEAL.
SEE YOU AT THE SPRINGS!
OPEN
NATURAL HOT SPRING

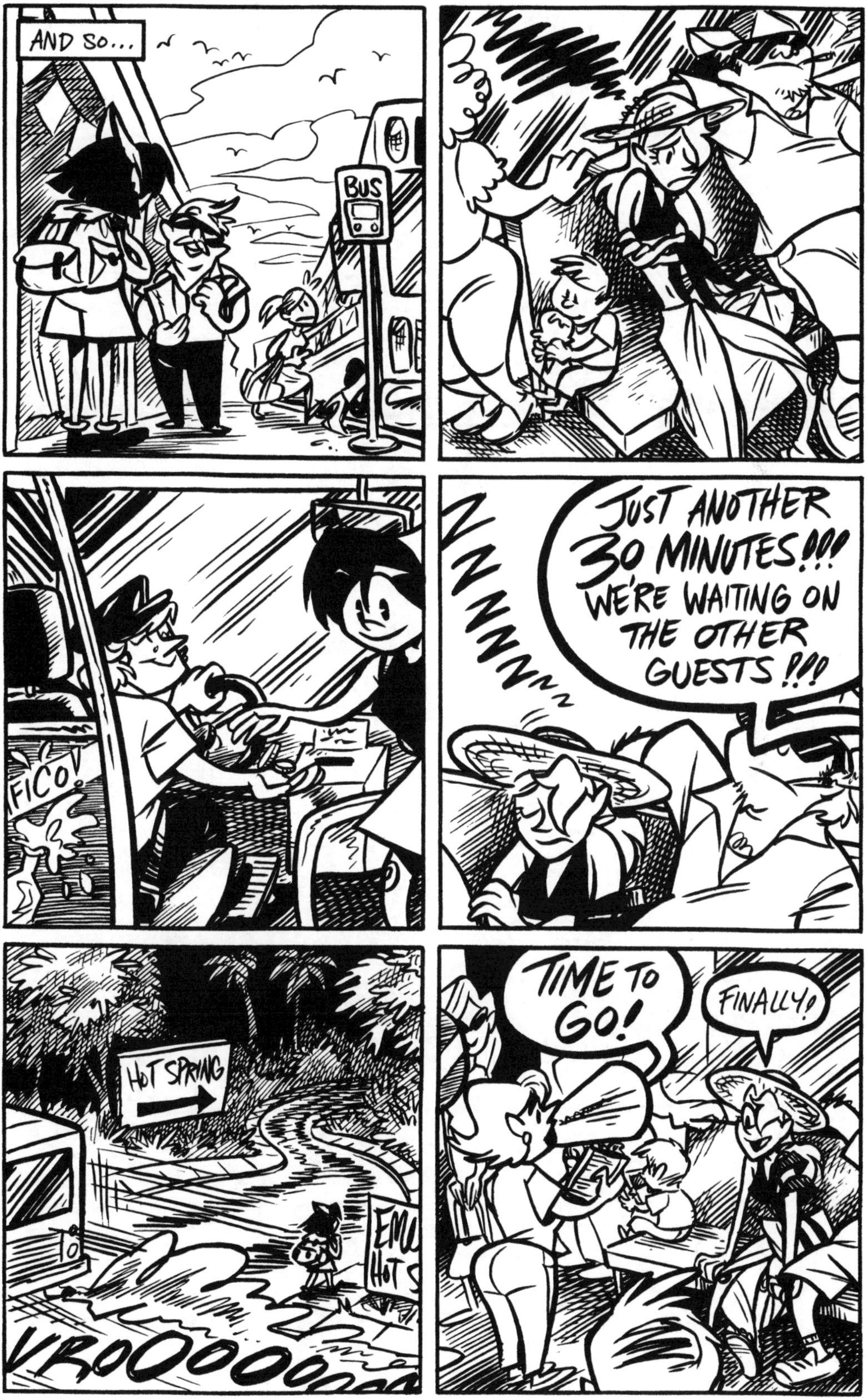
AND SO...
BUS
JUST ANOTHER 30 MINUTES!!! WE'RE WAITING ON THE OTHER GUESTS!!!
HOT SPRING
VROOOOOO
TIME TO GO!
FINALLY!

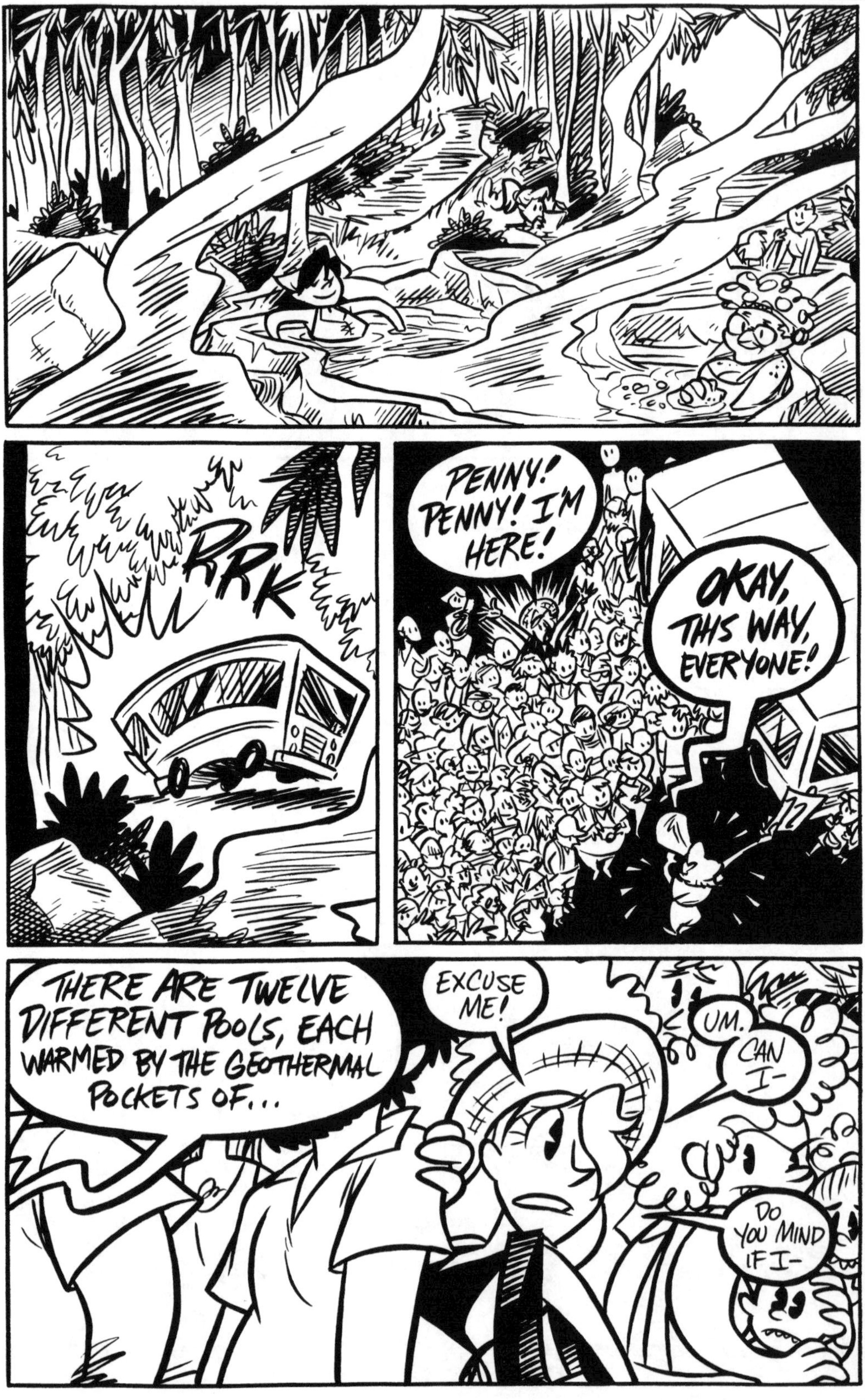
RRK
PENNY! PENNY! I'M HERE!
OKAY, THIS WAY, EVERYONE!
THERE ARE TWELVE DIFFERENT POOLS, EACH WARMED BY THE GEOTHERMAL POCKETS OF...
EXCUSE ME!
UM. CAN I-
DO YOU MIND IF I-

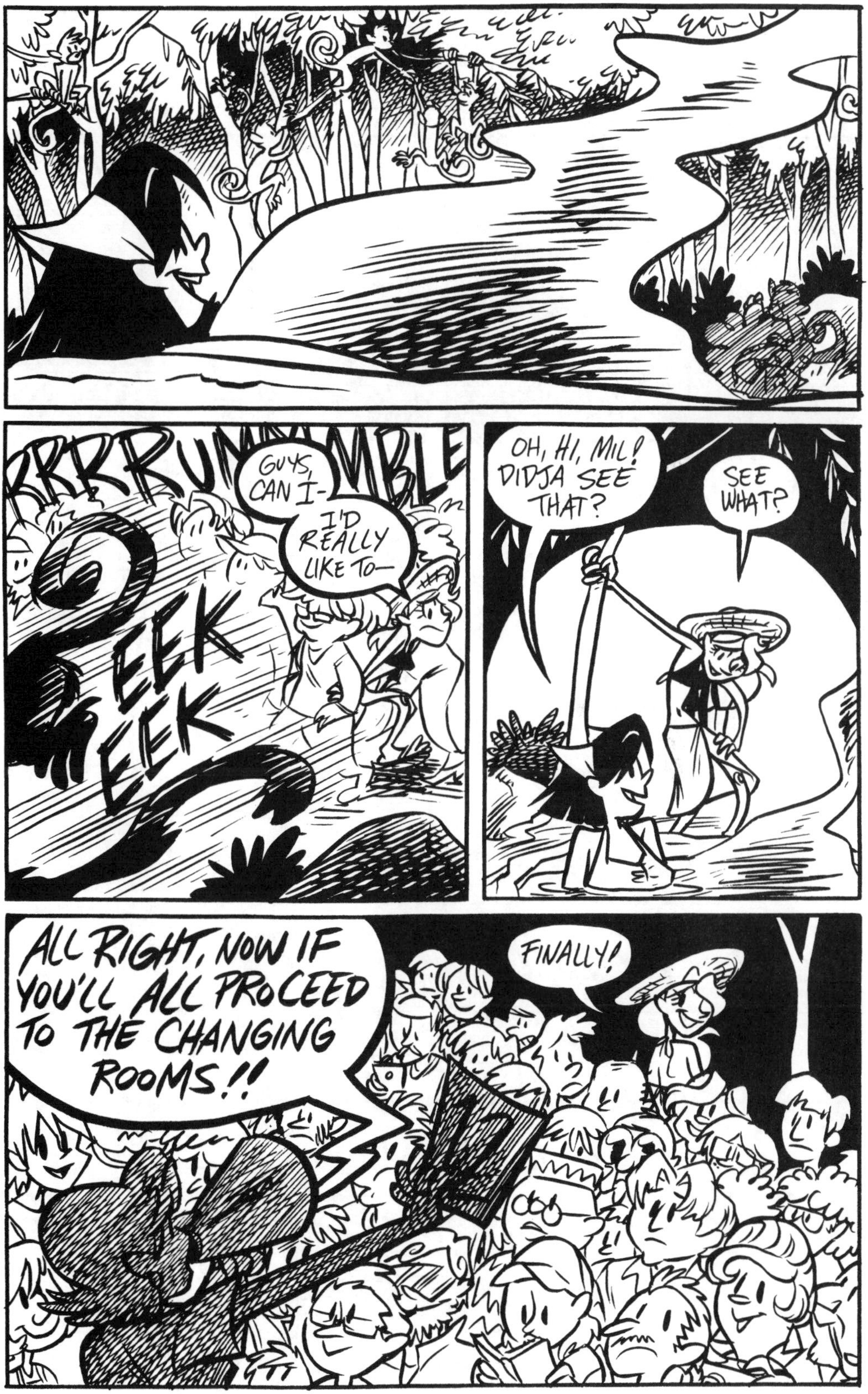
RRRRUMMMMBLE
GUYS, CAN I-
I'D REALLY LIKE TO—
EEK EEK
OH, HI, MIL! DIDJA SEE THAT?
SEE WHAT?
ALL RIGHT, NOW IF YOU'LL ALL PROCEED TO THE CHANGING ROOMS!!
FINALLY!

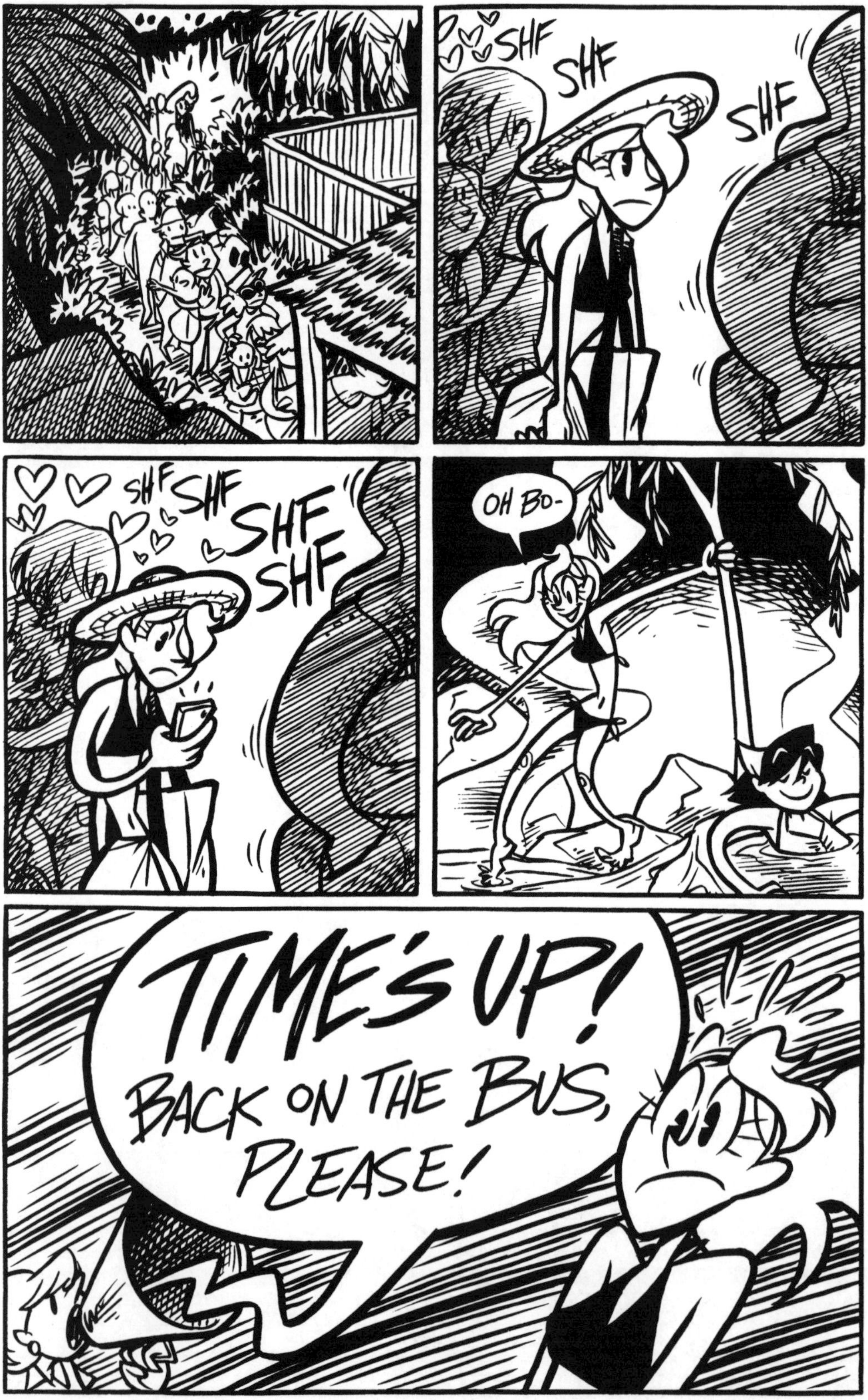
SHF
SHF
SHF
SHF
SHF
SHF
SHF
OH BO-
TIME'S UP!
BACK ON THE BUS, PLEASE!

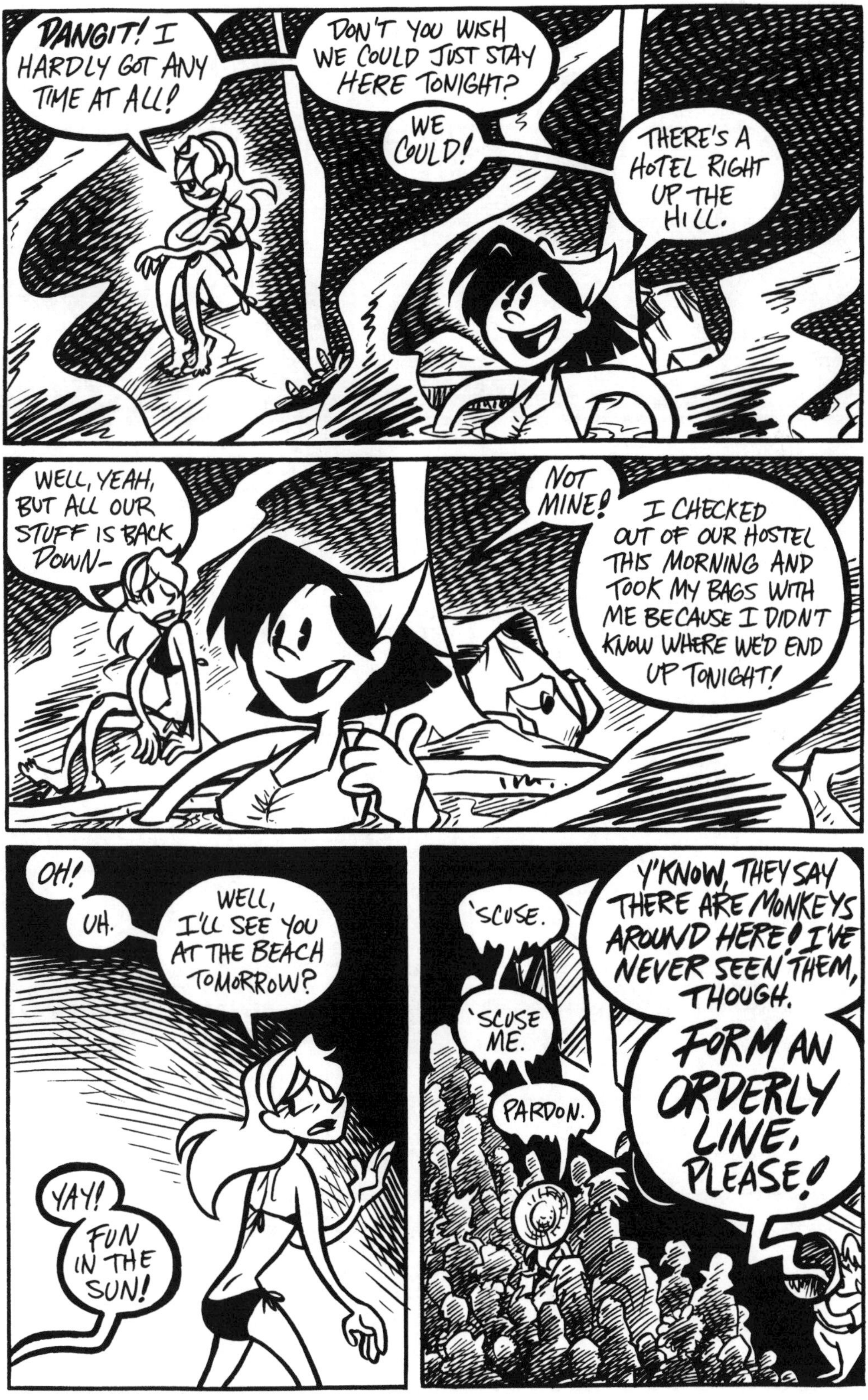
DANGIT! I HARDLY GOT ANY TIME AT ALL!
DON'T YOU WISH WE COULD JUST STAY HERE TONIGHT?
WE COULD!
THERE'S A HOTEL RIGHT UP THE HILL.
WELL, YEAH, BUT ALL OUR STUFF IS BACK DOWN-
NOT MINE!
I CHECKED OUT OF OUR HOSTEL THIS MORNING AND TOOK MY BAGS WITH ME BECAUSE I DIDN'T KNOW WHERE WE'D END UP TONIGHT!
OH!
UH.
WELL, I'LL SEE YOU AT THE BEACH TOMORROW?
YAY!
FUN IN THE SUN!
Y'KNOW, THEY SAY THERE ARE MONKEYS AROUND HERE! I'VE NEVER SEEN THEM, THOUGH.
FORM AN ORDERLY LINE, PLEASE!
'SCUSE.
'SCUSE ME.
PARDON.

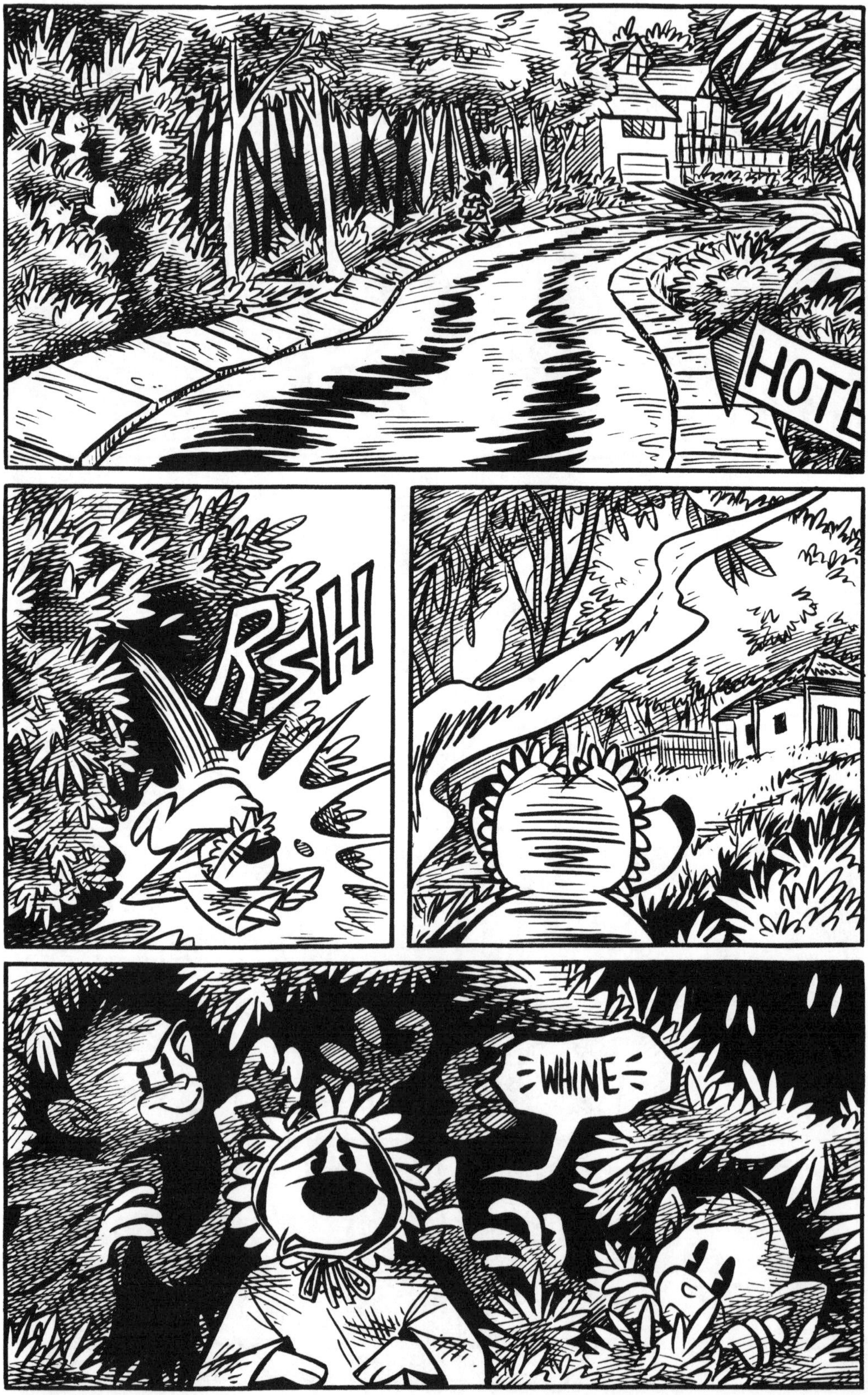
HOTE
RSH
WHINE

Chapter Eight
Shopping

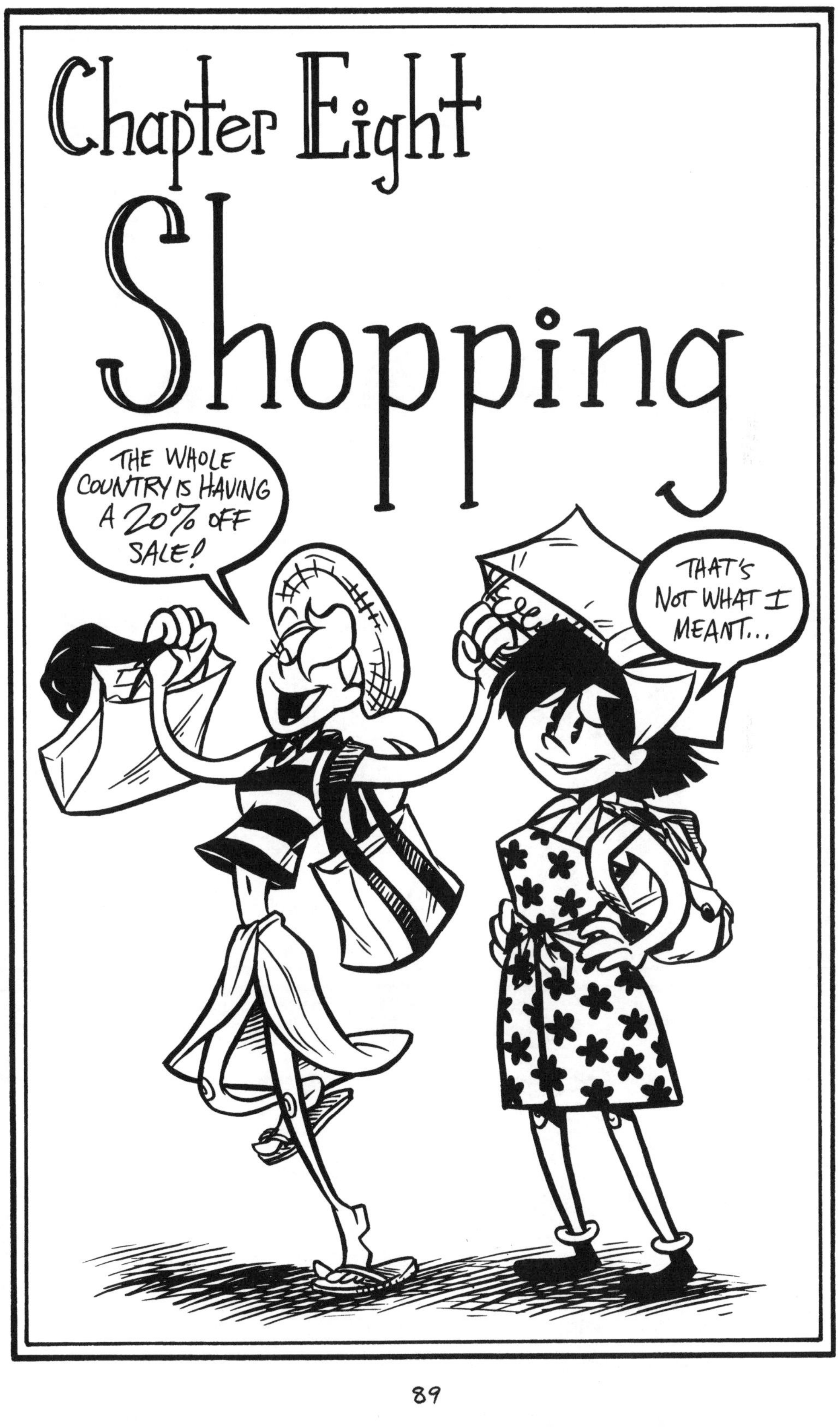

THE WHOLE COUNTRY IS HAVING A 20% OFF SALE!
THAT'S NOT WHAT I MEANT...

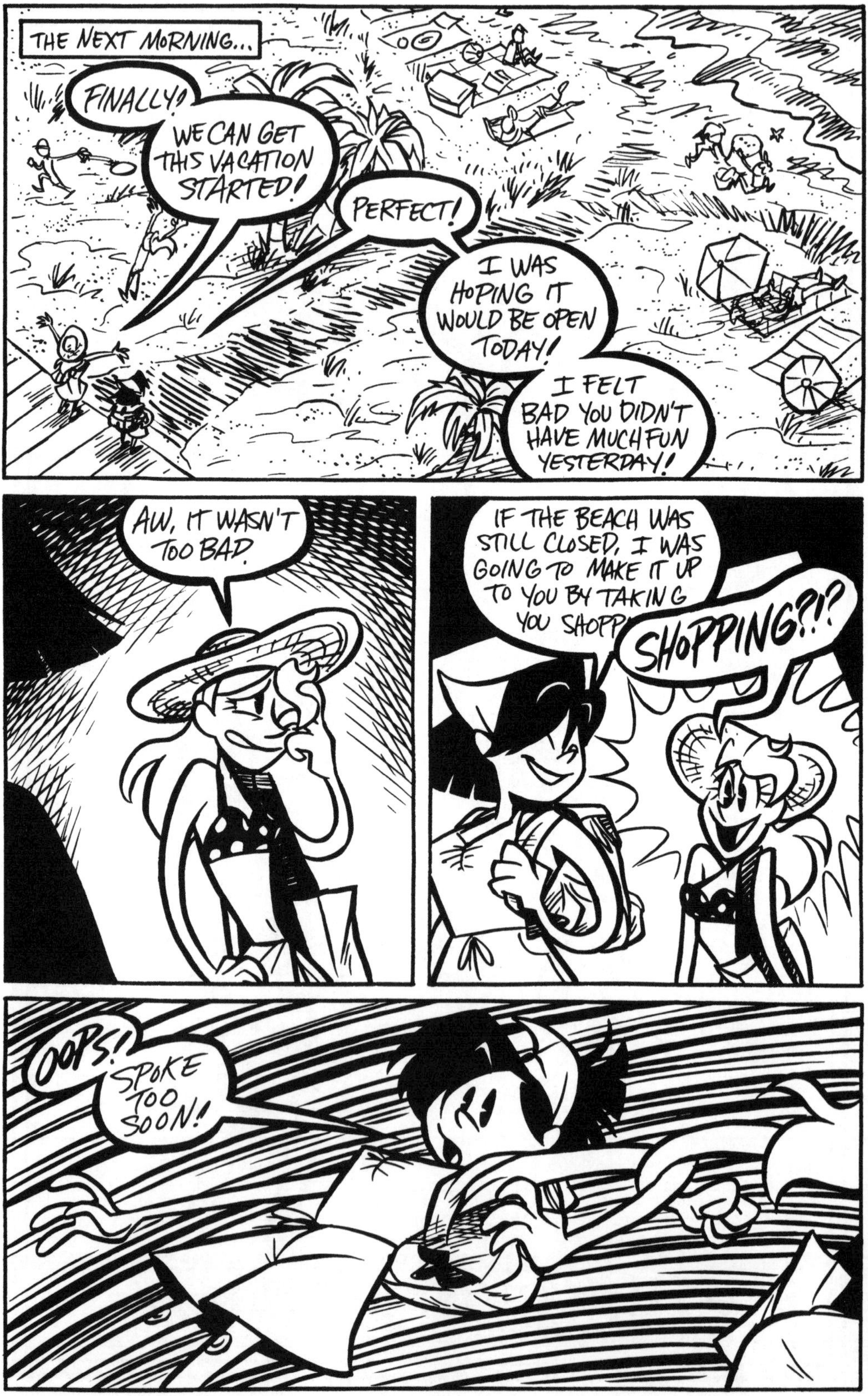
THE NEXT MORNING...
FINALLY!
WE CAN GET THIS VACATION STARTED!
PERFECT!
I WAS HOPING IT WOULD BE OPEN TODAY!
I FELT BAD YOU DIDN'T HAVE MUCH FUN YESTERDAY!
AW, IT WASN'T TOO BAD.
IF THE BEACH WAS STILL CLOSED, I WAS GOING TO MAKE IT UP TO YOU BY TAKING YOU SHOPP
SHOPPING?!?
OOPS!
SPOKE TOO SOON!

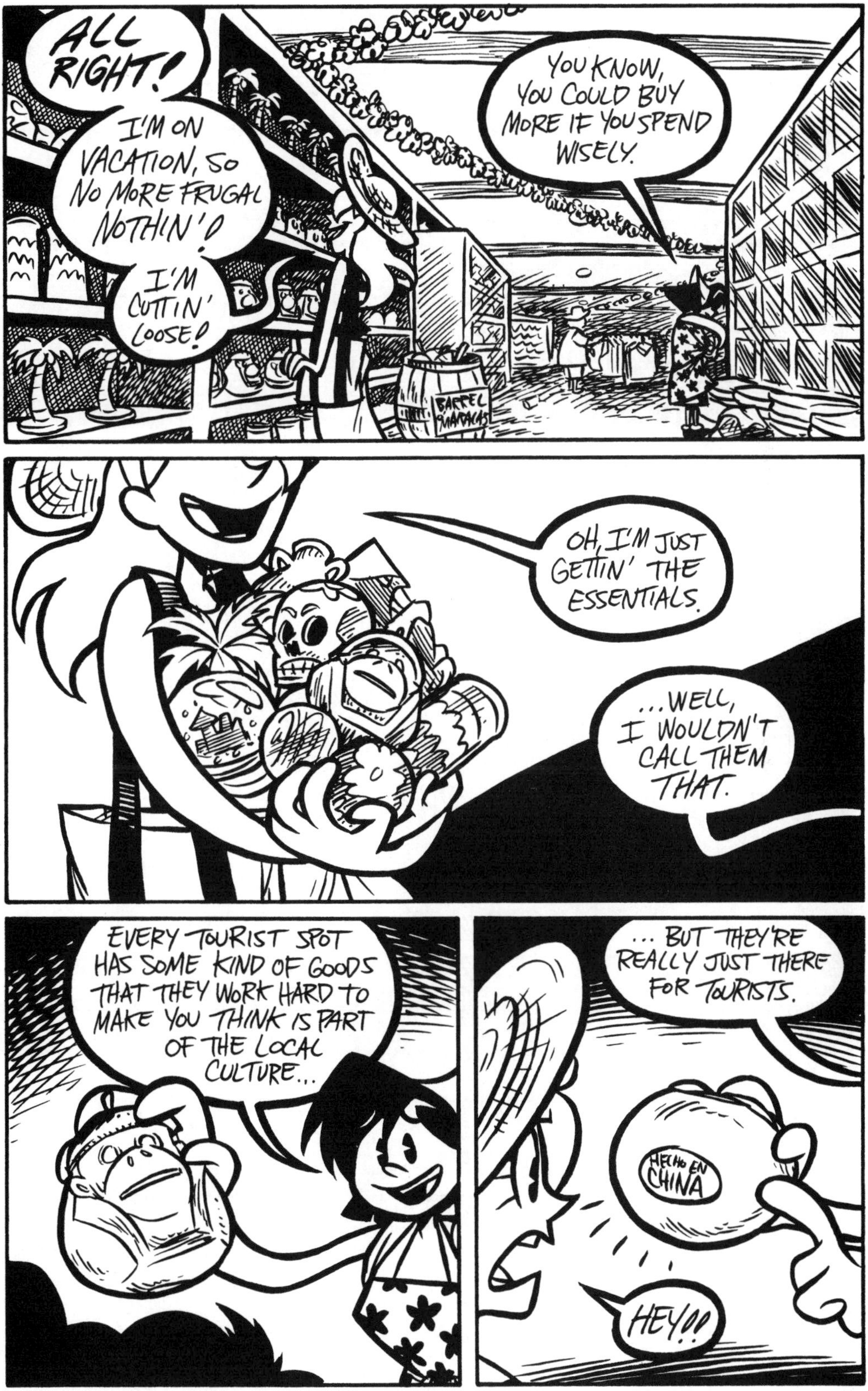
ALL RIGHT!
I'M ON VACATION, SO NO MORE FRUGAL NOTHIN'!
I'M CUTTIN' LOOSE!
YOU KNOW, YOU COULD BUY MORE IF YOU SPEND WISELY.
BARREL O' MARACAS
OH, I'M JUST GETTIN' THE ESSENTIALS.
...WELL, I WOULDN'T CALL THEM THAT.
EVERY TOURIST SPOT HAS SOME KIND OF GOODS THAT THEY WORK HARD TO MAKE YOU THINK IS PART OF THE LOCAL CULTURE...
... BUT THEY'RE REALLY JUST THERE FOR TOURISTS.
HECHO EN CHINA
HEY!!

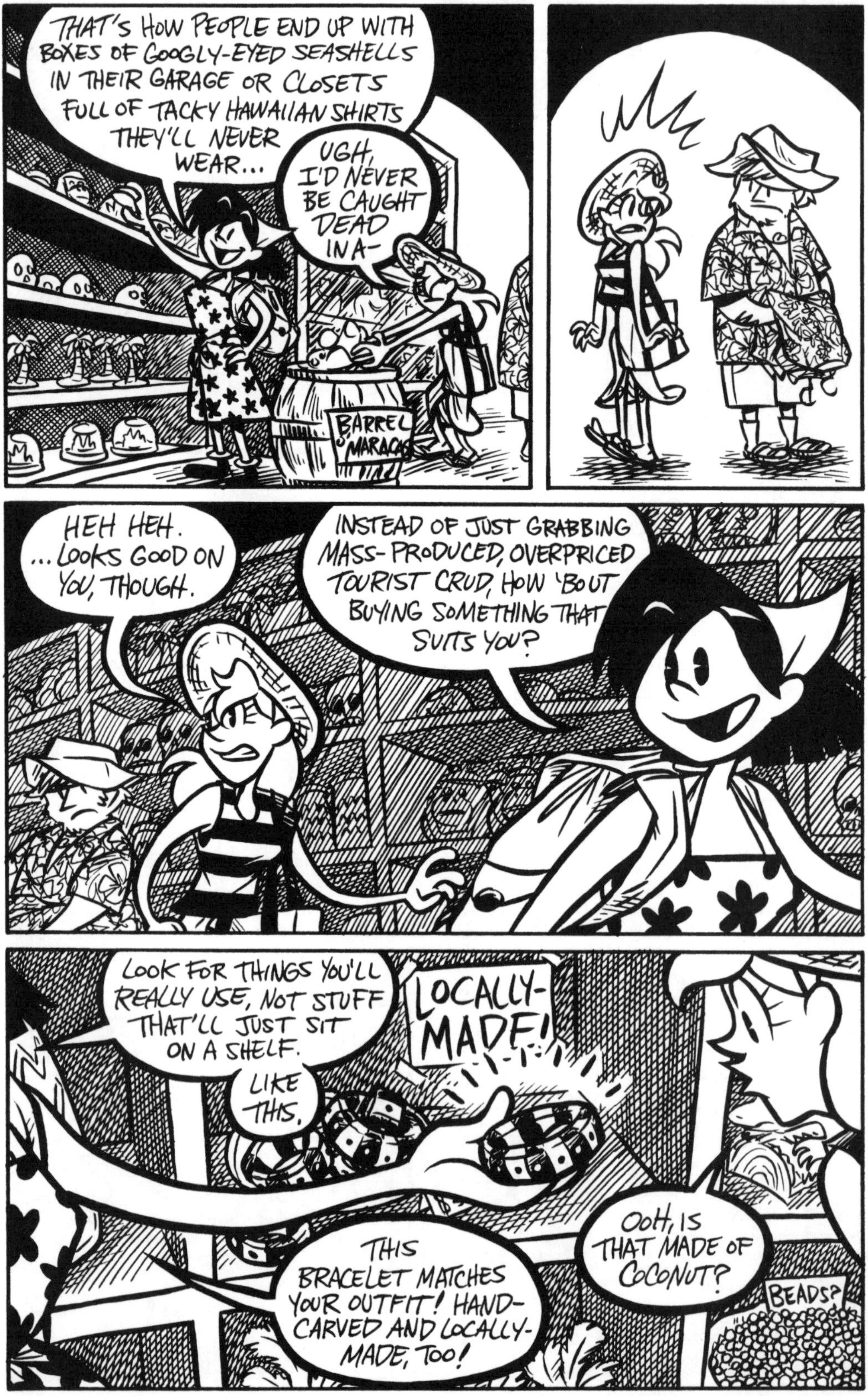
THAT'S HOW PEOPLE END UP WITH BOXES OF GOOGLY-EYED SEASHELLS IN THEIR GARAGE OR CLOSETS FULL OF TACKY HAWAIIAN SHIRTS THEY'LL NEVER WEAR...
UGH, I'D NEVER BE CAUGHT DEAD IN A-
BARREL O' MARACAS
HEH HEH. ...LOOKS GOOD ON YOU, THOUGH.
INSTEAD OF JUST GRABBING MASS-PRODUCED, OVERPRICED TOURIST CRUD, HOW 'BOUT BUYING SOMETHING THAT SUITS YOU?
LOOK FOR THINGS YOU'LL REALLY USE, NOT STUFF THAT'LL JUST SIT ON A SHELF.
LIKE THIS.
LOCALLY-MADE!
THIS BRACELET MATCHES YOUR OUTFIT! HAND-CARVED AND LOCALLY-MADE, TOO!
OOH, IS THAT MADE OF COCONUT?
BEADS?

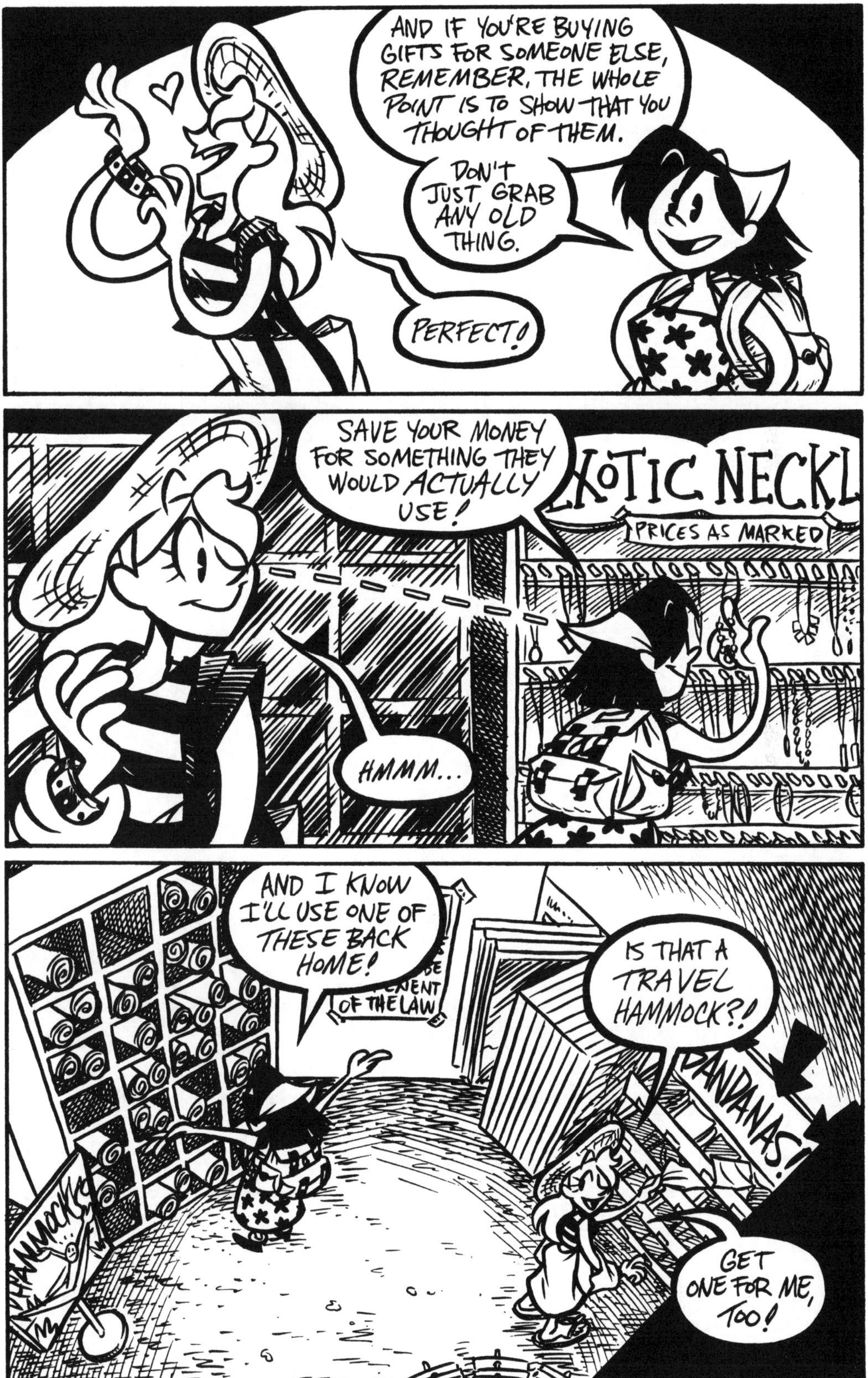
AND IF YOU'RE BUYING GIFTS FOR SOMEONE ELSE, REMEMBER, THE WHOLE POINT IS TO SHOW THAT YOU THOUGHT OF THEM.
DON'T JUST GRAB ANY OLD THING.
PERFECT!
SAVE YOUR MONEY FOR SOMETHING THEY WOULD ACTUALLY USE!
XOTIC NECKL
PRICES AS MARKED
HMMM...
AND I KNOW I'LL USE ONE OF THESE BACK HOME!
OF THE LAW
IS THAT A TRAVEL HAMMOCK?!
BANDANAS!
HAMMOCKS
GET ONE FOR ME, TOO!

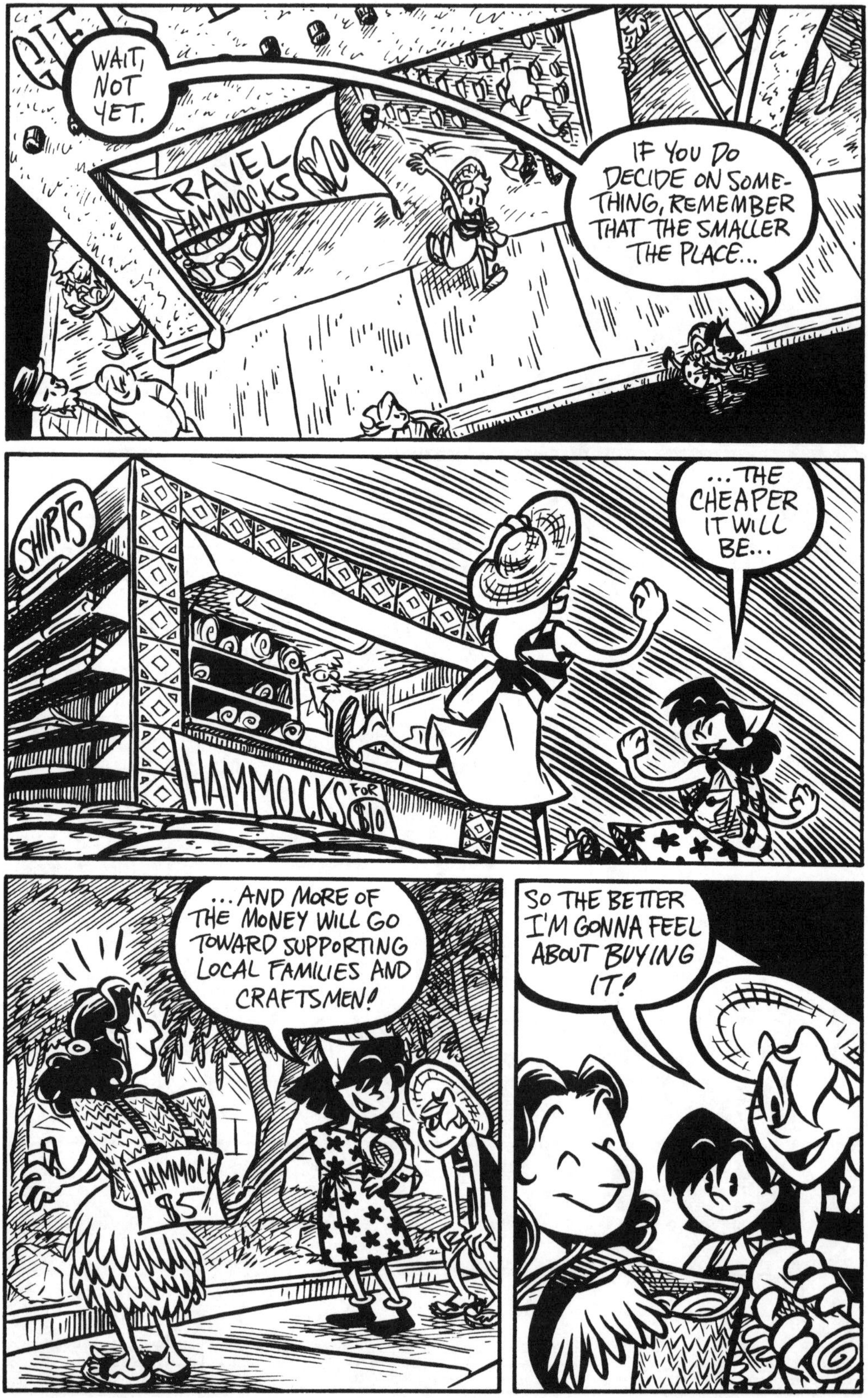
WAIT, NOT YET.
TRAVEL HAMMOCKS $20
IF YOU DO DECIDE ON SOMETHING, REMEMBER THAT THE SMALLER THE PLACE...
SHIRTS
...THE CHEAPER IT WILL BE...
HAMMOCKS FOR $10
...AND MORE OF THE MONEY WILL GO TOWARD SUPPORTING LOCAL FAMILIES AND CRAFTSMEN!
HAMMOCK $5
SO THE BETTER I'M GONNA FEEL ABOUT BUYING IT!

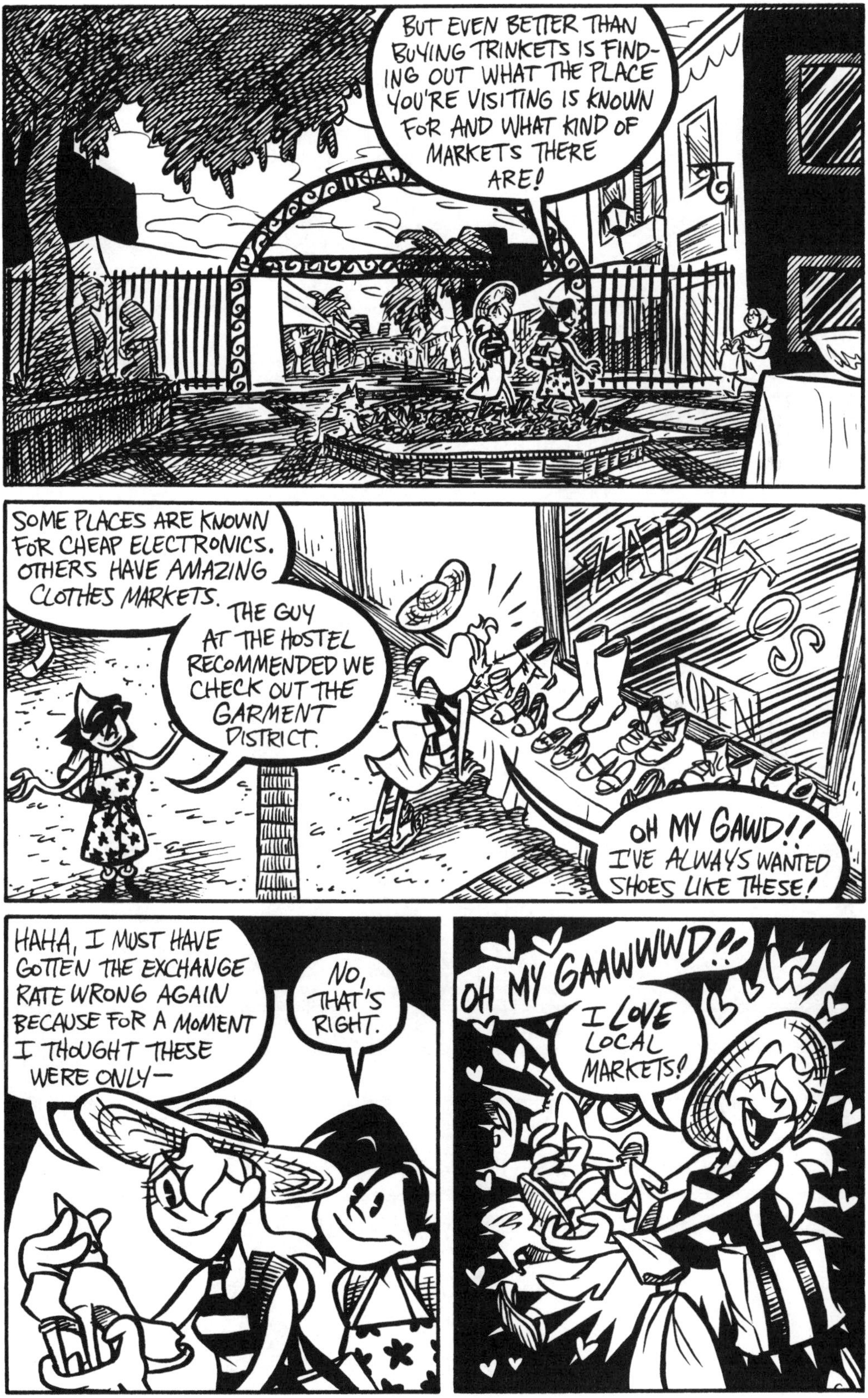
BUT EVEN BETTER THAN BUYING TRINKETS IS FINDING OUT WHAT THE PLACE YOU'RE VISITING IS KNOWN FOR AND WHAT KIND OF MARKETS THERE ARE!
SOME PLACES ARE KNOWN FOR CHEAP ELECTRONICS. OTHERS HAVE AMAZING CLOTHES MARKETS.
THE GUY AT THE HOSTEL RECOMMENDED WE CHECK OUT THE GARMENT DISTRICT.
ZAPATOS
OPEN
OH MY GAWD!! I'VE ALWAYS WANTED SHOES LIKE THESE!
HAHA, I MUST HAVE GOTTEN THE EXCHANGE RATE WRONG AGAIN BECAUSE FOR A MOMENT I THOUGHT THESE WERE ONLY—
NO, THAT'S RIGHT.
OH MY GAAWWWD!!
I LOVE LOCAL MARKETS!

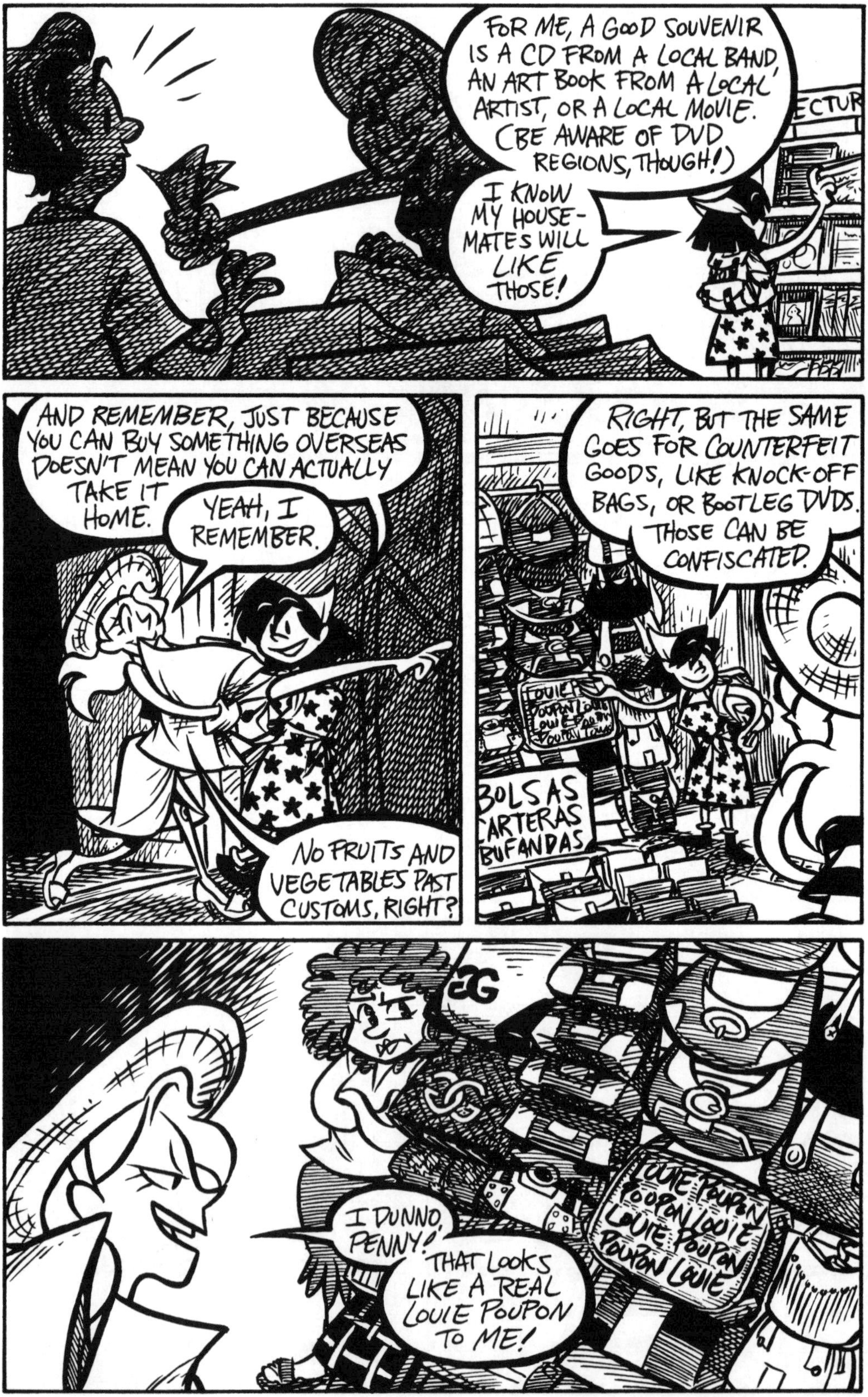
FOR ME, A GOOD SOUVENIR IS A CD FROM A LOCAL BAND, AN ART BOOK FROM A LOCAL ARTIST, OR A LOCAL MOVIE. (BE AWARE OF DVD REGIONS, THOUGH!)
I KNOW MY HOUSE-MATES WILL LIKE THOSE!
AND REMEMBER, JUST BECAUSE YOU CAN BUY SOMETHING OVERSEAS DOESN'T MEAN YOU CAN ACTUALLY TAKE IT HOME.
YEAH, I REMEMBER.
NO FRUITS AND VEGETABLES PAST CUSTOMS, RIGHT?
RIGHT, BUT THE SAME GOES FOR COUNTERFEIT GOODS, LIKE KNOCK-OFF BAGS, OR BOOTLEG DVDS. THOSE CAN BE CONFISCATED.
BOLSAS
CARTERAS
BUFANDAS
LOUIE POUPON LOUIE POUPON LOUIE POUPON
I DUNNO, PENNY!
THAT LOOKS LIKE A REAL LOUIE POUPON TO ME!

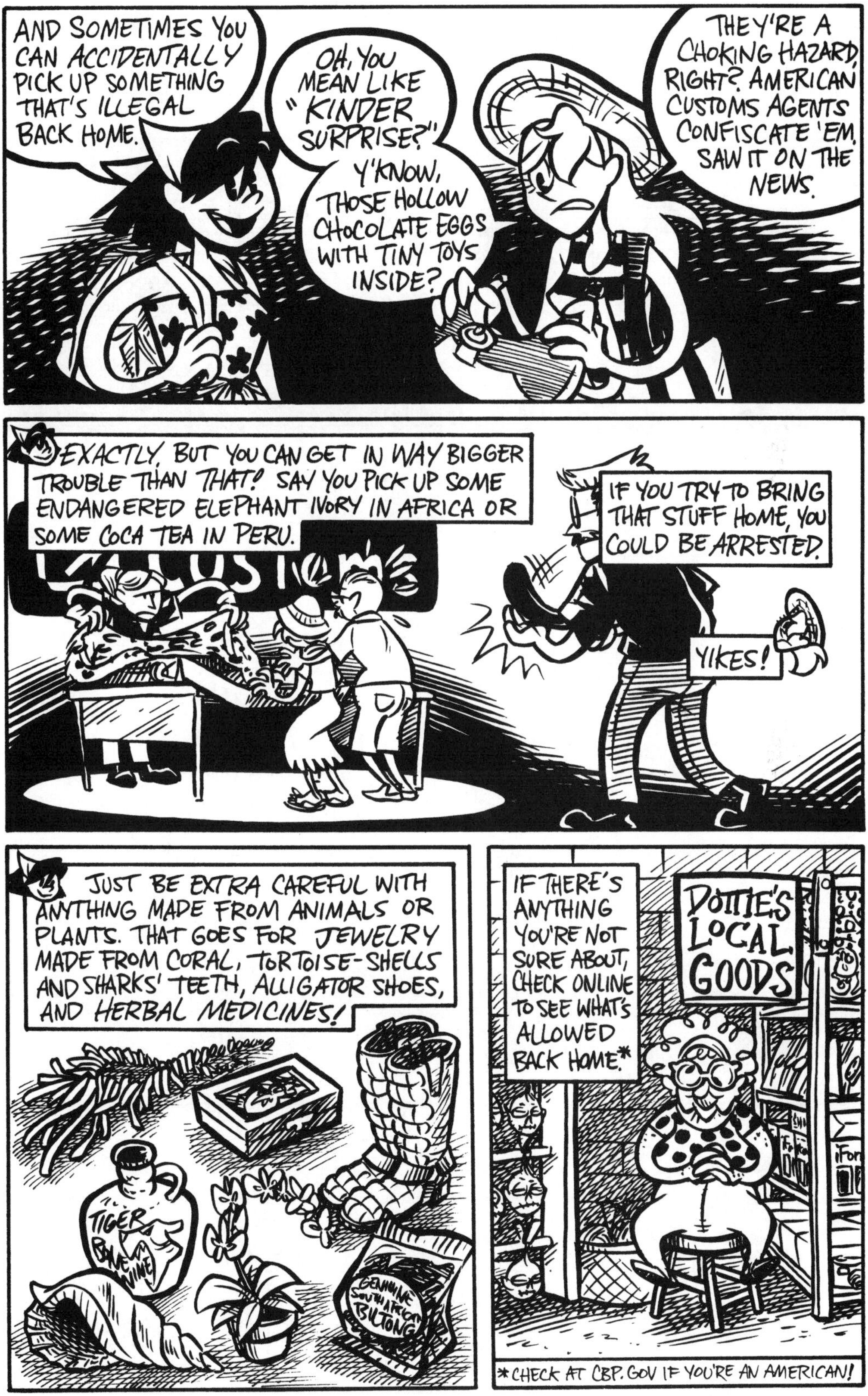
AND SOMETIMES YOU CAN ACCIDENTALLY PICK UP SOMETHING THAT'S ILLEGAL BACK HOME.
OH, YOU MEAN LIKE "KINDER SURPRISE?"
Y'KNOW, THOSE HOLLOW CHOCOLATE EGGS WITH TINY TOYS INSIDE?
THEY'RE A CHOKING HAZARD, RIGHT? AMERICAN CUSTOMS AGENTS CONFISCATE 'EM. SAW IT ON THE NEWS.
EXACTLY, BUT YOU CAN GET IN WAY BIGGER TROUBLE THAN THAT! SAY YOU PICK UP SOME ENDANGERED ELEPHANT IVORY IN AFRICA OR SOME COCA TEA IN PERU.
IF YOU TRY TO BRING THAT STUFF HOME, YOU COULD BE ARRESTED.
YIKES!
JUST BE EXTRA CAREFUL WITH ANYTHING MADE FROM ANIMALS OR PLANTS. THAT GOES FOR JEWELRY MADE FROM CORAL, TORTOISE-SHELLS AND SHARKS' TEETH, ALLIGATOR SHOES, AND HERBAL MEDICINES!
TIGER BONE WINE
GENUINE SOUTH AFRICAN BILTONG
IF THERE'S ANYTHING YOU'RE NOT SURE ABOUT, CHECK ONLINE TO SEE WHAT'S ALLOWED BACK HOME.*
DOTTIE'S LOCAL GOODS
*CHECK AT CBP.GOV IF YOU'RE AN AMERICAN!

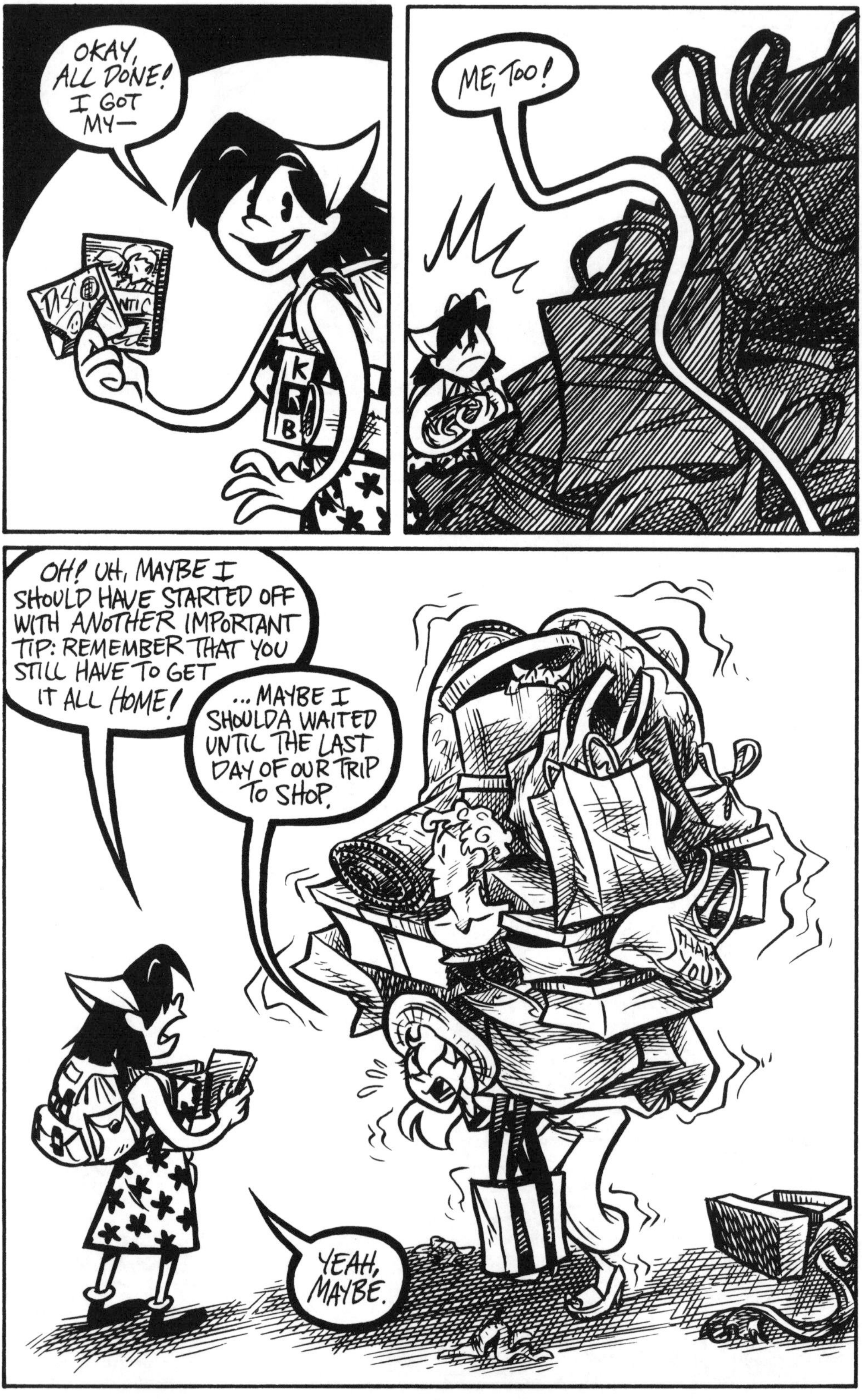
OKAY, ALL DONE! I GOT MY—
KRB
ME, TOO!
OH! UH, MAYBE I SHOULD HAVE STARTED OFF WITH ANOTHER IMPORTANT TIP: REMEMBER THAT YOU STILL HAVE TO GET IT ALL HOME!
...MAYBE I SHOULDA WAITED UNTIL THE LAST DAY OF OUR TRIP TO SHOP.
THANK YOU!
YEAH, MAYBE.

Chapter Nine
Staying Safe

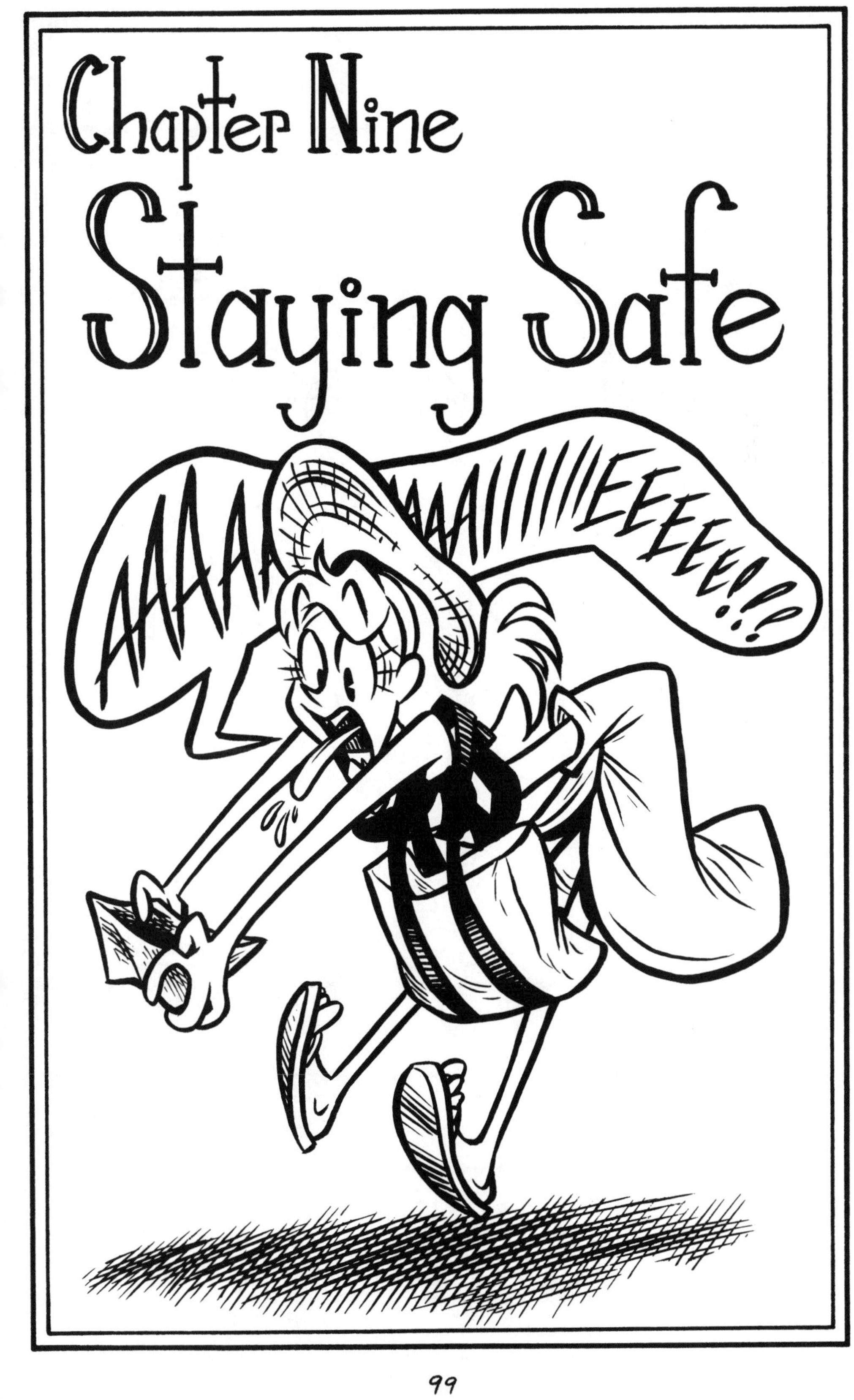
AAAA AAAIIIIIIIIEEEEEE!!!

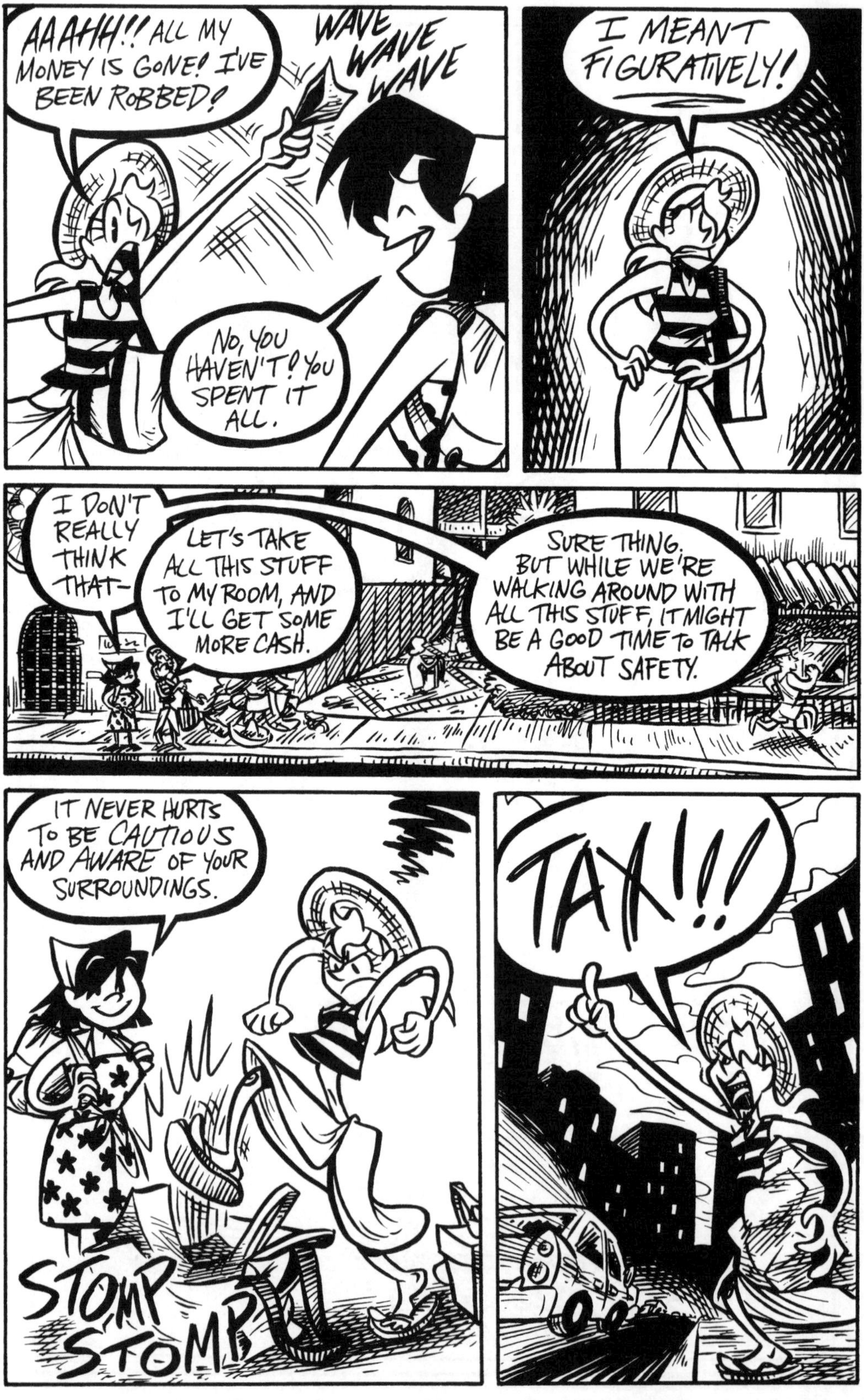
AAAHH!! ALL MY MONEY IS GONE! I'VE BEEN ROBBED!
WAVE WAVE WAVE
NO, YOU HAVEN'T! YOU SPENT IT ALL.
I MEANT FIGURATIVELY!
I DON'T REALLY THINK THAT-
LET'S TAKE ALL THIS STUFF TO MY ROOM, AND I'LL GET SOME MORE CASH.
SURE THING. BUT WHILE WE'RE WALKING AROUND WITH ALL THIS STUFF, IT MIGHT BE A GOOD TIME TO TALK ABOUT SAFETY.
IT NEVER HURTS TO BE CAUTIOUS AND AWARE OF YOUR SURROUNDINGS.
STOMP STOMP
TAX!!!

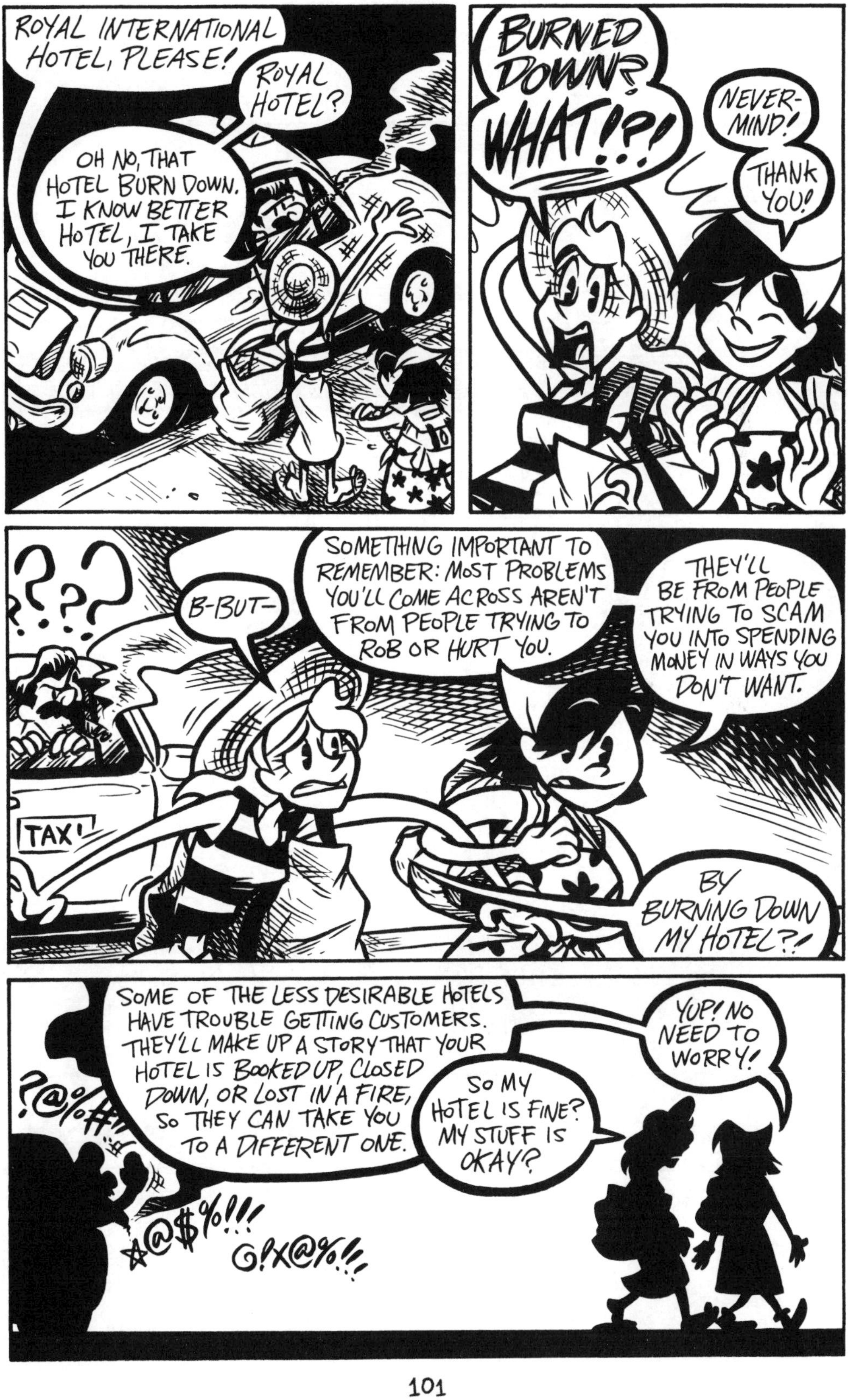
ROYAL INTERNATIONAL HOTEL, PLEASE!
ROYAL HOTEL?
OH NO, THAT HOTEL BURN DOWN. I KNOW BETTER HOTEL, I TAKE YOU THERE.
BURNED DOWN? WHAT!?!
NEVER-MIND!
THANK YOU!
B-BUT-
SOMETHING IMPORTANT TO REMEMBER: MOST PROBLEMS YOU'LL COME ACROSS AREN'T FROM PEOPLE TRYING TO ROB OR HURT YOU.
THEY'LL BE FROM PEOPLE TRYING TO SCAM YOU INTO SPENDING MONEY IN WAYS YOU DON'T WANT.
TAXI
BY BURNING DOWN MY HOTEL?!
SOME OF THE LESS DESIRABLE HOTELS HAVE TROUBLE GETTING CUSTOMERS. THEY'LL MAKE UP A STORY THAT YOUR HOTEL IS BOOKED UP, CLOSED DOWN, OR LOST IN A FIRE, SO THEY CAN TAKE YOU TO A DIFFERENT ONE.
SO MY HOTEL IS FINE? MY STUFF IS OKAY?
YUP! NO NEED TO WORRY!
?@%#!!
☆@$%!!!
©!X@%!!!

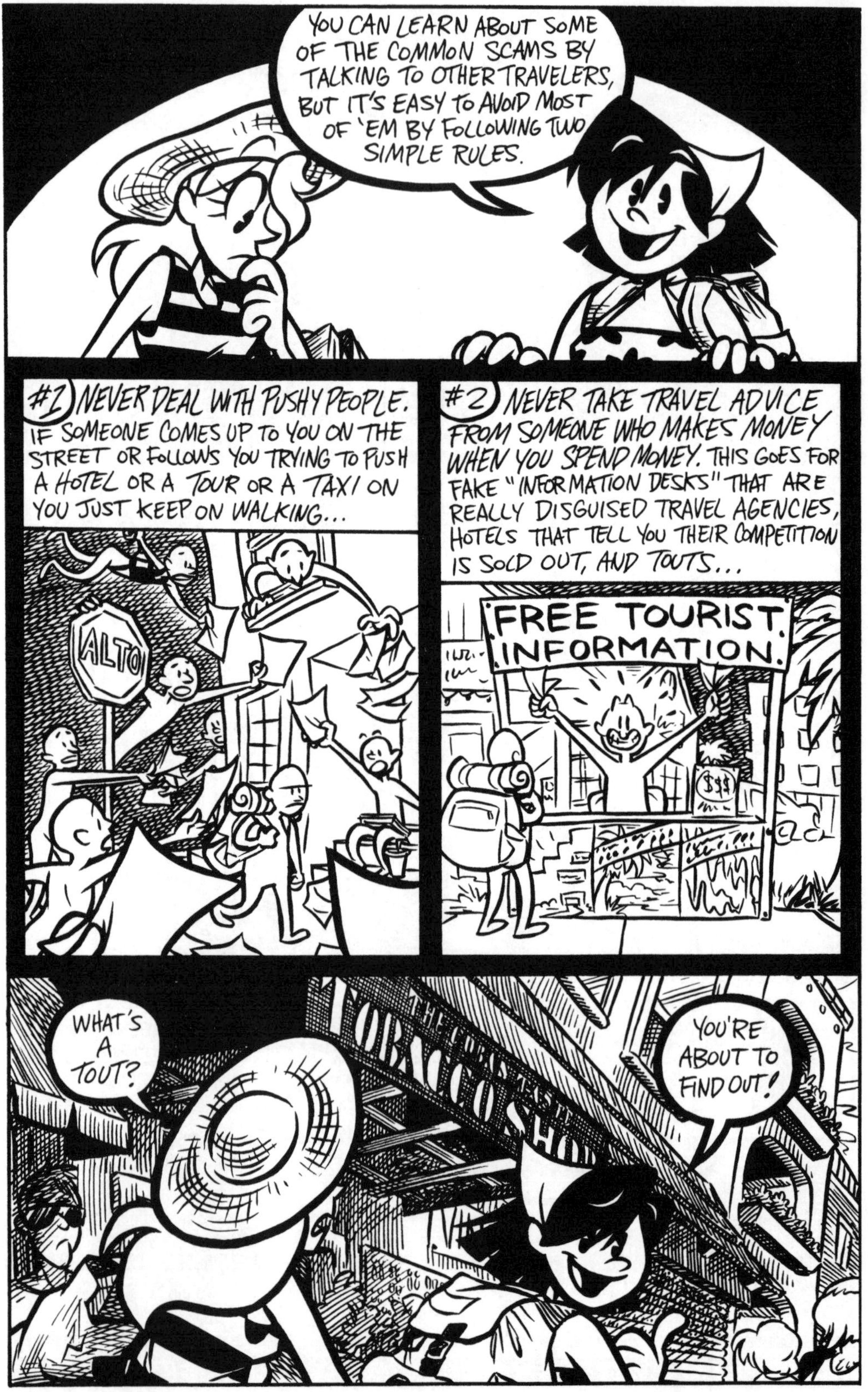
YOU CAN LEARN ABOUT SOME OF THE COMMON SCAMS BY TALKING TO OTHER TRAVELERS, BUT IT'S EASY TO AVOID MOST OF 'EM BY FOLLOWING TWO SIMPLE RULES.
#1 NEVER DEAL WITH PUSHY PEOPLE. IF SOMEONE COMES UP TO YOU ON THE STREET OR FOLLOWS YOU TRYING TO PUSH A HOTEL OR A TOUR OR A TAXI ON YOU JUST KEEP ON WALKING...
ALTO
#2 NEVER TAKE TRAVEL ADVICE FROM SOMEONE WHO MAKES MONEY WHEN YOU SPEND MONEY. THIS GOES FOR FAKE "INFORMATION DESKS" THAT ARE REALLY DISGUISED TRAVEL AGENCIES, HOTELS THAT TELL YOU THEIR COMPETITION IS SOLD OUT, AND TOUTS...
FREE TOURIST INFORMATION
$$$
WHAT'S A TOUT?
YOU'RE ABOUT TO FIND OUT!
TOBACCO SHO

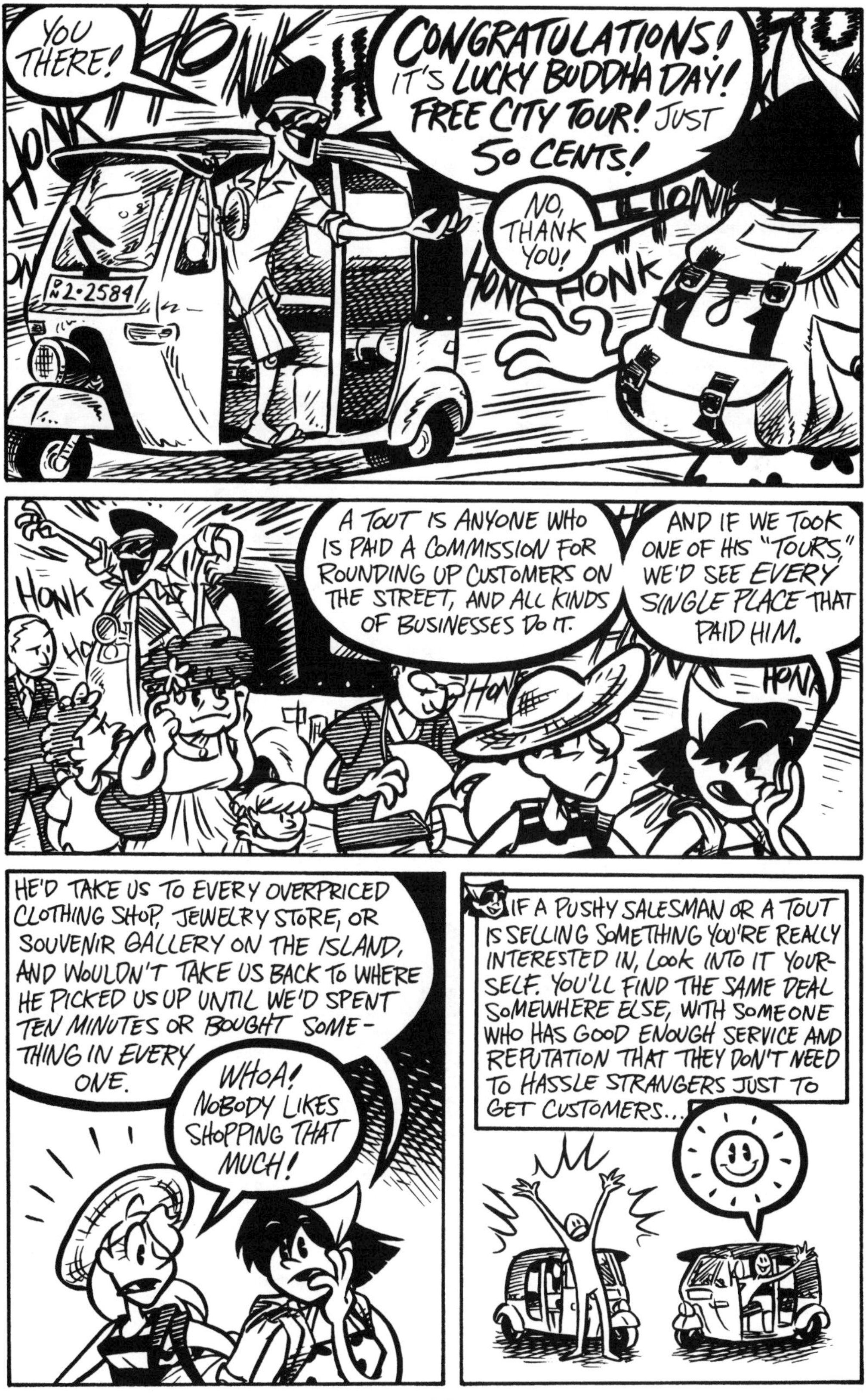
YOU THERE!
HONK
CONGRATULATIONS! IT'S LUCKY BUDDHA DAY! FREE CITY TOUR! JUST 50 CENTS!
NO, THANK YOU!
HONK HONK
A TOUT IS ANYONE WHO IS PAID A COMMISSION FOR ROUNDING UP CUSTOMERS ON THE STREET, AND ALL KINDS OF BUSINESSES DO IT.
AND IF WE TOOK ONE OF HIS "TOURS," WE'D SEE EVERY SINGLE PLACE THAT PAID HIM.
HE'D TAKE US TO EVERY OVERPRICED CLOTHING SHOP, JEWELRY STORE, OR SOUVENIR GALLERY ON THE ISLAND, AND WOULDN'T TAKE US BACK TO WHERE HE PICKED US UP UNTIL WE'D SPENT TEN MINUTES OR BOUGHT SOMETHING IN EVERY ONE.
WHOA! NOBODY LIKES SHOPPING THAT MUCH!
IF A PUSHY SALESMAN OR A TOUT IS SELLING SOMETHING YOU'RE REALLY INTERESTED IN, LOOK INTO IT YOURSELF. YOU'LL FIND THE SAME DEAL SOMEWHERE ELSE, WITH SOMEONE WHO HAS GOOD ENOUGH SERVICE AND REPUTATION THAT THEY DON'T NEED TO HASSLE STRANGERS JUST TO GET CUSTOMERS...

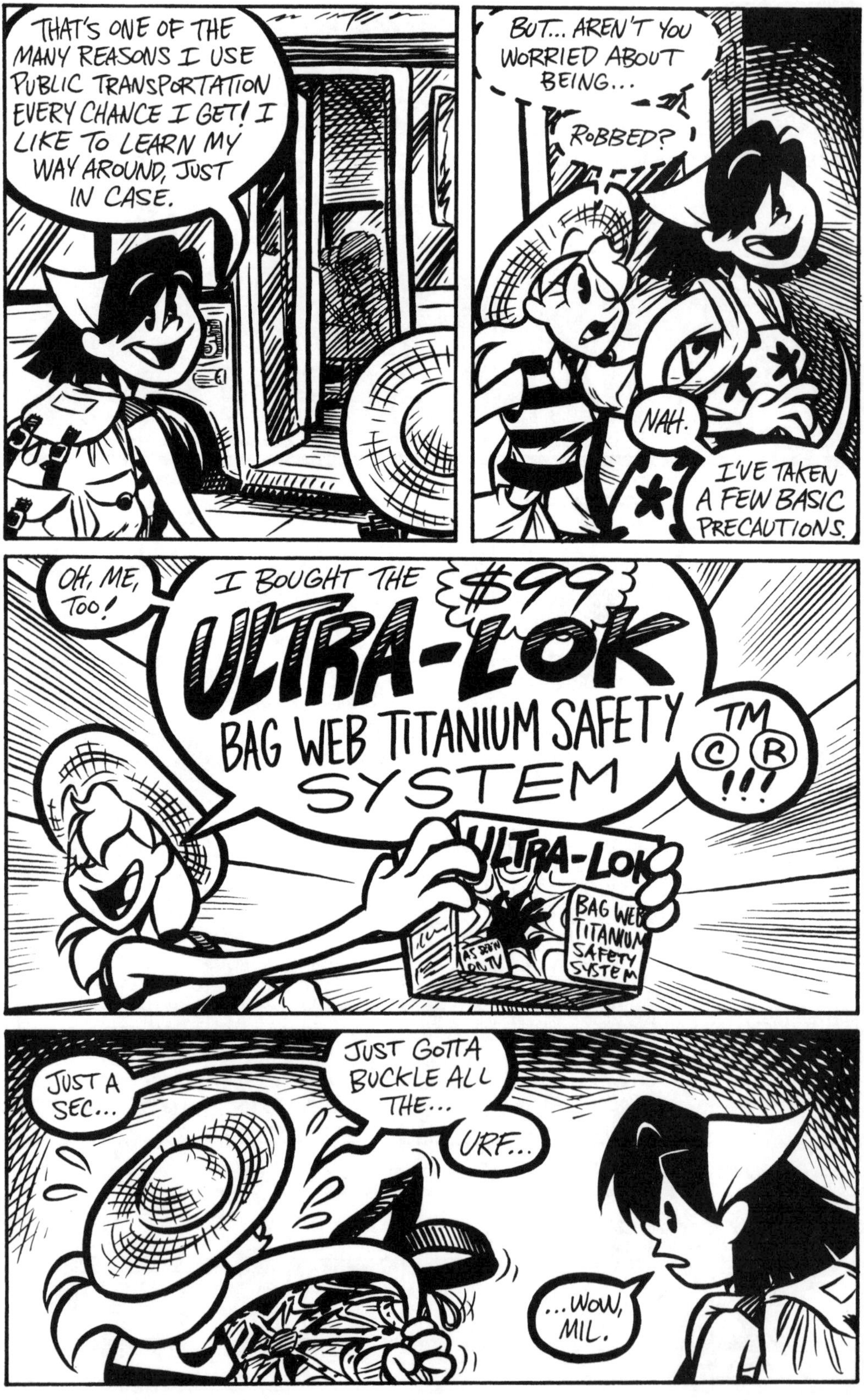
THAT'S ONE OF THE MANY REASONS I USE PUBLIC TRANSPORTATION EVERY CHANCE I GET! I LIKE TO LEARN MY WAY AROUND, JUST IN CASE.
BUT... AREN'T YOU WORRIED ABOUT BEING...
ROBBED?
NAH.
I'VE TAKEN A FEW BASIC PRECAUTIONS.
OH, ME, TOO!
I BOUGHT THE $99 ULTRA-LOK BAG WEB TITANIUM SAFETY SYSTEM
TM © ® !!!
ULTRA-LOK
BAG WEB TITANIUM SAFETY SYSTEM
AS SEEN ON TV
JUST A SEC...
JUST GOTTA BUCKLE ALL THE...
URF...
...WOW, MIL.

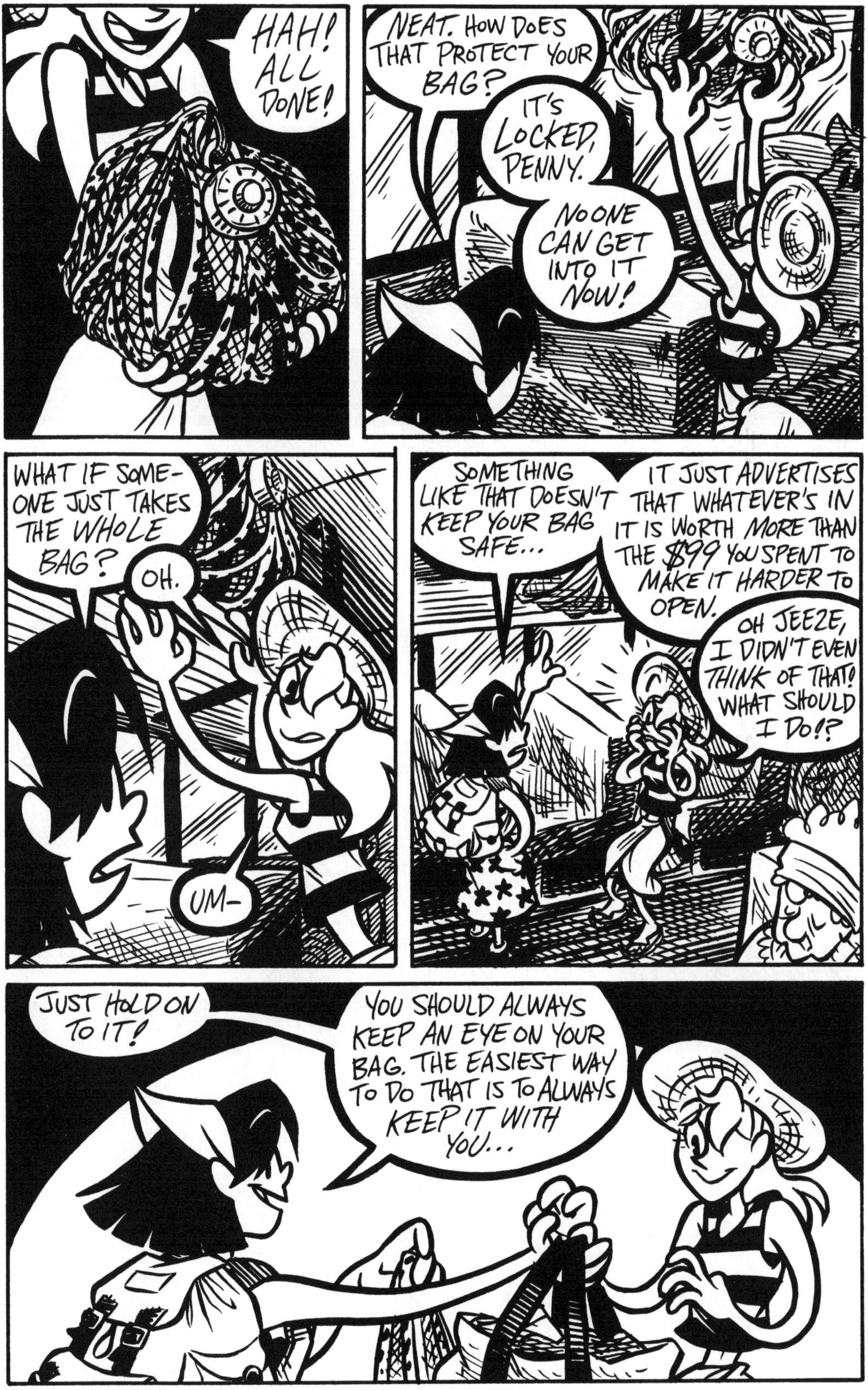
HAH! ALL DONE!
NEAT. HOW DOES THAT PROTECT YOUR BAG?
IT'S LOCKED, PENNY.
NO ONE CAN GET INTO IT NOW!
WHAT IF SOME-ONE JUST TAKES THE WHOLE BAG?
OH.
UM-
SOMETHING LIKE THAT DOESN'T KEEP YOUR BAG SAFE...
IT JUST ADVERTISES THAT WHATEVER'S IN IT IS WORTH MORE THAN THE $99 YOU SPENT TO MAKE IT HARDER TO OPEN.
OH JEEZE, I DIDN'T EVEN THINK OF THAT! WHAT SHOULD I DO!?
JUST HOLD ON TO IT!
YOU SHOULD ALWAYS KEEP AN EYE ON YOUR BAG. THE EASIEST WAY TO DO THAT IS TO ALWAYS KEEP IT WITH YOU...

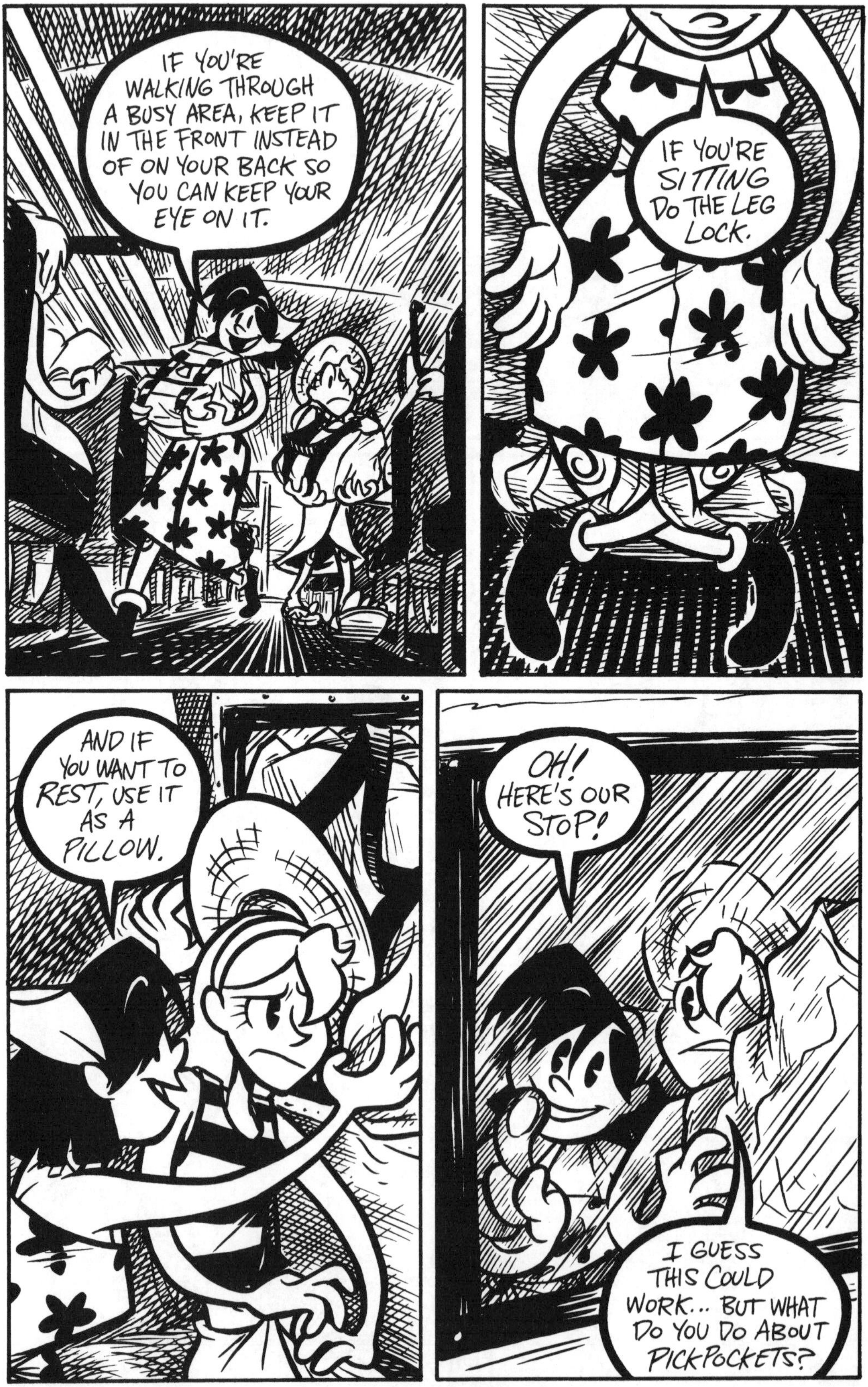
IF YOU'RE WALKING THROUGH A BUSY AREA, KEEP IT IN THE FRONT INSTEAD OF ON YOUR BACK SO YOU CAN KEEP YOUR EYE ON IT.
IF YOU'RE SITTING DO THE LEG LOCK.
AND IF YOU WANT TO REST, USE IT AS A PILLOW.
OH! HERE'S OUR STOP!
I GUESS THIS COULD WORK... BUT WHAT DO YOU DO ABOUT PICKPOCKETS?

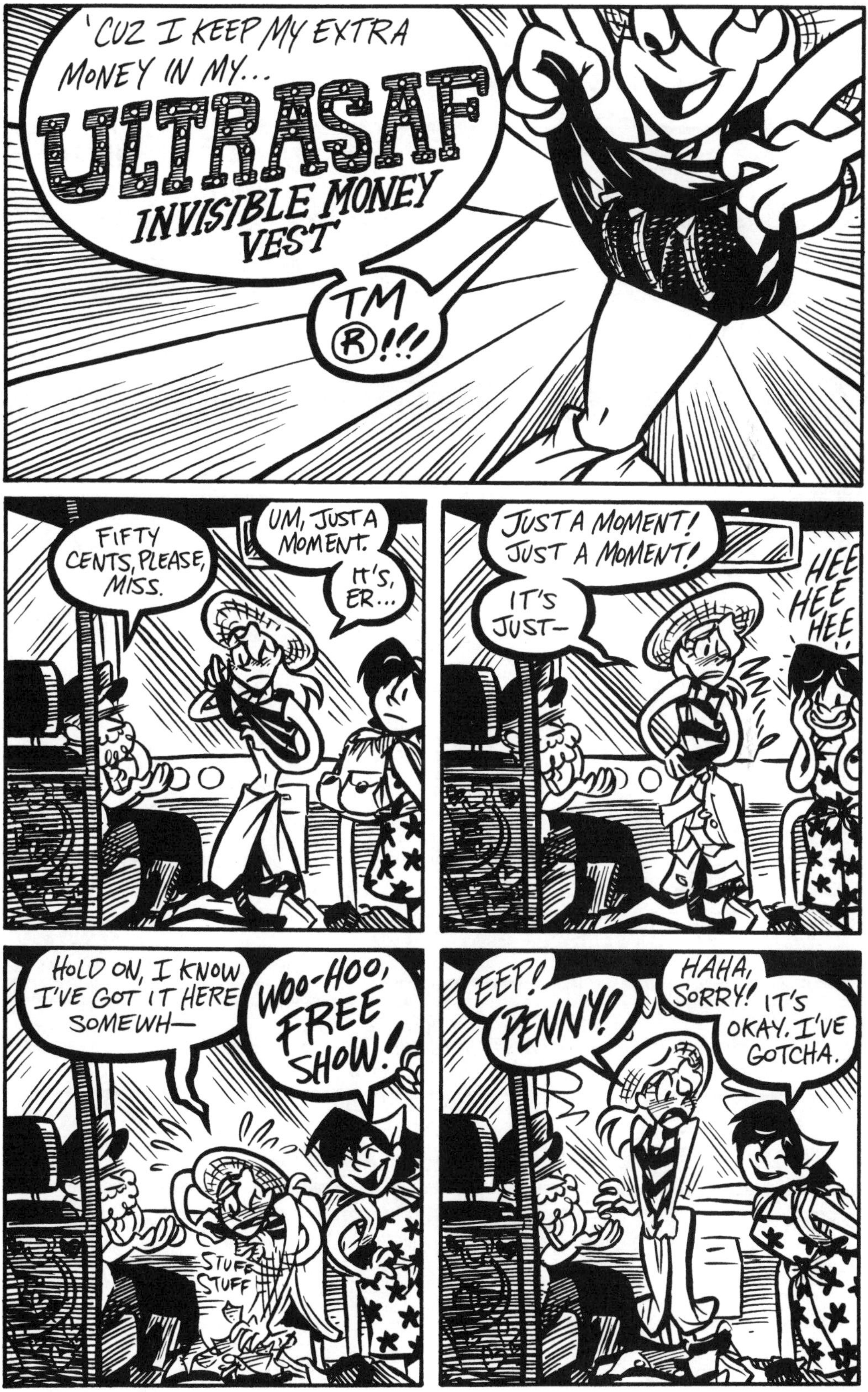
'CUZ I KEEP MY EXTRA MONEY IN MY...
ULTRASAF
INVISIBLE MONEY VEST
TM ®!!!
FIFTY CENTS, PLEASE, MISS.
UM, JUST A MOMENT.
IT'S, ER...
JUST A MOMENT! JUST A MOMENT!
IT'S JUST—
HEE HEE HEE!
HOLD ON, I KNOW I'VE GOT IT HERE SOMEWH—
WOO-HOO, FREE SHOW!
STUFF STUFF
EEP!
PENNY!
HAHA, SORRY!
IT'S OKAY. I'VE GOTCHA.

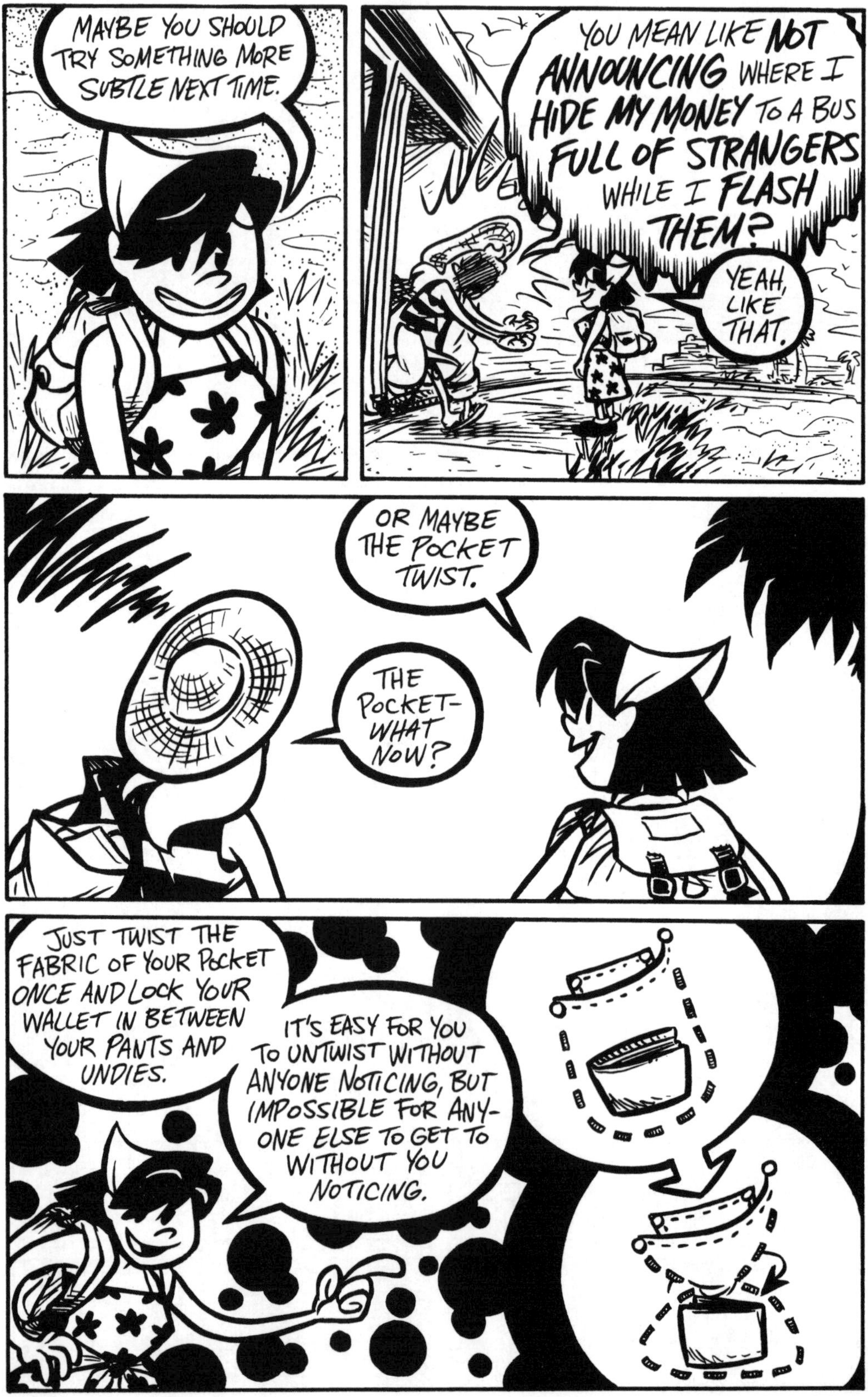
MAYBE YOU SHOULD TRY SOMETHING MORE SUBTLE NEXT TIME.
YOU MEAN LIKE NOT ANNOUNCING WHERE I HIDE MY MONEY TO A BUS FULL OF STRANGERS WHILE I FLASH THEM?
YEAH, LIKE THAT.
OR MAYBE THE POCKET TWIST.
THE POCKET-WHAT NOW?
JUST TWIST THE FABRIC OF YOUR POCKET ONCE AND LOCK YOUR WALLET IN BETWEEN YOUR PANTS AND UNDIES.
IT'S EASY FOR YOU TO UNTWIST WITHOUT ANYONE NOTICING, BUT IMPOSSIBLE FOR ANY-ONE ELSE TO GET TO WITHOUT YOU NOTICING.

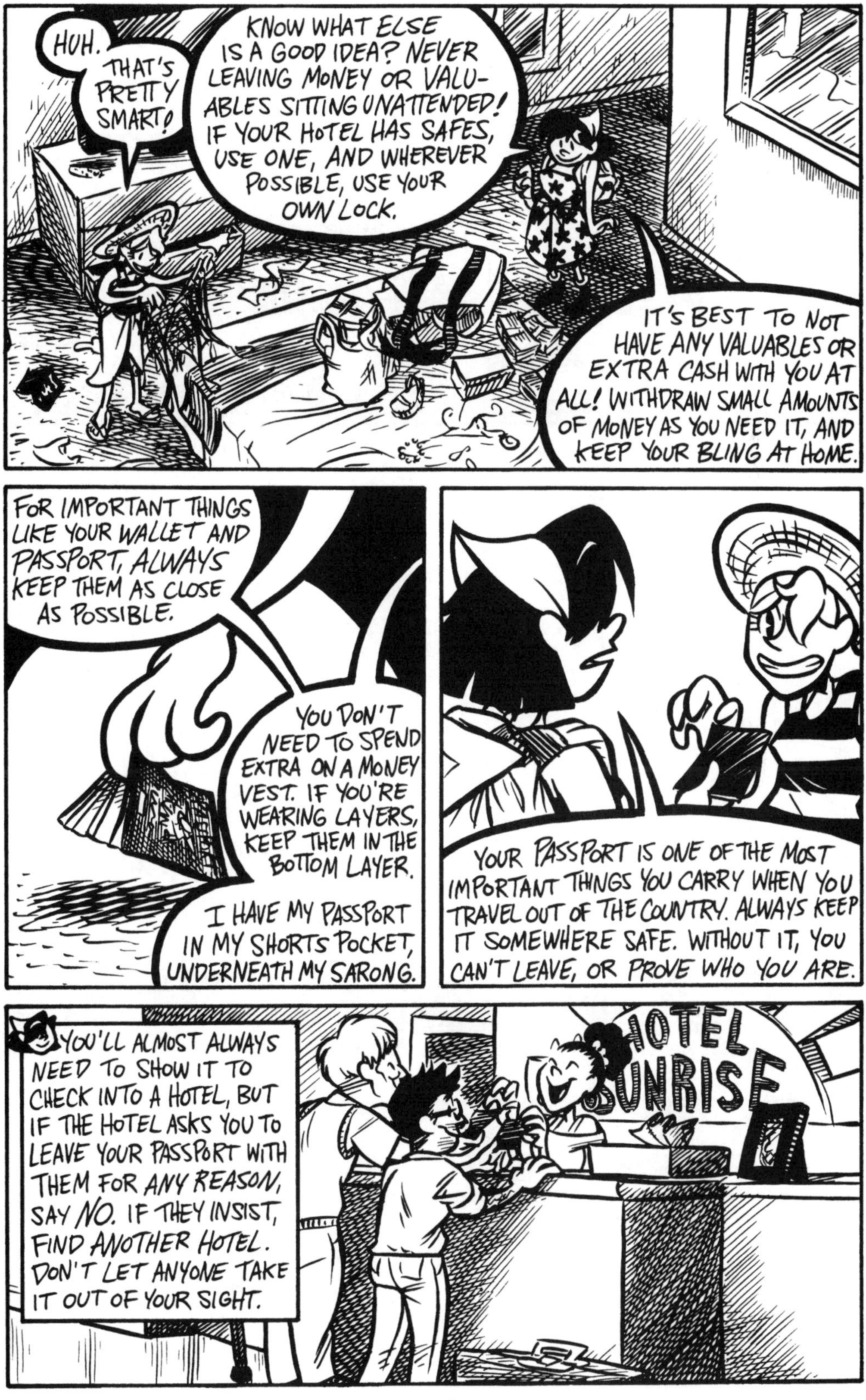
HUH.
THAT'S PRETTY SMART!
KNOW WHAT ELSE IS A GOOD IDEA? NEVER LEAVING MONEY OR VALUABLES SITTING UNATTENDED! IF YOUR HOTEL HAS SAFES, USE ONE, AND WHEREVER POSSIBLE, USE YOUR OWN LOCK.
IT'S BEST TO NOT HAVE ANY VALUABLES OR EXTRA CASH WITH YOU AT ALL! WITHDRAW SMALL AMOUNTS OF MONEY AS YOU NEED IT, AND KEEP YOUR BLING AT HOME.
FOR IMPORTANT THINGS LIKE YOUR WALLET AND PASSPORT, ALWAYS KEEP THEM AS CLOSE AS POSSIBLE.
YOU DON'T NEED TO SPEND EXTRA ON A MONEY VEST. IF YOU'RE WEARING LAYERS, KEEP THEM IN THE BOTTOM LAYER.
I HAVE MY PASSPORT IN MY SHORTS POCKET, UNDERNEATH MY SARONG.
YOUR PASSPORT IS ONE OF THE MOST IMPORTANT THINGS YOU CARRY WHEN YOU TRAVEL OUT OF THE COUNTRY. ALWAYS KEEP IT SOMEWHERE SAFE. WITHOUT IT, YOU CAN'T LEAVE, OR PROVE WHO YOU ARE.
YOU'LL ALMOST ALWAYS NEED TO SHOW IT TO CHECK INTO A HOTEL, BUT IF THE HOTEL ASKS YOU TO LEAVE YOUR PASSPORT WITH THEM FOR ANY REASON, SAY NO. IF THEY INSIST, FIND ANOTHER HOTEL. DON'T LET ANYONE TAKE IT OUT OF YOUR SIGHT.
HOTEL SUNRISE

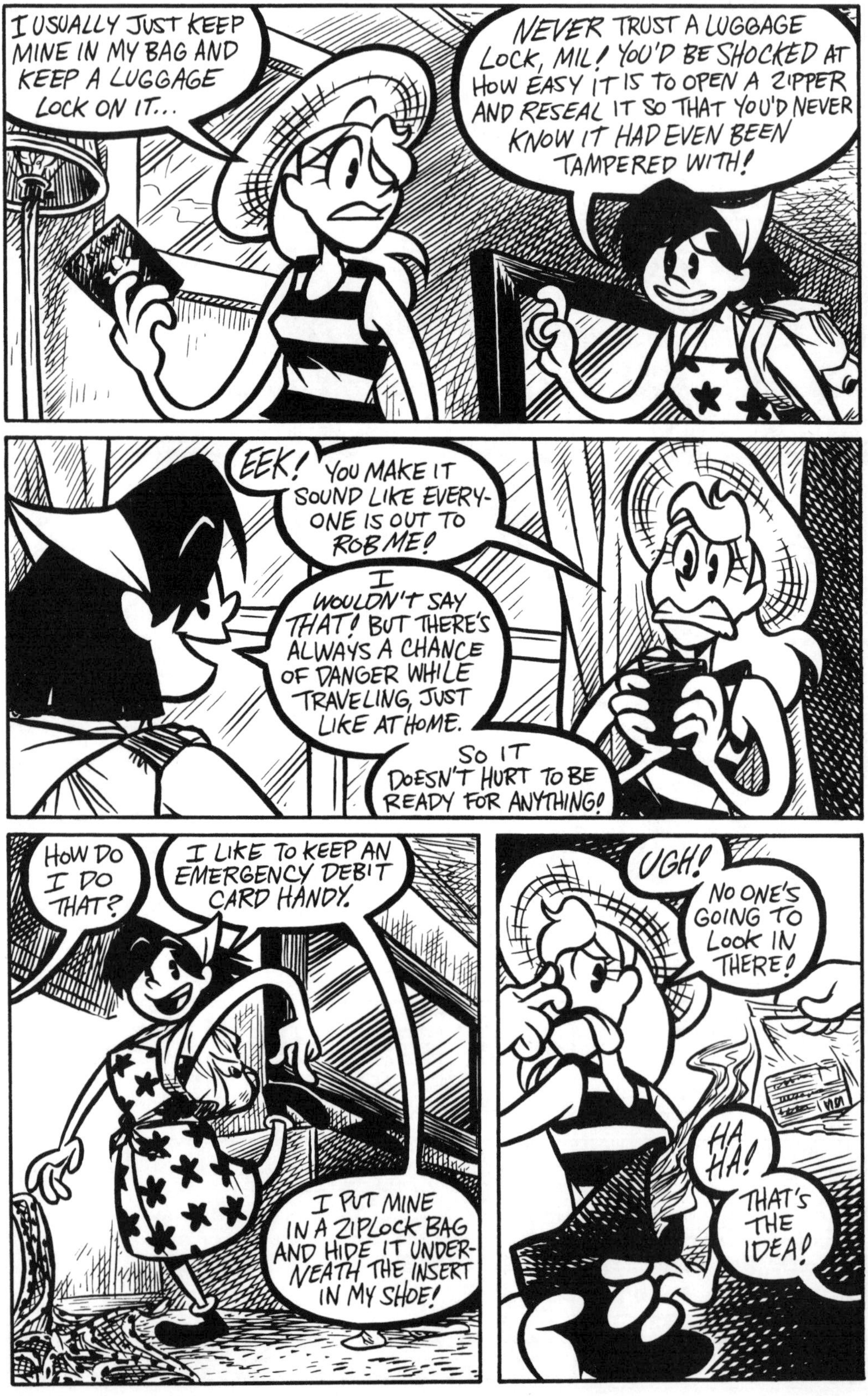
I USUALLY JUST KEEP MINE IN MY BAG AND KEEP A LUGGAGE LOCK ON IT...
NEVER TRUST A LUGGAGE LOCK, MIL! YOU'D BE SHOCKED AT HOW EASY IT IS TO OPEN A ZIPPER AND RESEAL IT SO THAT YOU'D NEVER KNOW IT HAD EVEN BEEN TAMPERED WITH!
EEK!
YOU MAKE IT SOUND LIKE EVERYONE IS OUT TO ROB ME!
I WOULDN'T SAY THAT! BUT THERE'S ALWAYS A CHANCE OF DANGER WHILE TRAVELING, JUST LIKE AT HOME.
SO IT DOESN'T HURT TO BE READY FOR ANYTHING!
HOW DO I DO THAT?
I LIKE TO KEEP AN EMERGENCY DEBIT CARD HANDY.
I PUT MINE IN A ZIPLOCK BAG AND HIDE IT UNDERNEATH THE INSERT IN MY SHOE!
UGH!
NO ONE'S GOING TO LOOK IN THERE!
HA HA!
THAT'S THE IDEA!

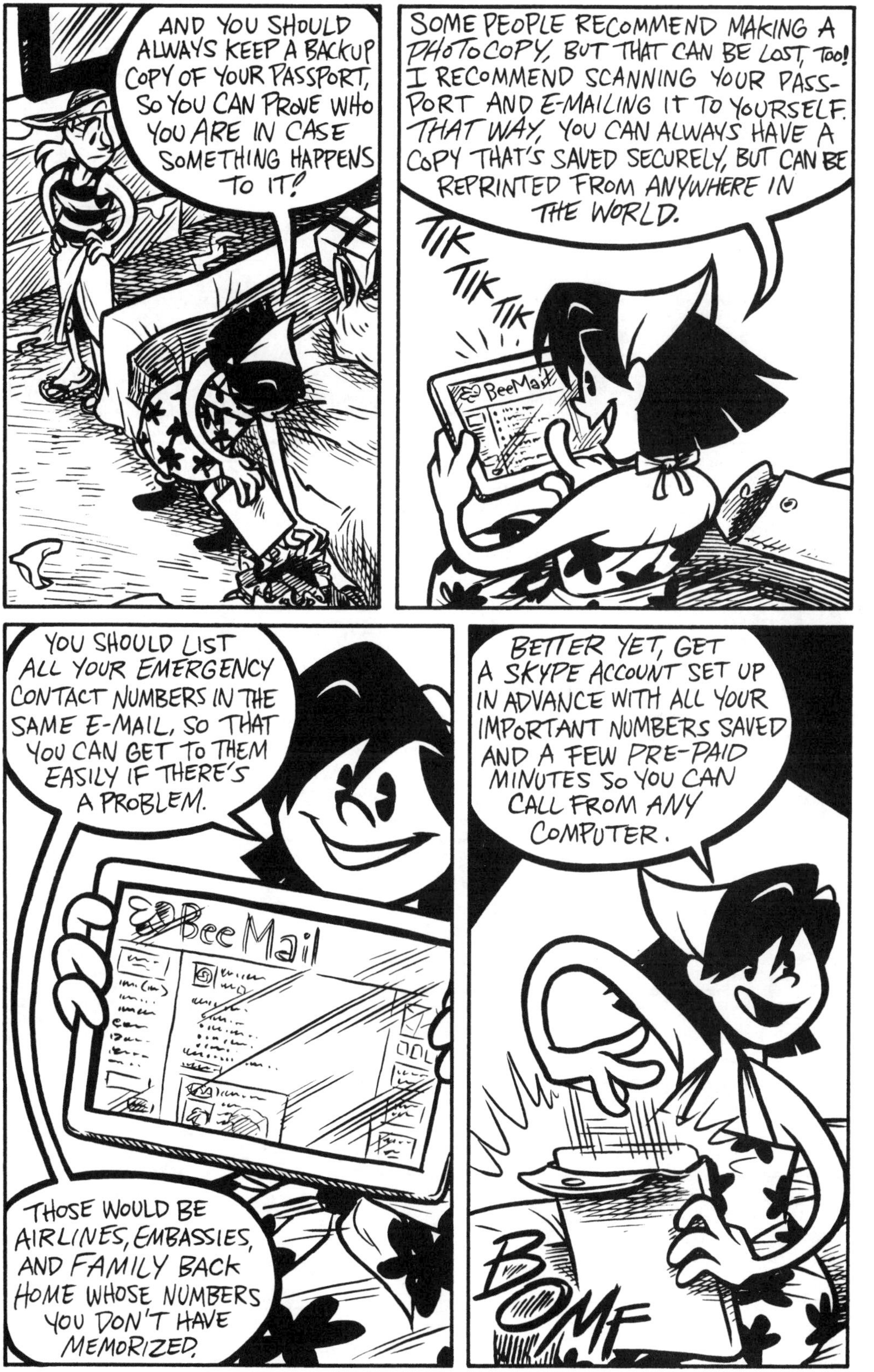
AND YOU SHOULD ALWAYS KEEP A BACKUP COPY OF YOUR PASSPORT, SO YOU CAN PROVE WHO YOU ARE IN CASE SOMETHING HAPPENS TO IT!
SOME PEOPLE RECOMMEND MAKING A PHOTOCOPY, BUT THAT CAN BE LOST, TOO! I RECOMMEND SCANNING YOUR PASSPORT AND E-MAILING IT TO YOURSELF. THAT WAY, YOU CAN ALWAYS HAVE A COPY THAT'S SAVED SECURELY, BUT CAN BE REPRINTED FROM ANYWHERE IN THE WORLD.
TIK TIK TIK
BeeMail
YOU SHOULD LIST ALL YOUR EMERGENCY CONTACT NUMBERS IN THE SAME E-MAIL, SO THAT YOU CAN GET TO THEM EASILY IF THERE'S A PROBLEM.
Bee Mail
THOSE WOULD BE AIRLINES, EMBASSIES, AND FAMILY BACK HOME WHOSE NUMBERS YOU DON'T HAVE MEMORIZED.
BETTER YET, GET A SKYPE ACCOUNT SET UP IN ADVANCE WITH ALL YOUR IMPORTANT NUMBERS SAVED AND A FEW PRE-PAID MINUTES SO YOU CAN CALL FROM ANY COMPUTER.
BOMF

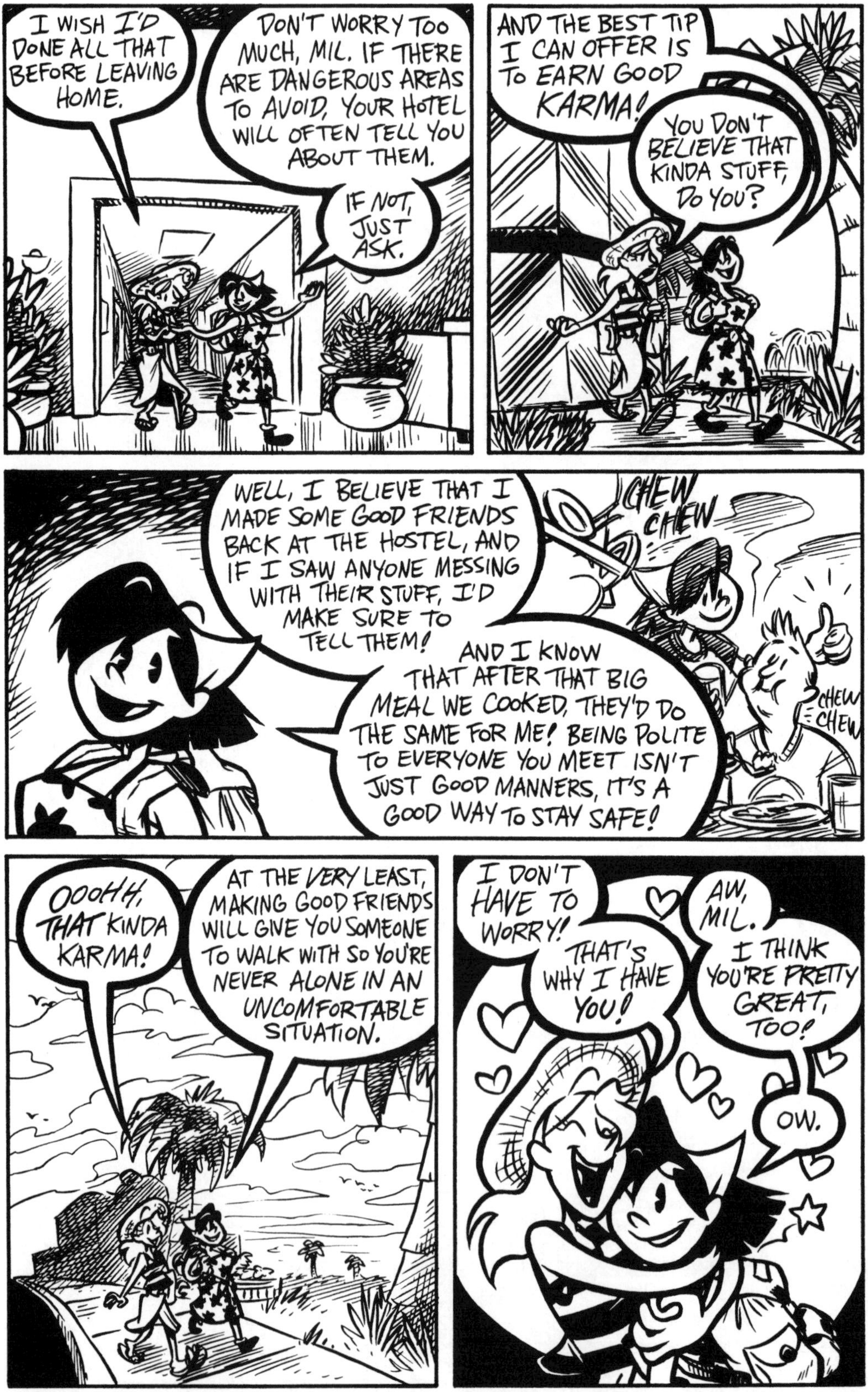

I WISH I'D DONE ALL THAT BEFORE LEAVING HOME.
DON'T WORRY TOO MUCH, MIL. IF THERE ARE DANGEROUS AREAS TO AVOID, YOUR HOTEL WILL OFTEN TELL YOU ABOUT THEM.
IF NOT, JUST ASK.
AND THE BEST TIP I CAN OFFER IS TO EARN GOOD KARMA!
YOU DON'T BELIEVE THAT KINDA STUFF, DO YOU?
WELL, I BELIEVE THAT I MADE SOME GOOD FRIENDS BACK AT THE HOSTEL, AND IF I SAW ANYONE MESSING WITH THEIR STUFF, I'D MAKE SURE TO TELL THEM!
AND I KNOW THAT AFTER THAT BIG MEAL WE COOKED, THEY'D DO THE SAME FOR ME! BEING POLITE TO EVERYONE YOU MEET ISN'T JUST GOOD MANNERS, IT'S A GOOD WAY TO STAY SAFE!
CHEW CHEW
CHEW CHEW
OOOHH, THAT KINDA KARMA!
AT THE VERY LEAST, MAKING GOOD FRIENDS WILL GIVE YOU SOMEONE TO WALK WITH SO YOU'RE NEVER ALONE IN AN UNCOMFORTABLE SITUATION.
I DON'T HAVE TO WORRY!
THAT'S WHY I HAVE YOU!
AW, MIL.
I THINK YOU'RE PRETTY GREAT, TOO!
OW.

Chapter Ten
Living and Working Abroad

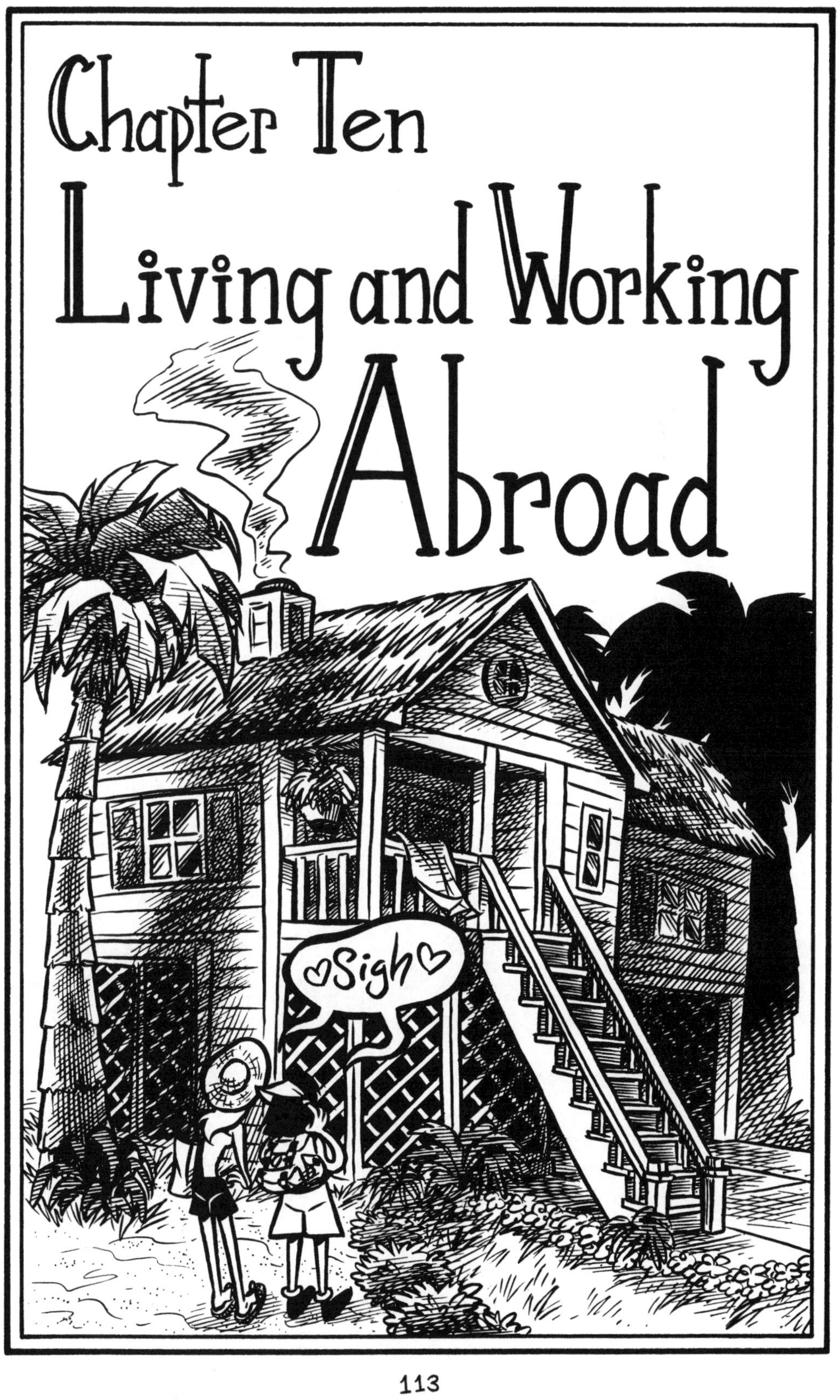

♡Sigh♡

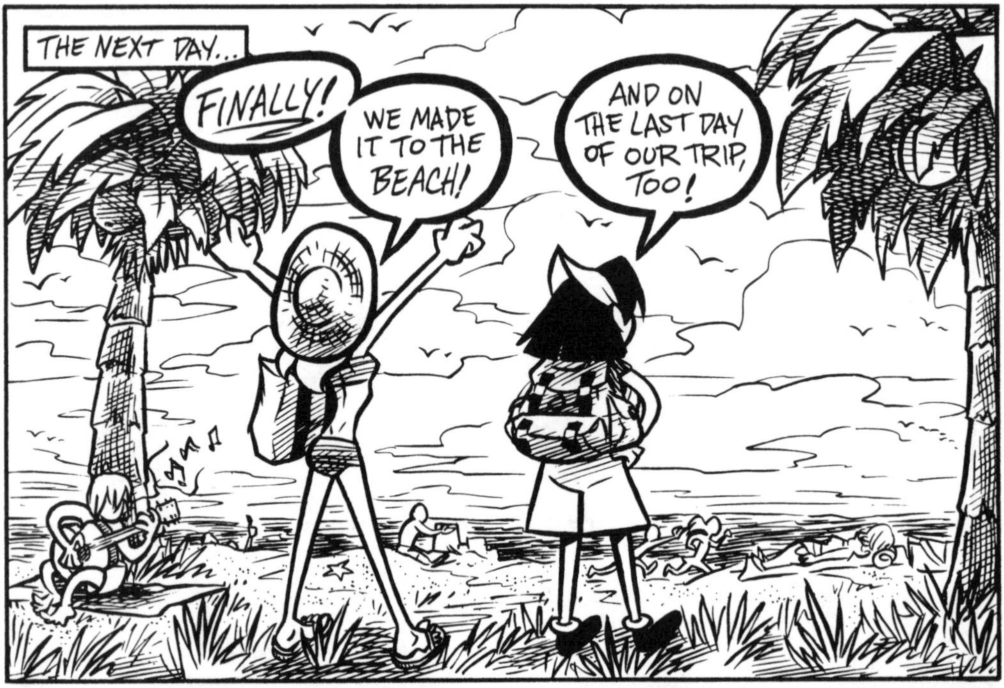
THE NEXT DAY...
FINALLY!
WE MADE IT TO THE BEACH!
AND ON THE LAST DAY OF OUR TRIP, TOO!

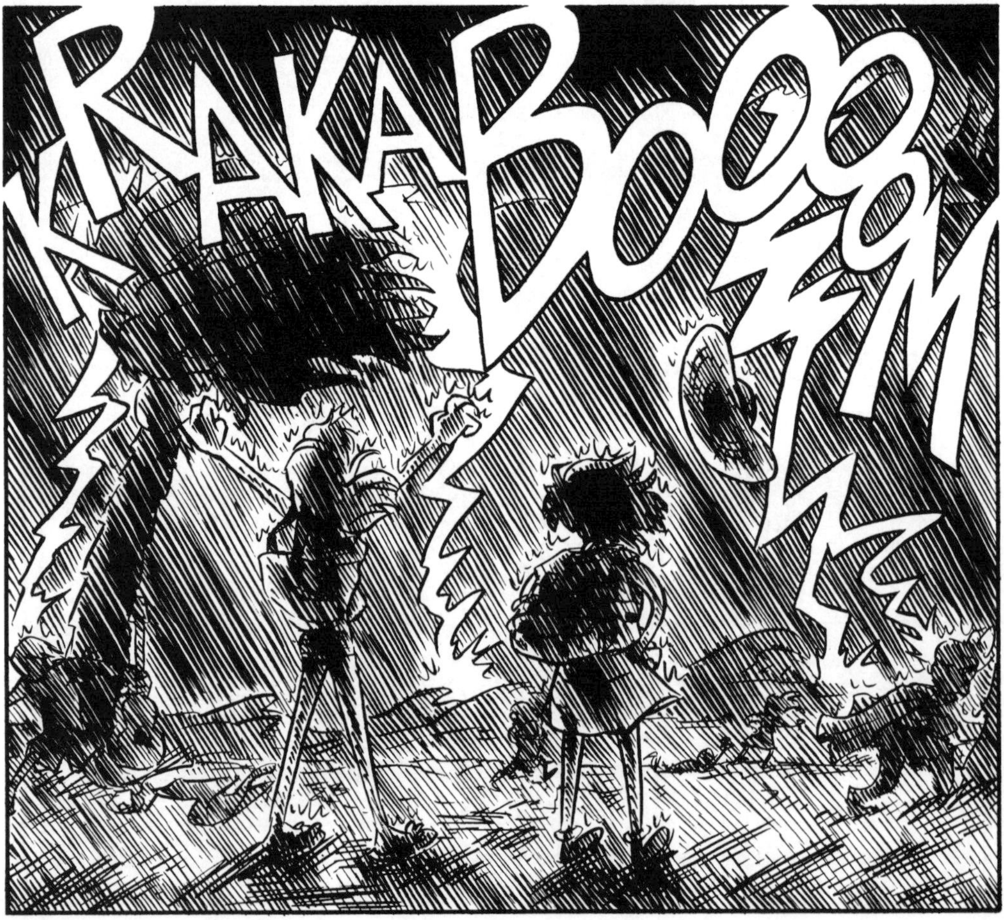
KRAKABOOOOM

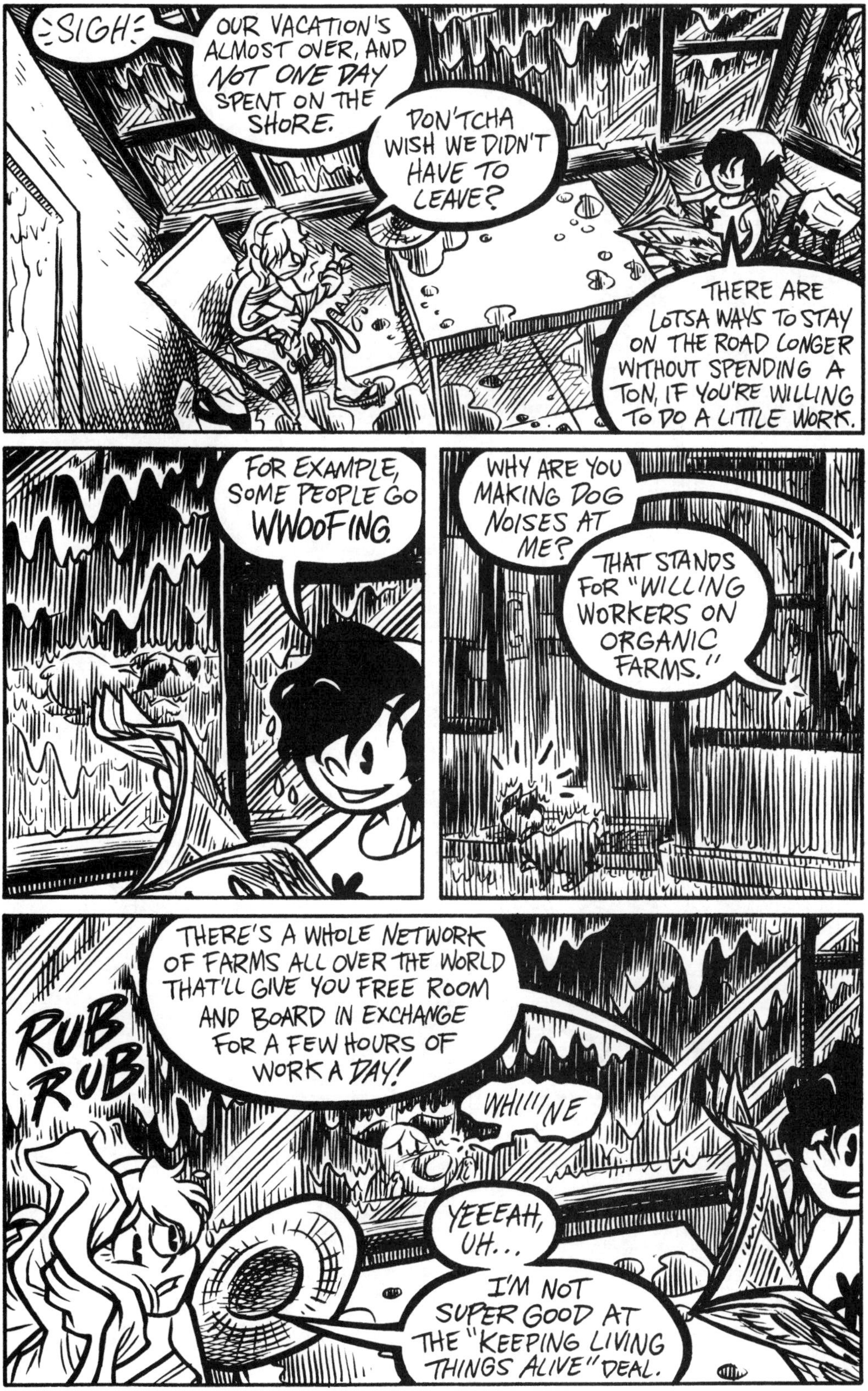
SIGH
OUR VACATION'S ALMOST OVER, AND NOT ONE DAY SPENT ON THE SHORE.
DON'TCHA WISH WE DIDN'T HAVE TO LEAVE?
THERE ARE LOTSA WAYS TO STAY ON THE ROAD LONGER WITHOUT SPENDING A TON, IF YOU'RE WILLING TO DO A LITTLE WORK.
FOR EXAMPLE, SOME PEOPLE GO WWOOFING.
WHY ARE YOU MAKING DOG NOISES AT ME?
THAT STANDS FOR "WILLING WORKERS ON ORGANIC FARMS."
THERE'S A WHOLE NETWORK OF FARMS ALL OVER THE WORLD THAT'LL GIVE YOU FREE ROOM AND BOARD IN EXCHANGE FOR A FEW HOURS OF WORK A DAY!
RUB RUB
WHIIIINE
YEEEAH, UH...
I'M NOT SUPER GOOD AT THE "KEEPING LIVING THINGS ALIVE" DEAL.

LOTS OF HOSTELS WILL OFFER YOU THE SAME DEAL! A FREE ROOM IN EXCHANGE FOR HELPING TAKE CARE OF OTHER GUESTS.

TOURISTS ARE LIVING THINGS, TOO, PENNY!

BRSH BRSH

RUMMAGE RUMMAGE

AND A LOT OF PEOPLE STAY OVERSEAS FOR LONG PERIODS DOING VOLUNTEER WORK, BUT THAT'S A LOT HARDER THAN YOU MIGHT THINK.

IT'S HARD ENOUGH TO WORK WHEN I DO GET PAID, SO I CAN IMAGINE!

WHAT I MEAN IS, WHEN YOU LOOK FOR VOLUNTEER WORK, MOST OF THE OPPORTUNITIES YOU'LL FIND WILL BE THROUGH FOR-PROFIT AGENCIES THAT CHARGE HUGE FEES TO JOIN. UNFORTUNATELY, MOST OF THAT MONEY GOES TO THE AGENCY, NOT THE COMMUNITY YOU'RE TRYING TO HELP.

TUTOR CHILDREN

WORK WITH MONKS! $1000 A WEEK

TEACH WEAVING WORKSHOP IN THE JUNGLE

IF YOU REALLY WANNA VOLUNTEER SOMEWHERE, CONTACT THE ORGANIZATION YOU'RE INTERESTED IN AND SEE WHAT THEY ACTUALLY NEED. THEY'RE OFTEN LOOKING FOR SKILLED LABOR, AND JUST A BUNCH OF RANDOM STRANGERS WITH SHOVELS ARE MORE LIKELY TO BE A LIABILITY THAN AN ASSET...

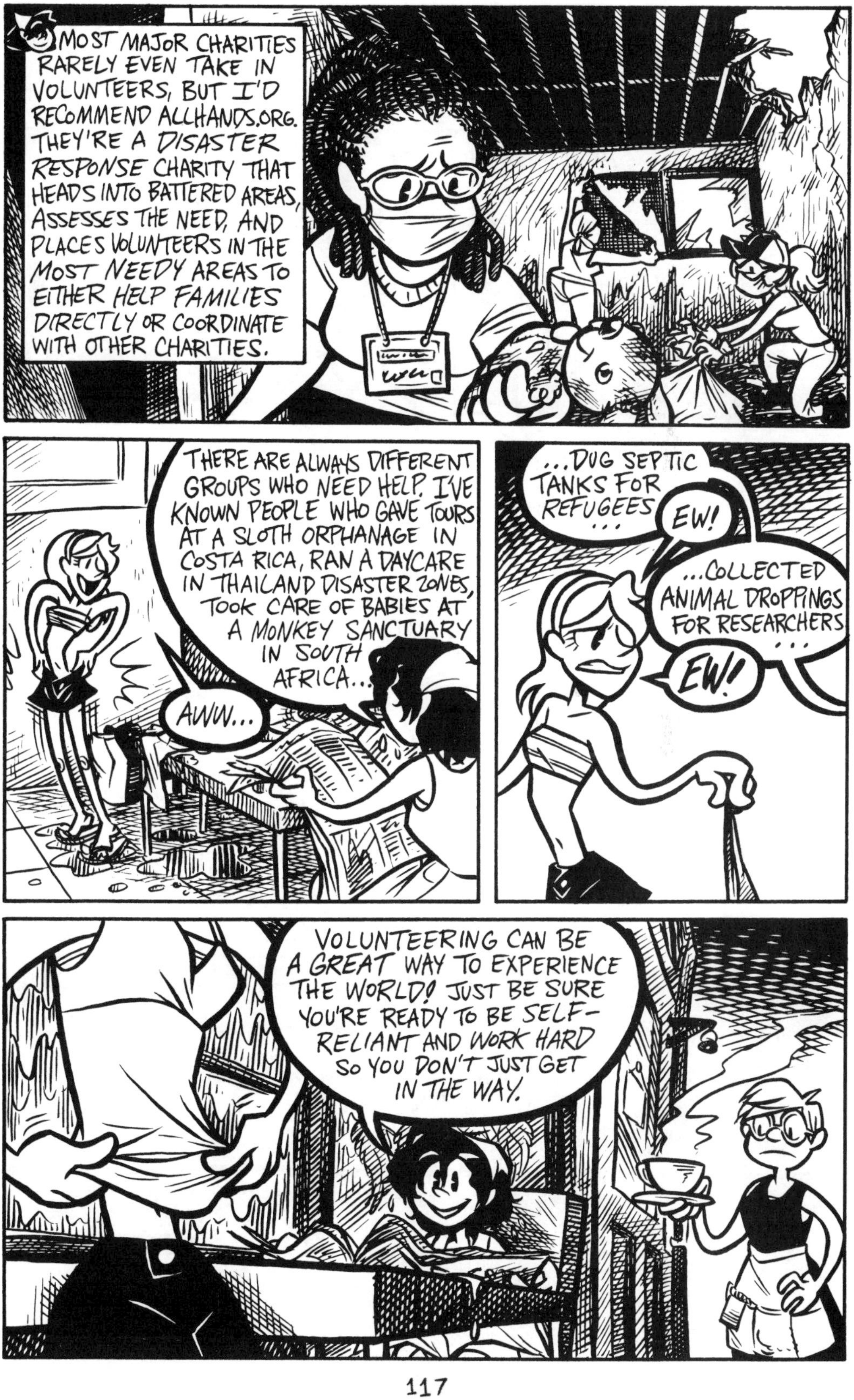
MOST MAJOR CHARITIES RARELY EVEN TAKE IN VOLUNTEERS, BUT I'D RECOMMEND ALLHANDS.ORG. THEY'RE A DISASTER RESPONSE CHARITY THAT HEADS INTO BATTERED AREAS, ASSESSES THE NEED, AND PLACES VOLUNTEERS IN THE MOST NEEDY AREAS TO EITHER HELP FAMILIES DIRECTLY OR COORDINATE WITH OTHER CHARITIES.
THERE ARE ALWAYS DIFFERENT GROUPS WHO NEED HELP. I'VE KNOWN PEOPLE WHO GAVE TOURS AT A SLOTH ORPHANAGE IN COSTA RICA, RAN A DAYCARE IN THAILAND DISASTER ZONES, TOOK CARE OF BABIES AT A MONKEY SANCTUARY IN SOUTH AFRICA...
AWW...
...DUG SEPTIC TANKS FOR REFUGEES...
EW!
...COLLECTED ANIMAL DROPPINGS FOR RESEARCHERS...
EW!
VOLUNTEERING CAN BE A GREAT WAY TO EXPERIENCE THE WORLD! JUST BE SURE YOU'RE READY TO BE SELF-RELIANT AND WORK HARD SO YOU DON'T JUST GET IN THE WAY.

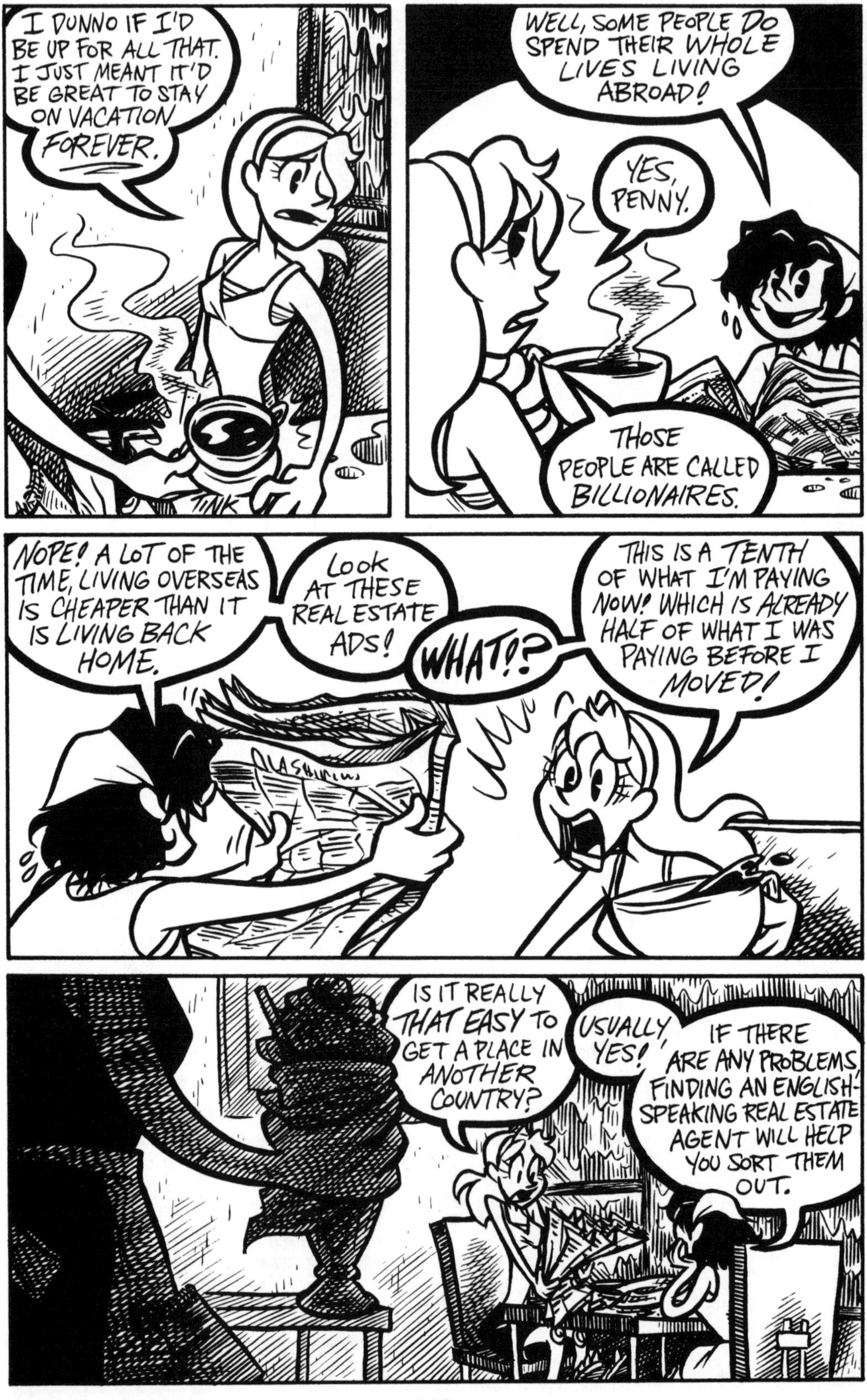

I DUNNO IF I'D BE UP FOR ALL THAT. I JUST MEANT IT'D BE GREAT TO STAY ON VACATION FOREVER.
TINK
WELL, SOME PEOPLE DO SPEND THEIR WHOLE LIVES LIVING ABROAD!
YES, PENNY.
THOSE PEOPLE ARE CALLED BILLIONAIRES.
NOPE! A LOT OF THE TIME, LIVING OVERSEAS IS CHEAPER THAN IT IS LIVING BACK HOME.
LOOK AT THESE REAL ESTATE ADS!
WHAT!?
THIS IS A TENTH OF WHAT I'M PAYING NOW! WHICH IS ALREADY HALF OF WHAT I WAS PAYING BEFORE I MOVED!
IS IT REALLY THAT EASY TO GET A PLACE IN ANOTHER COUNTRY?
USUALLY, YES!
IF THERE ARE ANY PROBLEMS, FINDING AN ENGLISH-SPEAKING REAL ESTATE AGENT WILL HELP YOU SORT THEM OUT.

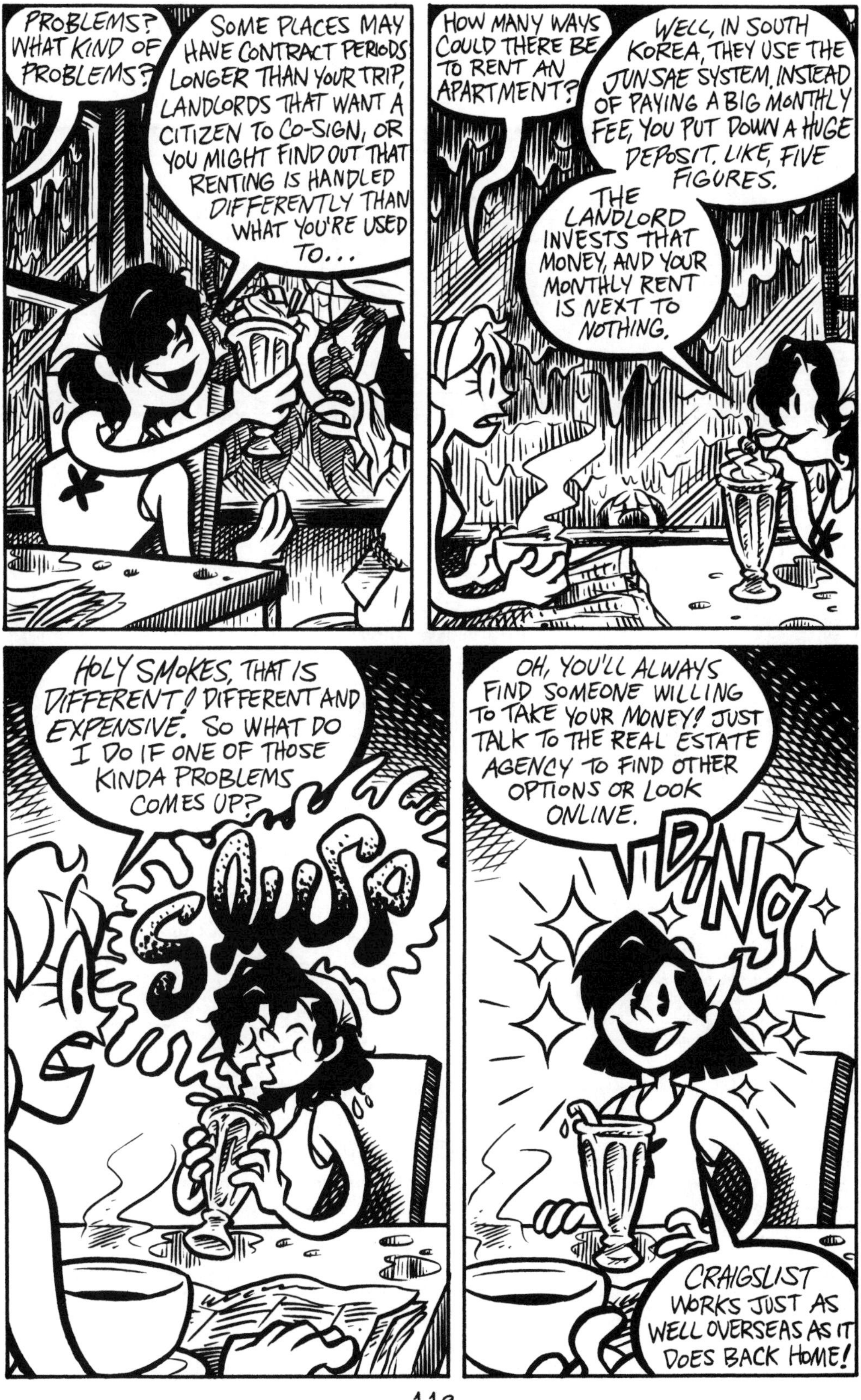
PROBLEMS? WHAT KIND OF PROBLEMS?
SOME PLACES MAY HAVE CONTRACT PERIODS LONGER THAN YOUR TRIP, LANDLORDS THAT WANT A CITIZEN TO CO-SIGN, OR YOU MIGHT FIND OUT THAT RENTING IS HANDLED DIFFERENTLY THAN WHAT YOU'RE USED TO...
HOW MANY WAYS COULD THERE BE TO RENT AN APARTMENT?
WELL, IN SOUTH KOREA, THEY USE THE JUNSAE SYSTEM. INSTEAD OF PAYING A BIG MONTHLY FEE, YOU PUT DOWN A HUGE DEPOSIT. LIKE, FIVE FIGURES.
THE LANDLORD INVESTS THAT MONEY, AND YOUR MONTHLY RENT IS NEXT TO NOTHING.
HOLY SMOKES, THAT IS DIFFERENT! DIFFERENT AND EXPENSIVE. SO WHAT DO I DO IF ONE OF THOSE KINDA PROBLEMS COMES UP?
SLURP
OH, YOU'LL ALWAYS FIND SOMEONE WILLING TO TAKE YOUR MONEY! JUST TALK TO THE REAL ESTATE AGENCY TO FIND OTHER OPTIONS OR LOOK ONLINE.
DING
CRAIGSLIST WORKS JUST AS WELL OVERSEAS AS IT DOES BACK HOME!

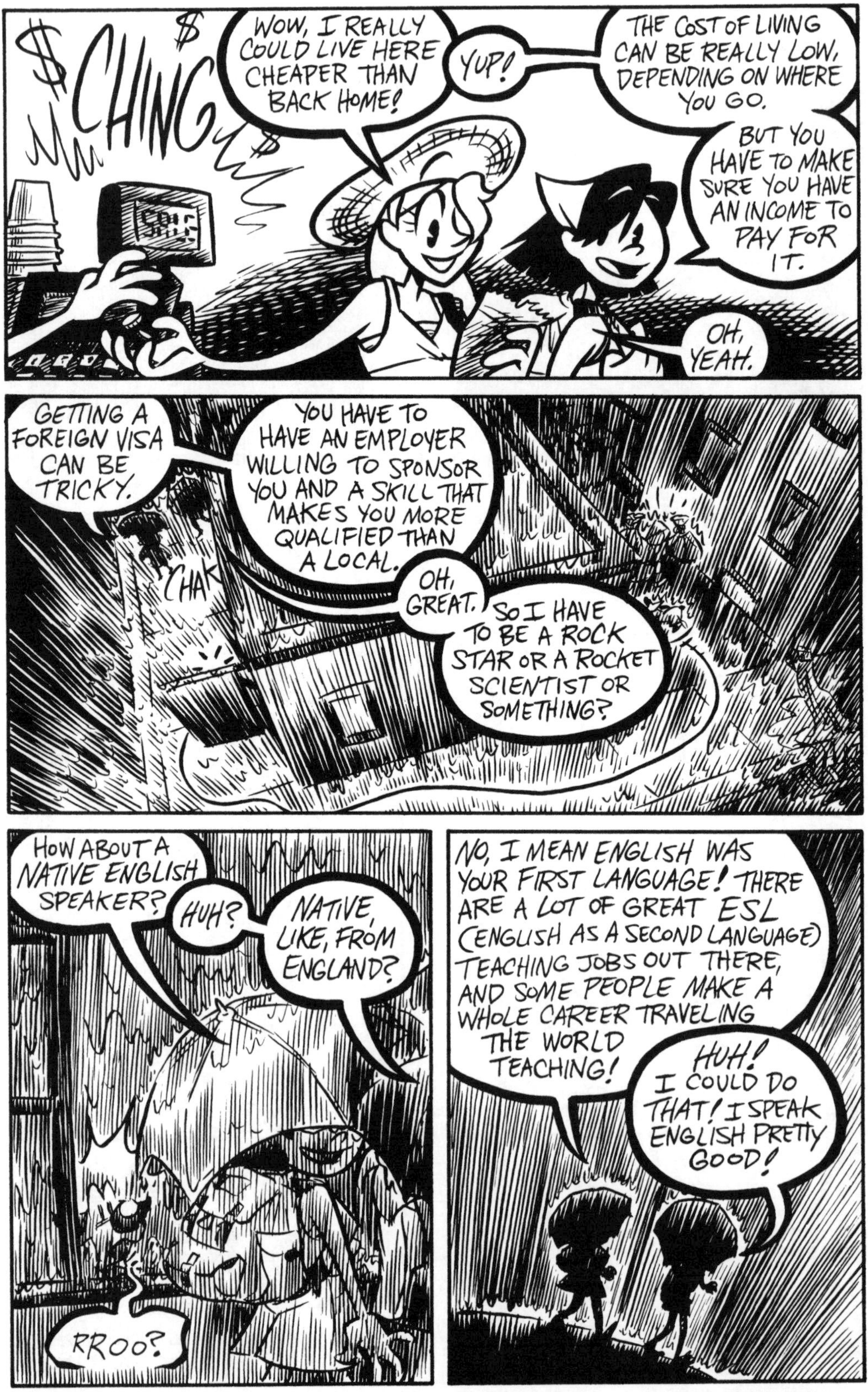
CHING
WOW, I REALLY COULD LIVE HERE CHEAPER THAN BACK HOME!
YUP!
THE COST OF LIVING CAN BE REALLY LOW, DEPENDING ON WHERE YOU GO.
BUT YOU HAVE TO MAKE SURE YOU HAVE AN INCOME TO PAY FOR IT.
OH, YEAH.
GETTING A FOREIGN VISA CAN BE TRICKY.
YOU HAVE TO HAVE AN EMPLOYER WILLING TO SPONSOR YOU AND A SKILL THAT MAKES YOU MORE QUALIFIED THAN A LOCAL.
CHAK
OH, GREAT.
SO I HAVE TO BE A ROCK STAR OR A ROCKET SCIENTIST OR SOMETHING?
HOW ABOUT A NATIVE ENGLISH SPEAKER?
HUH?
NATIVE, LIKE, FROM ENGLAND?
RROO?
NO, I MEAN ENGLISH WAS YOUR FIRST LANGUAGE! THERE ARE A LOT OF GREAT ESL (ENGLISH AS A SECOND LANGUAGE) TEACHING JOBS OUT THERE, AND SOME PEOPLE MAKE A WHOLE CAREER TRAVELING THE WORLD TEACHING!
HUH! I COULD DO THAT! I SPEAK ENGLISH PRETTY GOOD!

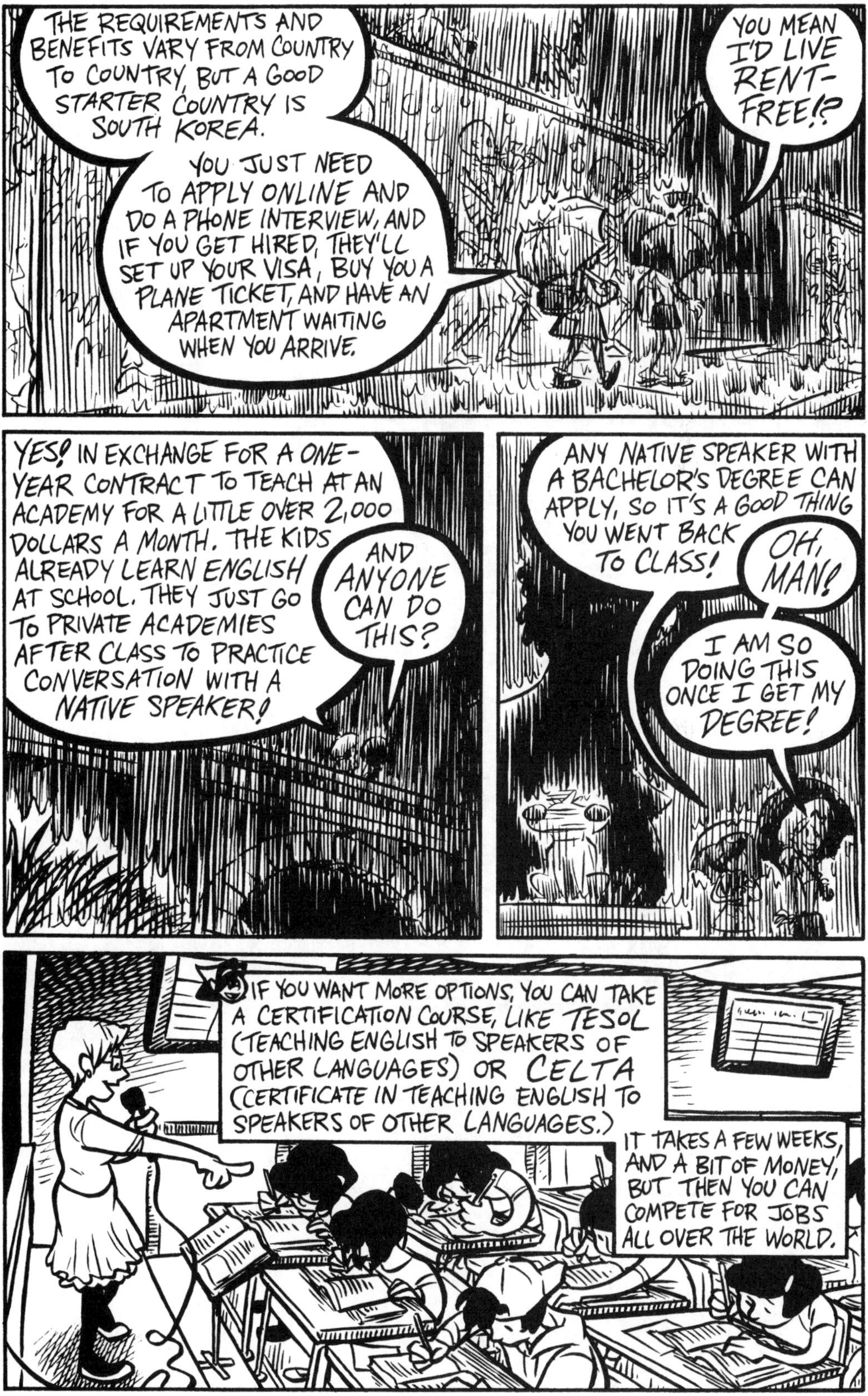

THE REQUIREMENTS AND BENEFITS VARY FROM COUNTRY TO COUNTRY, BUT A GOOD STARTER COUNTRY IS SOUTH KOREA.
YOU JUST NEED TO APPLY ONLINE AND DO A PHONE INTERVIEW, AND IF YOU GET HIRED, THEY'LL SET UP YOUR VISA, BUY YOU A PLANE TICKET, AND HAVE AN APARTMENT WAITING WHEN YOU ARRIVE.
YOU MEAN I'D LIVE RENT-FREE!?
YES! IN EXCHANGE FOR A ONE-YEAR CONTRACT TO TEACH AT AN ACADEMY FOR A LITTLE OVER 2,000 DOLLARS A MONTH. THE KIDS ALREADY LEARN ENGLISH AT SCHOOL. THEY JUST GO TO PRIVATE ACADEMIES AFTER CLASS TO PRACTICE CONVERSATION WITH A NATIVE SPEAKER!
AND ANYONE CAN DO THIS?
ANY NATIVE SPEAKER WITH A BACHELOR'S DEGREE CAN APPLY, SO IT'S A GOOD THING YOU WENT BACK TO CLASS!
OH, MAN!
I AM SO DOING THIS ONCE I GET MY DEGREE!
IF YOU WANT MORE OPTIONS, YOU CAN TAKE A CERTIFICATION COURSE, LIKE TESOL (TEACHING ENGLISH TO SPEAKERS OF OTHER LANGUAGES) OR CELTA (CERTIFICATE IN TEACHING ENGLISH TO SPEAKERS OF OTHER LANGUAGES.)
IT TAKES A FEW WEEKS, AND A BIT OF MONEY, BUT THEN YOU CAN COMPETE FOR JOBS ALL OVER THE WORLD.

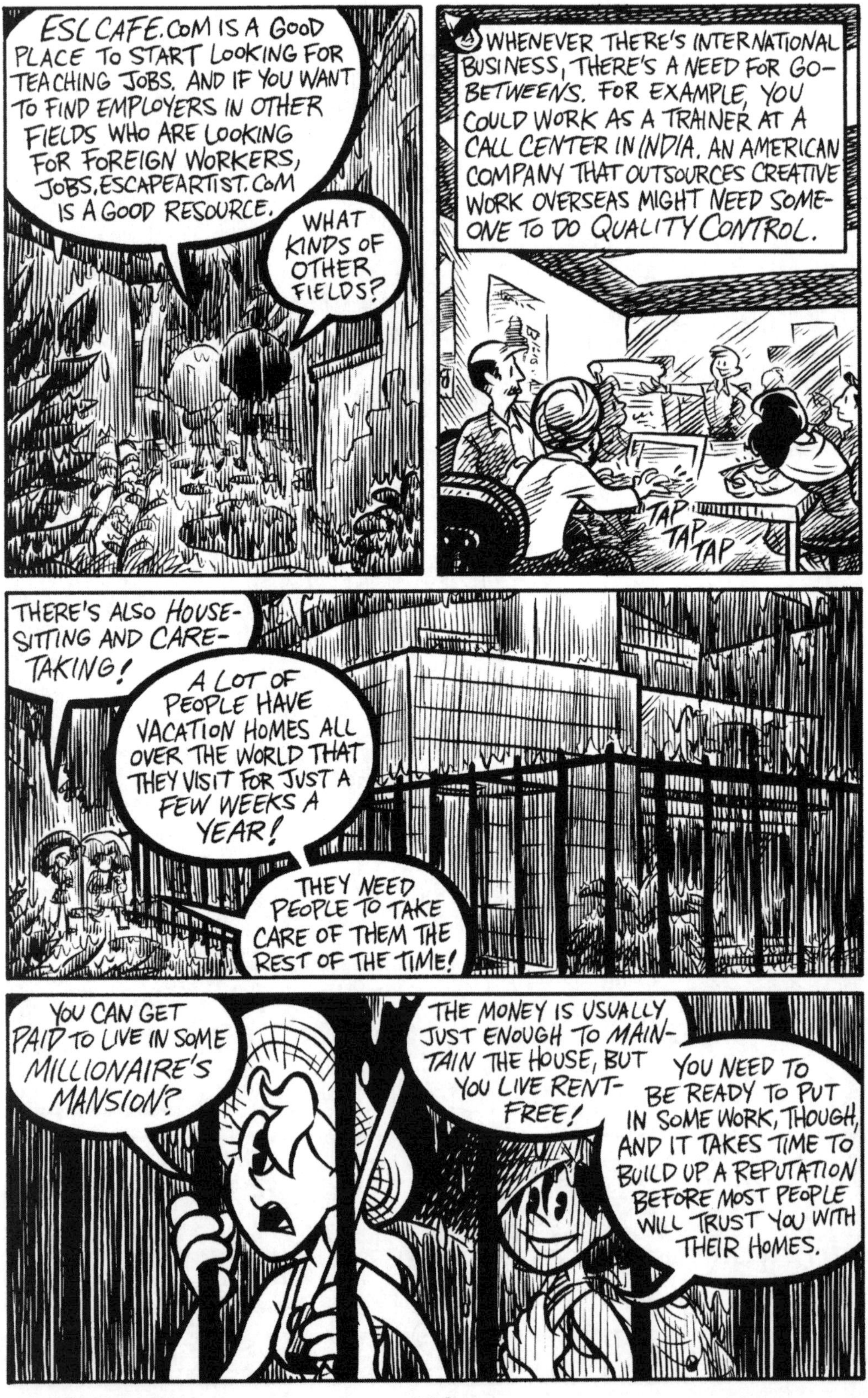
ESLCAFE.COM IS A GOOD PLACE TO START LOOKING FOR TEACHING JOBS. AND IF YOU WANT TO FIND EMPLOYERS IN OTHER FIELDS WHO ARE LOOKING FOR FOREIGN WORKERS, JOBS.ESCAPEARTIST.COM IS A GOOD RESOURCE.
WHAT KINDS OF OTHER FIELDS?
WHENEVER THERE'S INTERNATIONAL BUSINESS, THERE'S A NEED FOR GO-BETWEENS. FOR EXAMPLE, YOU COULD WORK AS A TRAINER AT A CALL CENTER IN INDIA. AN AMERICAN COMPANY THAT OUTSOURCES CREATIVE WORK OVERSEAS MIGHT NEED SOMEONE TO DO QUALITY CONTROL.
TAP TAP TAP
THERE'S ALSO HOUSE-SITTING AND CARE-TAKING!
A LOT OF PEOPLE HAVE VACATION HOMES ALL OVER THE WORLD THAT THEY VISIT FOR JUST A FEW WEEKS A YEAR!
THEY NEED PEOPLE TO TAKE CARE OF THEM THE REST OF THE TIME!
YOU CAN GET PAID TO LIVE IN SOME MILLIONAIRE'S MANSION?
THE MONEY IS USUALLY JUST ENOUGH TO MAINTAIN THE HOUSE, BUT YOU LIVE RENT-FREE!
YOU NEED TO BE READY TO PUT IN SOME WORK, THOUGH, AND IT TAKES TIME TO BUILD UP A REPUTATION BEFORE MOST PEOPLE WILL TRUST YOU WITH THEIR HOMES.

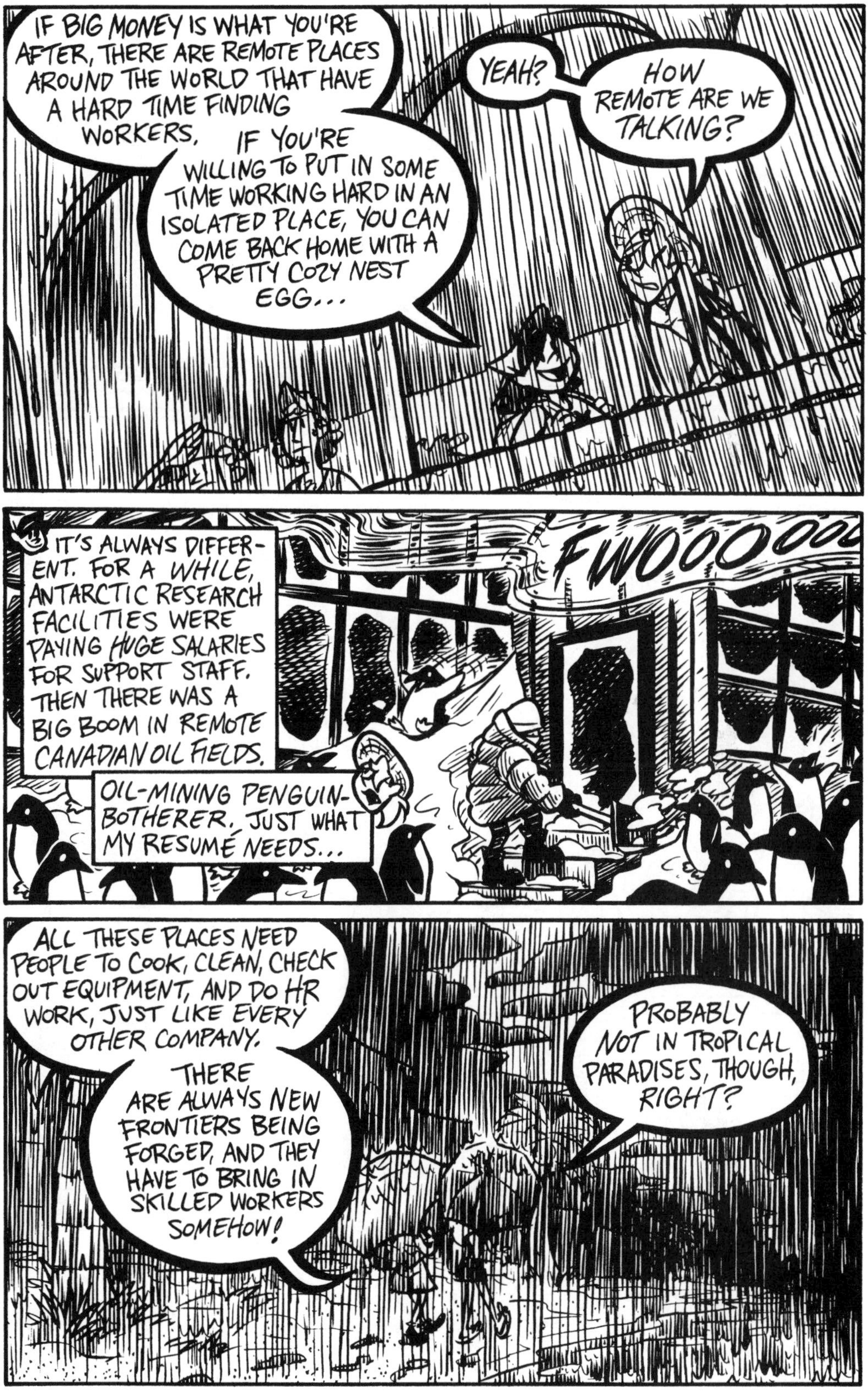

IF BIG MONEY IS WHAT YOU'RE AFTER, THERE ARE REMOTE PLACES AROUND THE WORLD THAT HAVE A HARD TIME FINDING WORKERS.
IF YOU'RE WILLING TO PUT IN SOME TIME WORKING HARD IN AN ISOLATED PLACE, YOU CAN COME BACK HOME WITH A PRETTY COZY NEST EGG...
YEAH?
HOW REMOTE ARE WE TALKING?
IT'S ALWAYS DIFFERENT. FOR A WHILE, ANTARCTIC RESEARCH FACILITIES WERE PAYING HUGE SALARIES FOR SUPPORT STAFF. THEN THERE WAS A BIG BOOM IN REMOTE CANADIAN OIL FIELDS.
FWOOOOOO
OIL-MINING PENGUIN-BOTHERER. JUST WHAT MY RESUMÉ NEEDS...
ALL THESE PLACES NEED PEOPLE TO COOK, CLEAN, CHECK OUT EQUIPMENT, AND DO HR WORK, JUST LIKE EVERY OTHER COMPANY.
THERE ARE ALWAYS NEW FRONTIERS BEING FORGED, AND THEY HAVE TO BRING IN SKILLED WORKERS SOMEHOW!
PROBABLY NOT IN TROPICAL PARADISES, THOUGH, RIGHT?

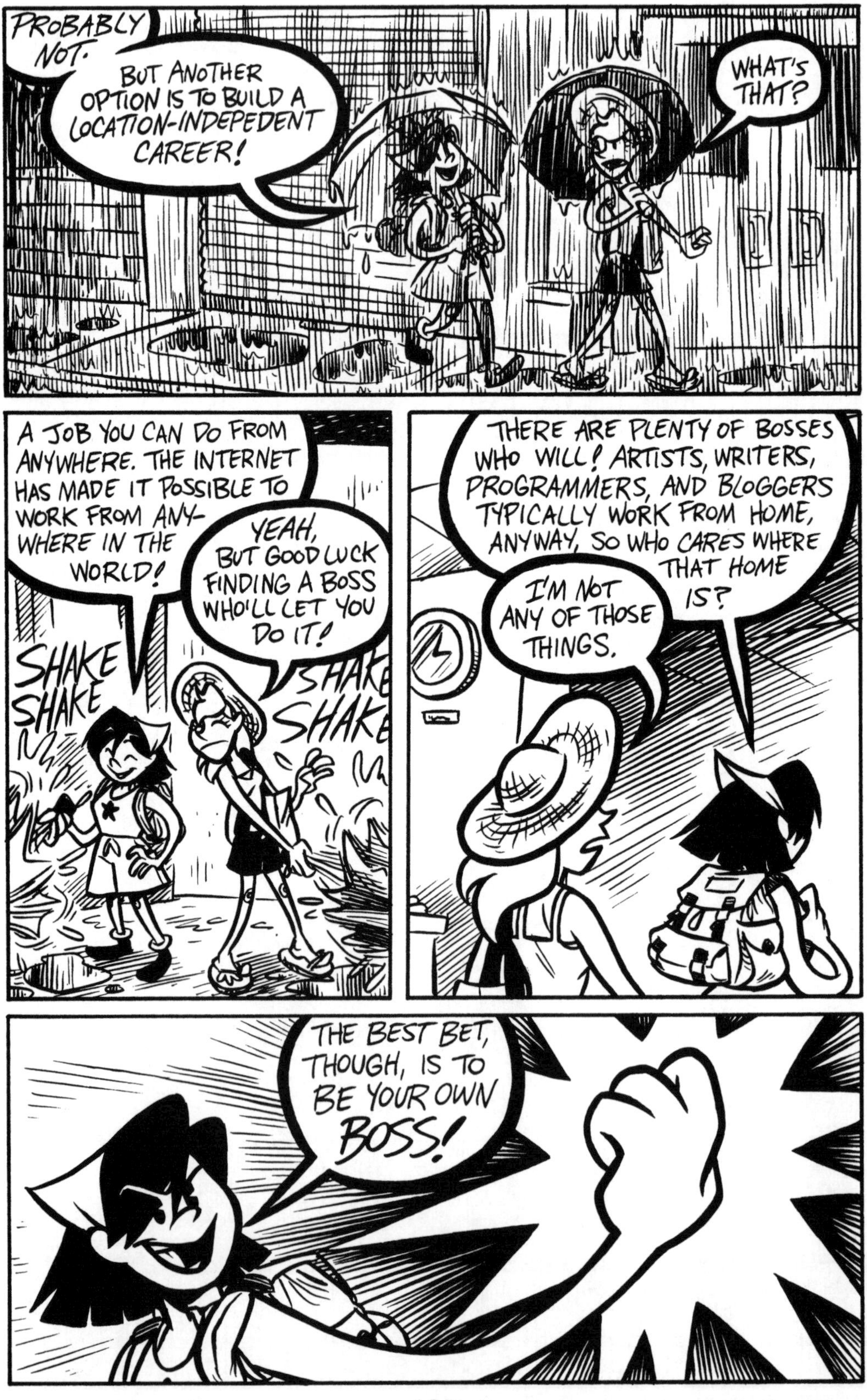
PROBABLY NOT.
BUT ANOTHER OPTION IS TO BUILD A LOCATION-INDEPEDENT CAREER!
WHAT'S THAT?
A JOB YOU CAN DO FROM ANYWHERE. THE INTERNET HAS MADE IT POSSIBLE TO WORK FROM ANY-WHERE IN THE WORLD!
YEAH, BUT GOOD LUCK FINDING A BOSS WHO'LL LET YOU DO IT!
SHAKE SHAKE
SHAKE SHAKE
THERE ARE PLENTY OF BOSSES WHO WILL! ARTISTS, WRITERS, PROGRAMMERS, AND BLOGGERS TYPICALLY WORK FROM HOME, ANYWAY, SO WHO CARES WHERE THAT HOME IS?
I'M NOT ANY OF THOSE THINGS.
THE BEST BET, THOUGH, IS TO BE YOUR OWN BOSS!

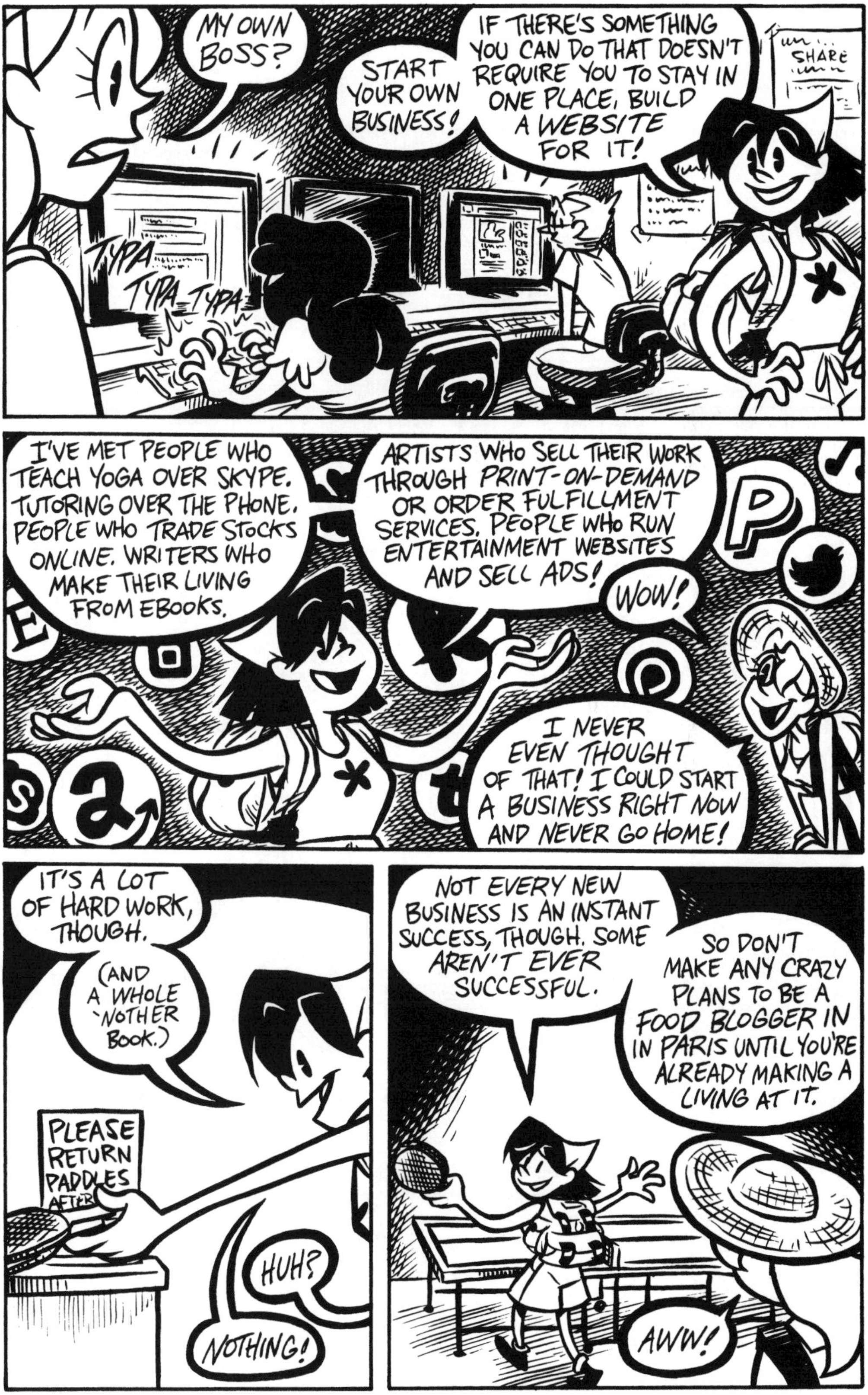
MY OWN BOSS?
START YOUR OWN BUSINESS!
IF THERE'S SOMETHING YOU CAN DO THAT DOESN'T REQUIRE YOU TO STAY IN ONE PLACE, BUILD A WEBSITE FOR IT!
SHARE
TYPA TYPA TYPA TYPA
I'VE MET PEOPLE WHO TEACH YOGA OVER SKYPE. TUTORING OVER THE PHONE. PEOPLE WHO TRADE STOCKS ONLINE. WRITERS WHO MAKE THEIR LIVING FROM EBOOKS.
ARTISTS WHO SELL THEIR WORK THROUGH PRINT-ON-DEMAND OR ORDER FULFILLMENT SERVICES. PEOPLE WHO RUN ENTERTAINMENT WEBSITES AND SELL ADS!
WOW!
I NEVER EVEN THOUGHT OF THAT! I COULD START A BUSINESS RIGHT NOW AND NEVER GO HOME!
IT'S A LOT OF HARD WORK, THOUGH.
(AND A WHOLE -NOTHER BOOK.)
PLEASE RETURN PADDLES AFTER
HUH?
NOTHING!
NOT EVERY NEW BUSINESS IS AN INSTANT SUCCESS, THOUGH. SOME AREN'T EVER SUCCESSFUL.
SO DON'T MAKE ANY CRAZY PLANS TO BE A FOOD BLOGGER IN IN PARIS UNTIL YOU'RE ALREADY MAKING A LIVING AT IT.
AWW!

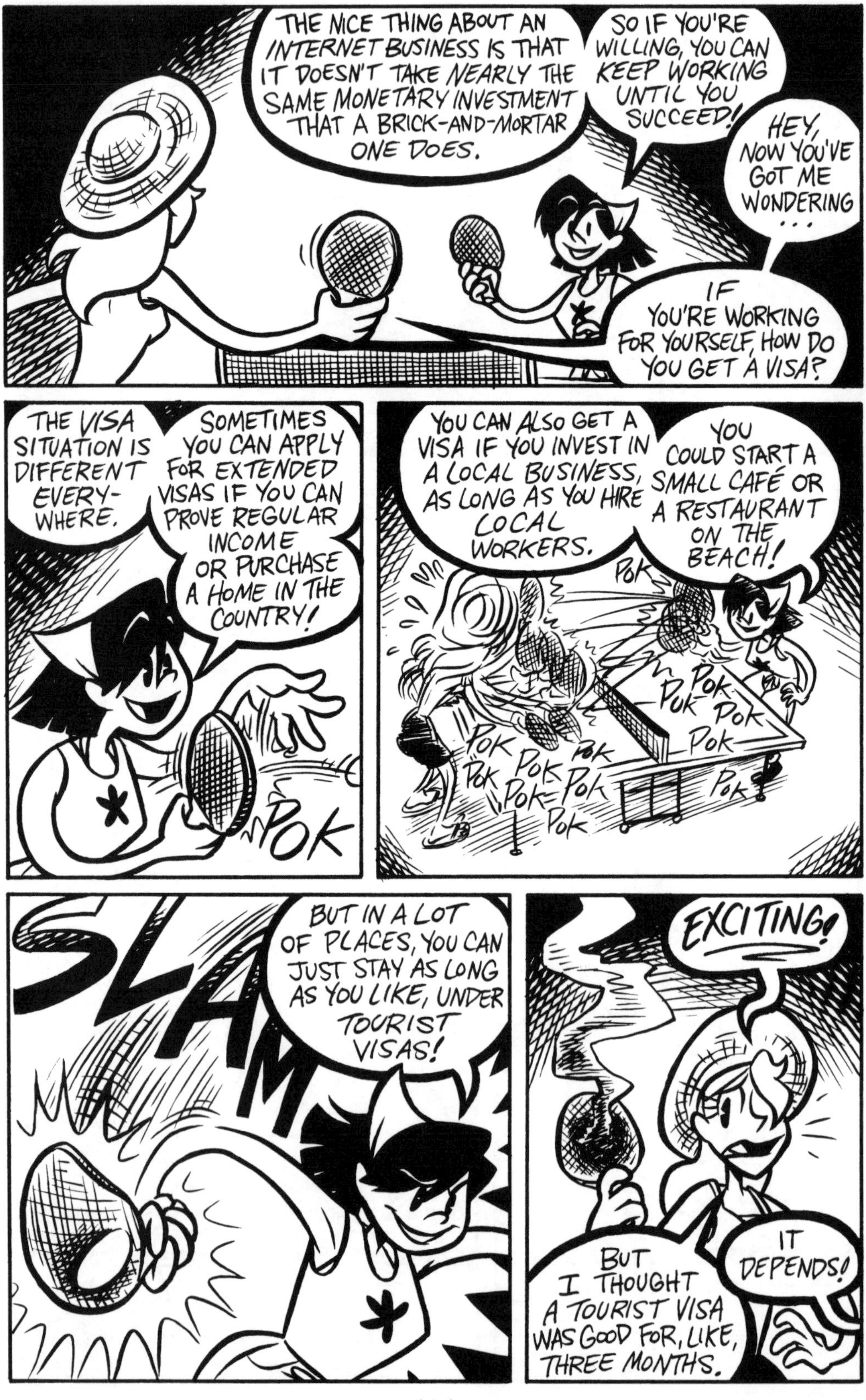
THE NICE THING ABOUT AN INTERNET BUSINESS IS THAT IT DOESN'T TAKE NEARLY THE SAME MONETARY INVESTMENT THAT A BRICK-AND-MORTAR ONE DOES.
SO IF YOU'RE WILLING, YOU CAN KEEP WORKING UNTIL YOU SUCCEED!
HEY, NOW YOU'VE GOT ME WONDERING...
IF YOU'RE WORKING FOR YOURSELF, HOW DO YOU GET A VISA?
THE VISA SITUATION IS DIFFERENT EVERY-WHERE.
SOMETIMES YOU CAN APPLY FOR EXTENDED VISAS IF YOU CAN PROVE REGULAR INCOME OR PURCHASE A HOME IN THE COUNTRY!
POK
YOU CAN ALSO GET A VISA IF YOU INVEST IN A LOCAL BUSINESS, AS LONG AS YOU HIRE LOCAL WORKERS.
YOU COULD START A SMALL CAFÉ OR A RESTAURANT ON THE BEACH!
POK POK POK POK POK POK POK POK POK POK POK POK POK POK
SLAM
BUT IN A LOT OF PLACES, YOU CAN JUST STAY AS LONG AS YOU LIKE, UNDER TOURIST VISAS!
EXCITING!
BUT I THOUGHT A TOURIST VISA WAS GOOD FOR, LIKE, THREE MONTHS.
IT DEPENDS!

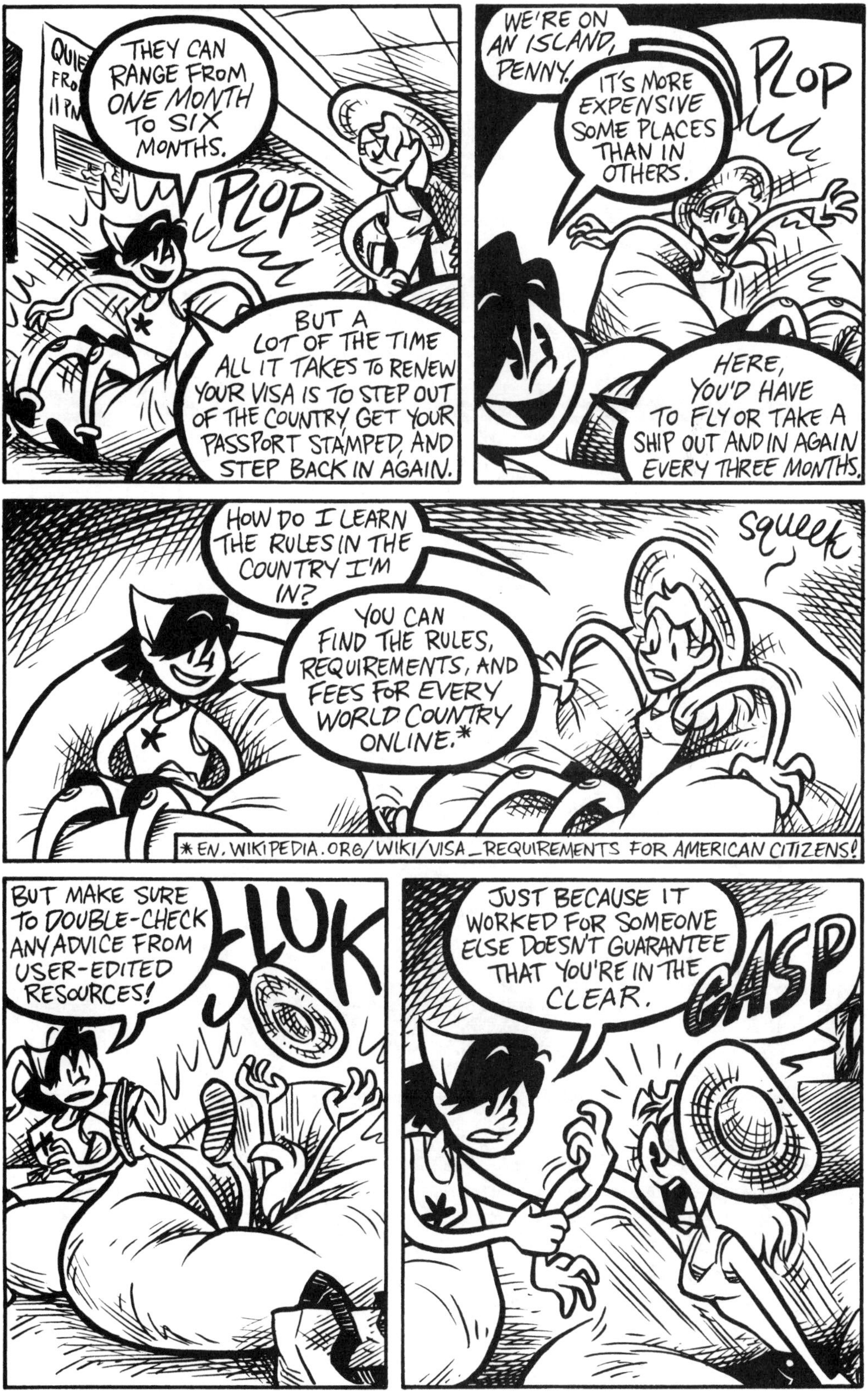
THEY CAN RANGE FROM ONE MONTH TO SIX MONTHS.
PLOP
BUT A LOT OF THE TIME ALL IT TAKES TO RENEW YOUR VISA IS TO STEP OUT OF THE COUNTRY, GET YOUR PASSPORT STAMPED, AND STEP BACK IN AGAIN.
WE'RE ON AN ISLAND, PENNY.
IT'S MORE EXPENSIVE SOME PLACES THAN IN OTHERS.
PLOP
HERE, YOU'D HAVE TO FLY OR TAKE A SHIP OUT AND IN AGAIN EVERY THREE MONTHS.
HOW DO I LEARN THE RULES IN THE COUNTRY I'M IN?
SQUEEK
YOU CAN FIND THE RULES, REQUIREMENTS, AND FEES FOR EVERY WORLD COUNTRY ONLINE.*
* EN.WIKIPEDIA.ORG/WIKI/VISA_REQUIREMENTS FOR AMERICAN CITIZENS!
BUT MAKE SURE TO DOUBLE-CHECK ANY ADVICE FROM USER-EDITED RESOURCES!
SLUK
JUST BECAUSE IT WORKED FOR SOMEONE ELSE DOESN'T GUARANTEE THAT YOU'RE IN THE CLEAR.
GASP

Chapter Eleven
In Conclusion

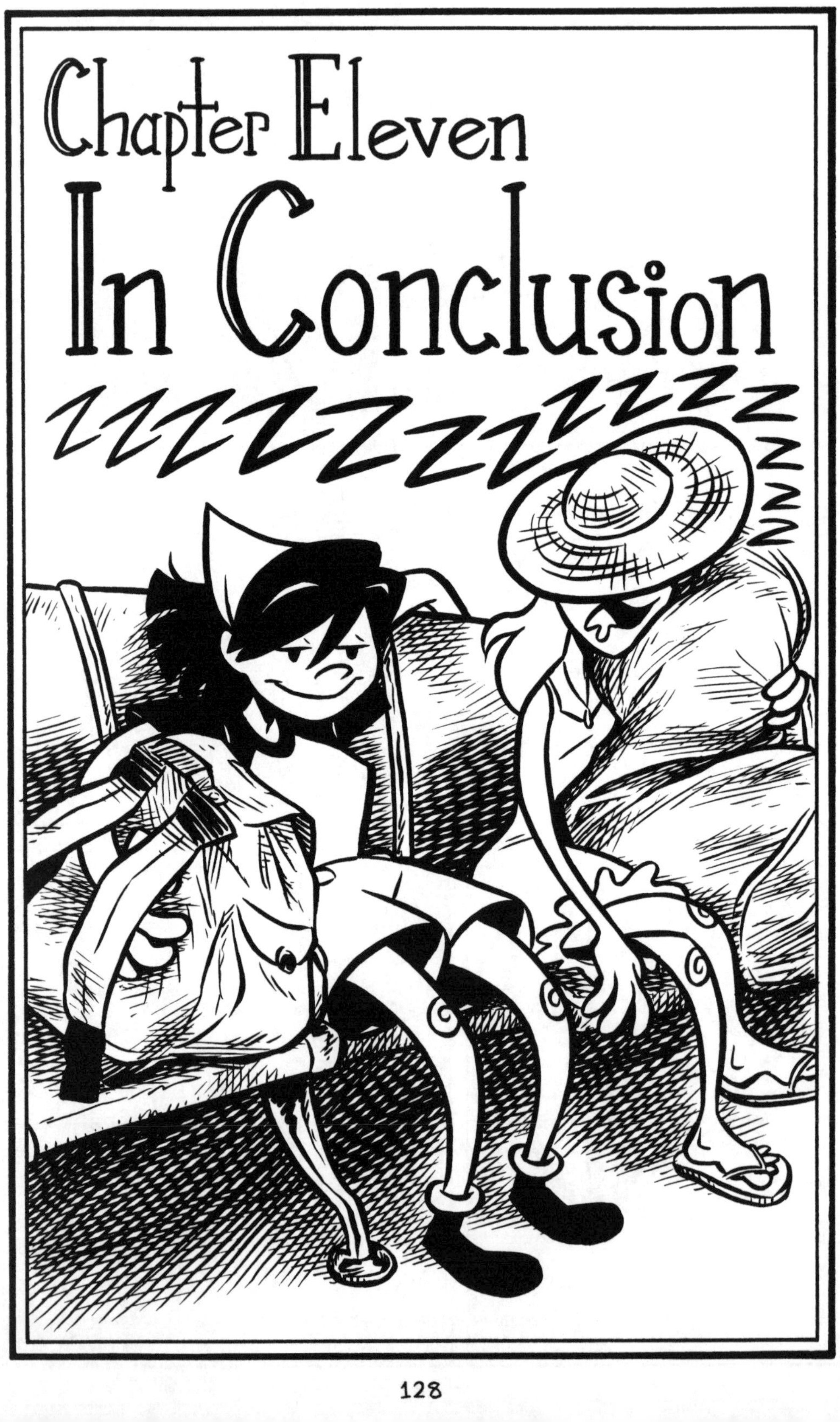

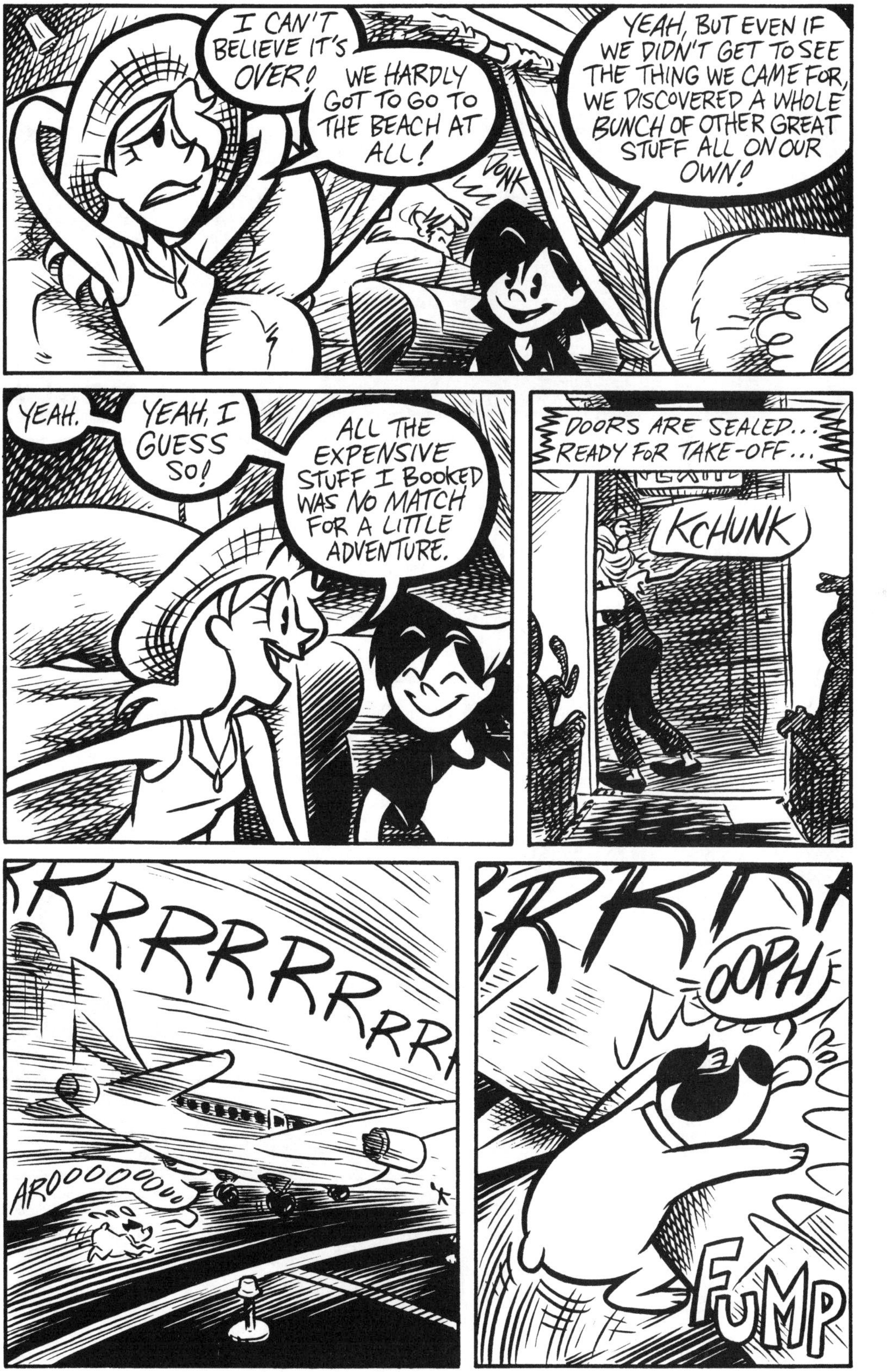
I CAN'T BELIEVE IT'S OVER!
WE HARDLY GOT TO GO TO THE BEACH AT ALL!
DONK
YEAH, BUT EVEN IF WE DIDN'T GET TO SEE THE THING WE CAME FOR, WE DISCOVERED A WHOLE BUNCH OF OTHER GREAT STUFF ALL ON OUR OWN!
YEAH.
YEAH, I GUESS SO!
ALL THE EXPENSIVE STUFF I BOOKED WAS NO MATCH FOR A LITTLE ADVENTURE.
DOORS ARE SEALED... READY FOR TAKE-OFF...
KCHUNK
RRRRRRRRRRR
AROOOOOOOO
RRRR
OOPH
FUMP

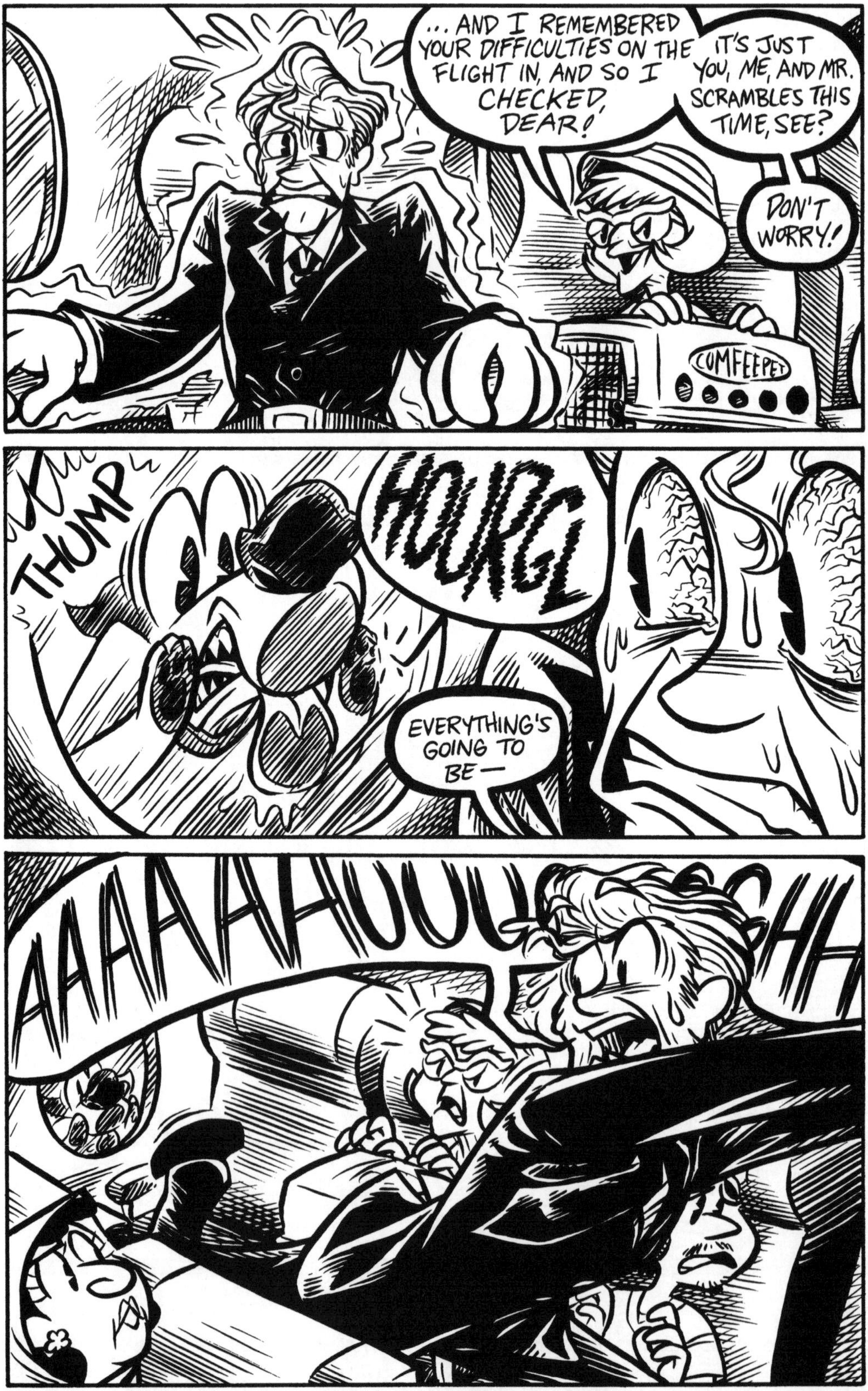
...AND I REMEMBERED YOUR DIFFICULTIES ON THE FLIGHT IN, AND SO I CHECKED, DEAR!
IT'S JUST YOU, ME, AND MR. SCRAMBLES THIS TIME, SEE?
DON'T WORRY!
THUMP
HOURGL
EVERYTHING'S GOING TO BE—
AAAAAHUUUGGHH

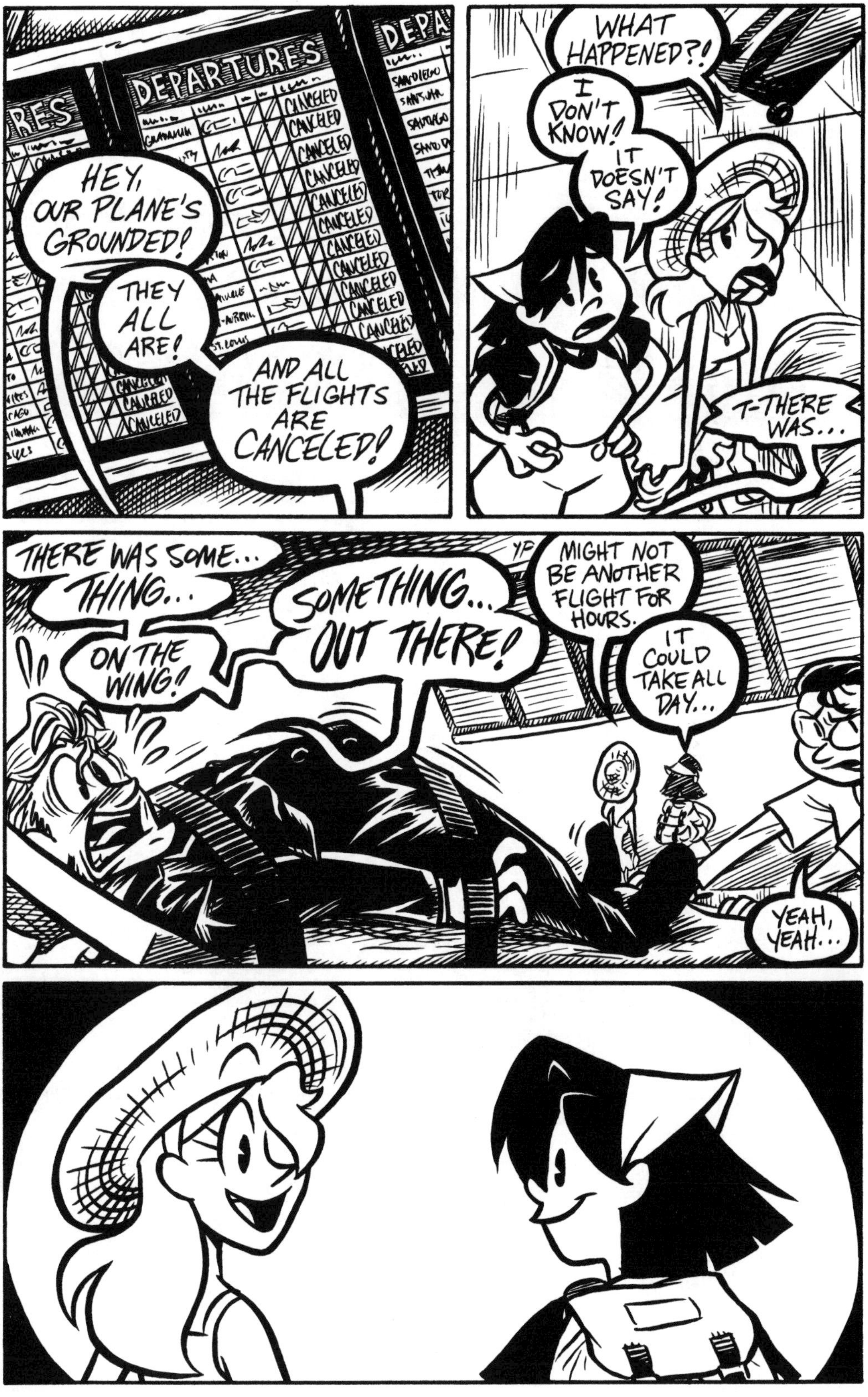
DEPARTURES
HEY, OUR PLANE'S GROUNDED!
THEY ALL ARE!
AND ALL THE FLIGHTS ARE CANCELED!
WHAT HAPPENED?!
I DON'T KNOW!
IT DOESN'T SAY!
T-THERE WAS...
THERE WAS SOME... THING...
ON THE WING!
SOMETHING... OUT THERE!
MIGHT NOT BE ANOTHER FLIGHT FOR HOURS.
IT COULD TAKE ALL DAY...
YEAH, YEAH...

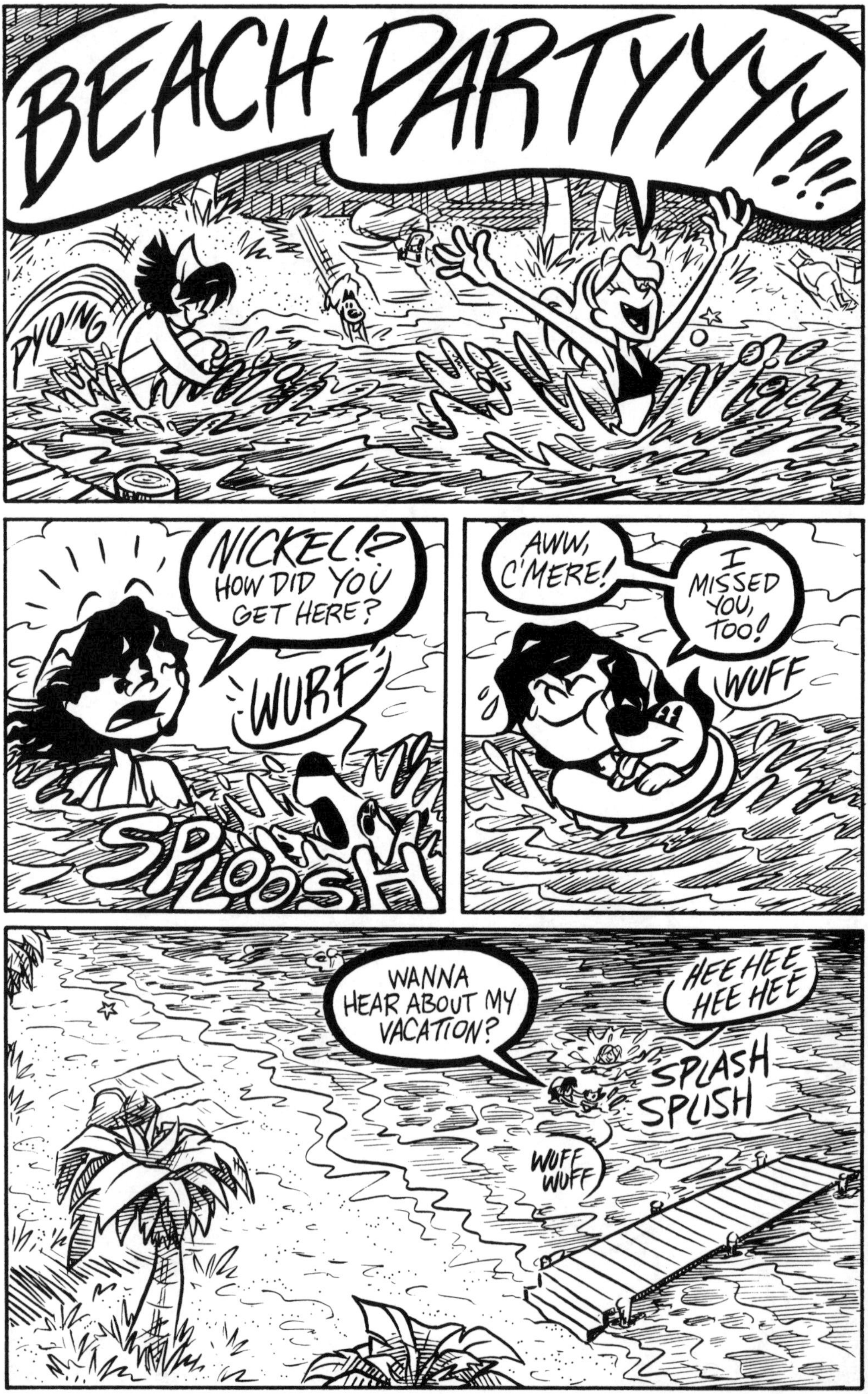
BEACH PARTYYY!!!
PYOING
NICKEL!? HOW DID YOU GET HERE?
WURF
SPLOOSH
AWW, C'MERE!
I MISSED YOU, TOO!
WUFF
WANNA HEAR ABOUT MY VACATION?
HEE HEE HEE HEE
SPLASH SPLISH
WUFF WUFF

SPECIAL THANKS

MINZOKU

N. CHAMBERS

CARLY DINGMAN

J KIM

GEORGE G OLIVE

SARAH CHAVIS

MICHAEL HANDLER

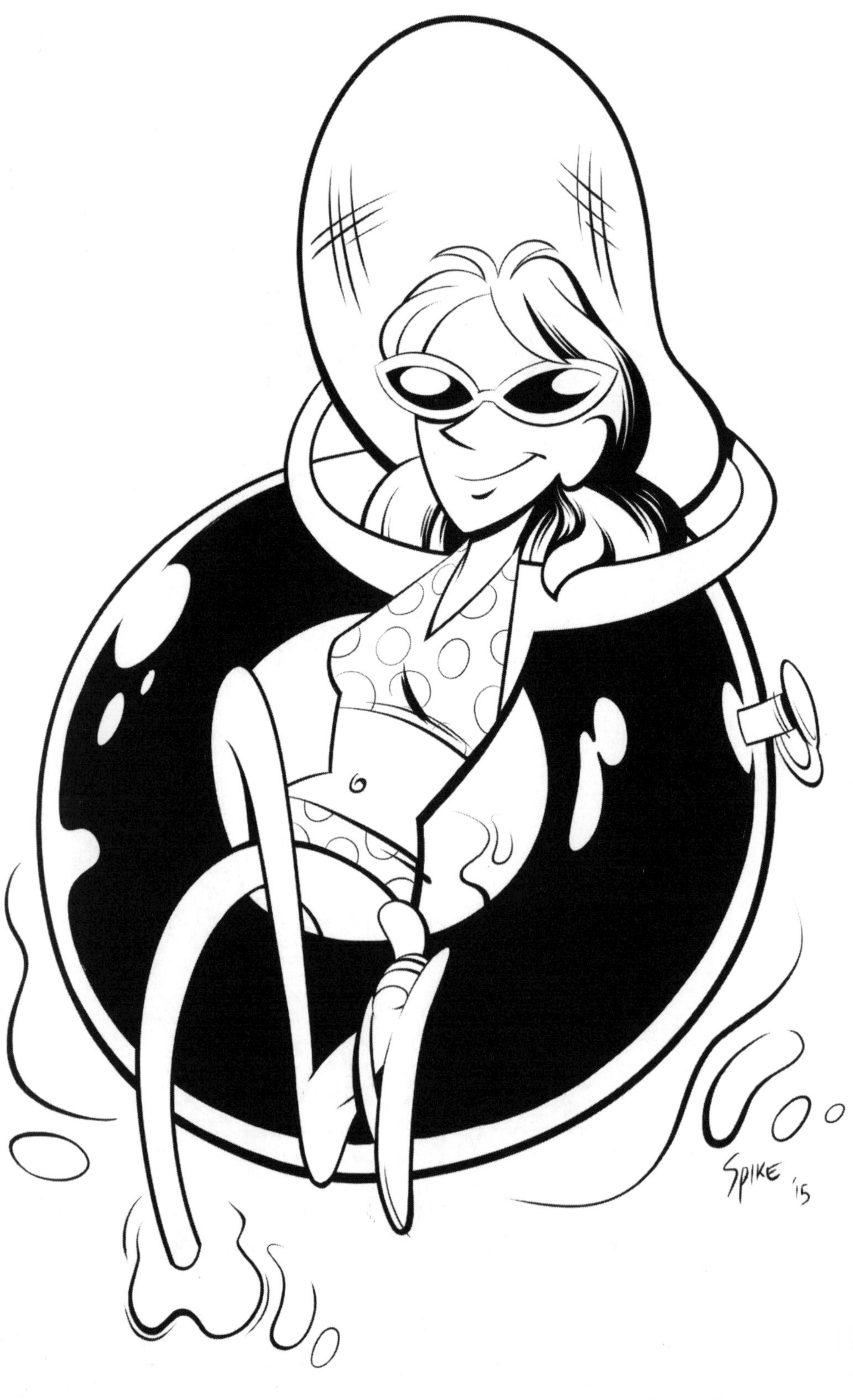
SPIKE '15